PORTFOLIO

UNFOLDING THE NAPKIN

Dan Roam is the bestselling author of *The Back of the Napkin: Solving Problems and Selling Ideas with Pictures*. Hailed by *Fast Company* magazine as the best innovation book of 2008 and by the *London Times* as "the business creativity book of the year." *The Back of the Napkin* has been translated into eighteen languages. As the president of Digital Roam Inc., Dan has helped leaders at Microsoft, Google, Wal-Mart, the Federal Reserve Bank, Boeing, and the United States Senate solve complex problems through visual thinking. Dan and his whiteboard have appeared on CNN, MSNBC, ABC News, Fox News, and NPR. Dan lives in San Francisco.

To attend one of Dan's "back of the napkin" workshops, please register at www.thebackofthenapkin.com.

UNFOLDING THE NAPKIN

The Hands-On Method
for Solving Complex Problems
with Simple Pictures

DAN ROAM

Portfolio

PORTFOLIO

Published by the Penguin Group

Penguin Group (USA) Inc., 375 Hudson Street, New York, New York 10014, U.S.A. • Penguin Group (Canada), 90 Eglinton Avenue East, Suite 700, Toronto, Ontario, Canada M4P 2Y3 (a division of Pearson Penguin Canada Inc.) • Penguin Books Ltd, 80 Strand, London WC2R 0RL, England • Penguin Ireland, 25 St. Stephen's Green, Dublin 2, Ireland (a division of Penguin Books Ltd) • Penguin Books Australia Ltd, 250 Camberwell Road, Camberwell, Victoria 3124, Australia (a division of Pearson Australia Group Pty Ltd) • Penguin Books India Pvt Ltd, 11 Community Centre, Panchsheel Park, New Delhi – 110 017, India • Penguin Group (NZ), 67 Apollo Drive, Rosedale, North Shore 0632, New Zealand (a division of Pearson New Zealand Ltd) • Penguin Books (South Africa) (Pty) Ltd, 24 Sturdee Avenue, Rosebank, Johannesburg 2196, South Africa

Penguin Books Ltd, Registered Offices:
80 Strand, London WC2R 0RL, England

First published in 2009 by Portfolio, a member of Penguin Group (USA) Inc.

10   9   8   7

Copyright © Dan Roam, 2009
All rights reserved

LIBRARY OF CONGRESS CATALOGING IN PUBLICATION DATA
Roam, Dan.
Unfolding the napkin : the hands-on method for solving complex problems
with simple pictures / Dan Roam.
       p.   cm.
Includes index.
ISBN 978-1-59184-319-1
1. Problem solving—Audio-visual aids. 2. Management—Audio-visual aids. I. Title.
HD30.29.R6258 2009
658.4'03—dc22   2009032657

Printed in the United States of America
Set in Dante MT with Felt Tip and Divine

Illustrations by the author
Designed by Daniel Lagin

For <u>Sophie</u> and <u>Celeste,</u>
the real masters of the magic wand.

CONTENTS

INTRODUCTION:
THE BACK OF THE NAPKIN, HANDS-ON | IX

DAY 1: LOOKING | 1

DAY 2: SEEING | 53

DAY 3: IMAGINING | 177

DAY 4: SHOWING | 243

APPENDIX: MY VISUAL ANSWERS TO
PARTICULARLY CHALLENGING EXERCISES | 271

INDEX | 277

YOUR SCRATCH PAPER | 281

INTRODUCTION:

THE BACK OF THE NAPKIN, HANDS-ON

Why a hands-on Back of the Napkin method?

Twenty-five years of helping business leaders around the world develop ideas has taught me three things:

1. There is no more powerful way to discover a new idea than to draw a simple picture.

2. There is no faster way to develop and test an idea than to draw a simple picture.

3. There is no more effective way to share an idea with other people than to draw a simple picture.

This book contains many tools, rules, and concepts, but in the end it's about just one thing: how you can draw that simple picture.

A guidebook for creating problem-solving pictures

This book is as a follow-up to *The Back of the Napkin: Solving Problems and Selling Ideas with Pictures*. In that book I talked about using simple pictures as a way to solve business problems and introduced a set of tools and rules to help anyone create problem-solving pictures.

I created this second book, *Unfolding the Napkin*, to help you see exactly how the visual problem-solving process works in the real world of business. Every tool and rule I introduced in *The Back of the Napkin* is here, only this time we'll work through them together, step-by-step, putting visual problem solving into everyday practice.

Think of *The Back of the Napkin* as an introduction to visual problem solving; think of *Unfolding the Napkin* as the hands-on guidebook.

The Back of the Napkin is the introduction to visual problem solving; this is the hands-on guidebook.

A self-contained four-day course

This book is set up as a four-day course on visual problem solving: my entire approach is spelled out picture by picture, taking us from "I can't draw" to "Here's the picture I drew that I think can save the world."

Why four days? Two reasons: First, experience tells me that's how long it takes to get through all the lessons in a meaningful way. Second, as we'll soon see, the visual thinking process naturally breaks into four steps, and addressing them one at a time helps the whole approach make sense.

But four days is a long time for businesspeople to stop what they normally do and learn something new. This workshop addresses that valid concern with two approaches: the carrot and the stick.

The Stick

The Carrot

(Both work fine)

The stick says, "Yes, there is a lot of material here, and, yes, it's all important. It simply takes four days to get through it all and make sure that it's going to stick. So buckle down and pick up your pens."

The happier approach, the carrot, says, "If we do this right, we won't have to 'stop what we normally do' at all." This book is set up so you can bring your real-world work with you. Rather than look only at hypothetical case studies, I'd like you to work on a few real problems from your office—that way you can see how visual thinking works and start to fix things at the same time.

▲

The stick says we've got a lot to cover; the carrot says we can make it part of our actual work.

Quick review: The Back of the Napkin on the back of a napkin

If you've read *The Back of the Napkin*, this book will need little introduction: it covers the same material in a more detailed and interactive way. If you haven't read *The Back of the Napkin*, here is a brief summary.

The Back of the Napkin on the back of a napkin: we can solve our problems with pictures.

I believe we can solve our business problems, whatever those problems might be, by creating simple pictures. *The Back of the Napkin* breaks that statement down into three essential questions: what problems can be solved with pictures, what pictures do the solving, and what people do the drawing.

The answers are as follows:

1. **What problems?** Any problem. Any problem that we have the ability to articulate at all, we have the ability to articulate abundantly more clearly through the use of a picture.

2. **What pictures?** Simple ones. If we can draw a square, a circle, a stick figure, and an arrow connecting them, we can draw any picture in this book.

3. **What people?** All of us. Because we are born visual thinkers (even if we don't think so, we are). The pictures we need are so simple that I believe that anyone who can see well enough to walk into a room can solve problems with pictures.

◀ What problems? All of them. What pictures? Simple ones. What people? All of us.

With these three questions answered, *The Back of the Napkin* introduces a process and a set of tools to help anyone quickly begin solving complex problems with simple pictures.

Kickoff: get ready for pictures

A year ago I attended a business meeting where I saw everything I believe about the power of pictures proven in a single day. It's a good illustration of how easy it can be to use pictures to think in business, but it's an even better example of where pictures could have been used to great effect but were not.

Last summer the executive committee at a large financial company—let's call it AmericanWay Financial*—invited me to run a visual-thinking workshop at their annual leadership meeting. AmericanWay had finished a record fiscal year, and the executive committee was looking for a thought-provoking session to take advantage of the positive energy. The committee thought solving problems with pictures sounded interesting, and I was happy to accept their invitation.

I looked forward to the workshop: financial executives tend to believe

*This is not the actual name of the company. All the stories in this book are true, but in some cases the companies asked that I not use their names. When I use a real company name, it means I received their approval.

there's only one kind of picture worth looking at (a stock chart), so the session would give me a chance to show a skeptical audience how to use all kinds of simple pictures to solve problems. It would also be an opportunity for me to learn more about the inner workings of a huge finance company.

THE DAY BUSINESS DIED

On the morning of my workshop, the American economy tanked. The week before, as 2008's financial crisis spread, Congress flip-flopped on voting up or down the U.S. Treasury's proposed $700 billion Wall Street bailout. Amid the uncertainty, the Dow lost 22 percent of its value, the index's worst week in history. But as the following week dawned—the week of my workshop— the bailout money began to flow. On Monday the market rallied as the Dow posted the biggest single-day advance in seventy-five years. Everyone heaved a huge sigh of relief, certain that the worst had passed.

Until Wednesday, that is.

As I woke that morning in the hotel room and opened my laptop for a final run-through of my presentation, I turned on the news. Already at that early hour the market was starting to bleed again. As I glanced back and forth between my computer and the TV, I wondered how focused my audience would be on what I had to show. The financial world was crashing down around us.

Then something dawned on me: by redrawing a handful of example sketches, I could change the workshop from a blue-sky exercise into a real-world "here's our new reality" visual-planning session. The same tools and rules of visual thinking would apply; I'd just need to change the questions I asked.

Using the drawing screen on my tablet computer, I reworked several sketches in my presentation. In thirty minutes I hot-wired a largely conceptual workshop into a practical one. Although I knew nothing about the specifics of AmericanWay's financials, I didn't need to: everyone else in the room would. Experience told me that if I just gave the executives the right frameworks and starting points, they would draw far better pictures of American-Way's present and future than I ever could.

As the workshop started, I demonstrated the tools of visual thinking, then asked the executives to break into small teams so they could draw their own ideas. By lunchtime dozens of pictures hung on the walls, showing what was going on in the market and, more importantly, what AmericanWay could do about it. In spite of the morning's rocky news, visual thinking was clearly a hit; the executives lingered in the room, pointing and talking as they walked from picture to picture.

But at lunch we heard more bad news. During the three hours that we'd been in the workshop, the Dow had dropped seven hundred points—enough to evaporate all the earnings of the previous days—and it was still on its way down. Not only was the crisis not over, there seemed to be nothing anyone could do to stop the plunge. After months of writhing, global finance as we knew it was over. That meant AmericanWay Financal might well be over too.

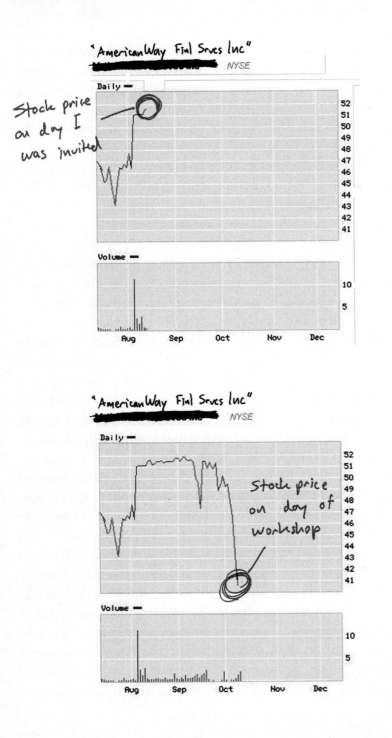

On the day I received the invitation, AmericanWay stock was trading at an all-time high.

By lunchtime on the day of the workshop, the American economy had tanked.

OKAY, BOSS, WHAT ARE WE GOING TO DO?

After lunch I took a seat in the back of the room. The next speaker was the CEO of the company. Given that Mike already had his entire executive team gathered together for the workshop, I wondered what approach he would take to addressing the eight-hundred-pound gorilla now sitting in the center of the room: the collapsing economy.

Would Mike cancel the whole event and send everyone back to their offices to shore up the barricades and put out the fires? Would he call together a small group of his most senior execs and whisk them away to a hidden room somewhere in the hotel, where they could quietly plot their next steps? Would he act as if nothing had happened and go ahead with the rest of the day's planned activities? As the sole nonemployee in the room, I was hoping to see an example of real leadership in a time of crisis.

That's what I saw. Tossing his prepared remarks aside, Mike walked to the stage, took a long look around the room, then delivered the most honest-to-goodness, hands-down, no-BS business speech I've ever heard. It was brilliant.

For an hour, Mike pulled no punches. He told his people that neither he nor anyone in the room had ever experienced a crisis of this speed and scale. He told them that although he couldn't promise that AmericanWay would even be in business in a year, he knew this team's good planning and near perfect execution in the previous years had left AmericanWay in the best possible position to weather the storm.

Mike said it was the people in the room that day who would share responsibility for whatever happened next at AmericanWay. If the company passed through this difficult time and came out on the other side, it would be because the people in this room made it so. And if the company failed, it would be because of the decisions of the people in this room.

That got everyone's attention, and then Mike got tactical. He outlined four strategies that he believed would clear AmericanWay's path to survival. First: pull back all offerings into the company's established market sweet spot; in other words, halt recent shifts upmarket and down-market and focus on the middle-market core. Second: acknowledge that AmericanWay was better positioned to be a "fast follower" in product development than the market leader; in other words, let somebody else make the investments required for risky innovations, then watch and copy only what worked. Third: develop a laser-sharp focus of customers' needs; in other words, stop listening to ourselves and start listening to our customers. Last: consolidate all business operations around the company's core infrastructure;

in other words, stop the costly duplication of processes at offices around the country.

It was a tough-love, no-nonsense talk, and it was exactly what everyone in that room needed to hear. Mike did what a CEO is supposed to: he rallied his troops, articulated a clear vision, and broke it down into bite-sized pieces that could be digested one by one. I'm not even an employee, but by the time we left the room I was ready to join him in kicking some financial butt.

But here was a problem with Mike's talk. A member of Mike's executive team took an informal poll the evening after the talk and was shocked by the results. Everybody felt great about Mike's clarity, passion, and honesty. The trouble was that an hour later nobody knew what they were actually supposed to do.

CHECKPOINT 1

We're going to continue this story, but before we do, it's time to get interactive. Let's do a quick check-in. *Without flipping back* to the text, take a moment and write down as many of Mike's underlying AmericanWay strategies as you can.

If you just felt your heart skip a beat or thought, "oh no!" welcome to the "business meeting club"—the club of smart people so overwhelmed by verbal data that we're hard pressed to know what to pay attention to. Let's do the exercise anyway. See how many of Mike's strategies you can recall.

How many could you recall? One? That's okay: believe it or not, that was the average among the people who were actually in the room. Two is not bad; three is remarkable. If you can remember all four, that is amazing. (If you remember five, something's up, because Mike only gave four.)

Yes, this is an unfair example. I didn't warn you in advance that there was going to be a test, nor did I indicate where in the story you really needed to pay attention. Then again, Mike didn't either. Remember, he just got up and talked. It was a great and inspiring talk, but I don't recall seeing many of the executives taking notes, and other than Mike, there wasn't anything to look at to make his points clear, distinct, and memorable.

Regardless how many of Mike's strategies you remembered, the lesson is this: while good speaking is engaging and inspiring, we need to recognize the limitations of words. Let's be clear: there's nothing wrong with words. What's wrong is that they're not enough.

IF WORDS AREN'T ENOUGH, WHAT SHOULD WE ADD?

The morning after the talk, I got a call from the executive who had taken the informal poll. He asked me to come to an impromptu meeting. When I arrived, six senior leaders from the previous day's workshop were drawing on flip charts. I was handed a transcript of Mike's talk, on which someone had already highlighted the four strategies. The poll taker asked if I would be willing to help them create a set of simple pictures to clarify Mike's message and give a stronger sense of direction for the executives.

He didn't have to ask me twice. For the next hour we sketched and talked. When we were done, we'd come up with these four pictures:

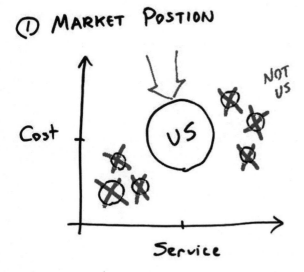

▲
Regroup at our middle-market sweet spot. Be willing to be a fast follower.

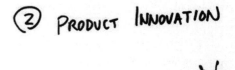

Throughout that day, these pictures were circulated to the executives. Because they were simple, clear, and visual, the feedback was overwhelmingly positive. Beyond being energized by an inspired talk, people could now see what Mike's words meant; they could literally see his vision.

This is where pictures come in. Whether drawing them, looking at them, or talking about them, pictures add enormously to our ability to think, to remember, and to do. If you already know that, this workbook will help you get even better at visual problem solving. If you're not sure or are afraid that you can't draw, this workbook will lay a foundation under your feet and give you all the tools you need to prove the power of pictures to yourself and to your colleagues.

▲
Listen to customers, not just to ourselves. Stop spending on being different companies.

Found in translation

Before we get this workshop started, let's do an exercise that will make the purpose of this workbook crystal clear.

When was the last time you visited a new city—a place where you didn't know the local people, didn't know your way around, and perhaps couldn't even read the street signs? There is a simple yet powerful lesson that we're going to expose here: thinking about how we find our way around an unfamiliar location will help us think about how we can find our way around an unfamiliar idea. Looking at how we navigate a *place* gives us insight into how to navigate a *problem*.

To show you what I mean, I'd like to invite you on a walk around Moscow. It's a city I've spent time in on business, and (in certain times of year) it's a wonderful place to walk. I vividly remember my first morning there—the thrill of setting off to explore a completely foreign city, mitigated by the terror of disappearing forever down a dark street—and I'd like to share the adventure with you.

Let's imagine that we're staying at the Saint George Hotel in central Moscow. We arrived the previous day and have awoken to a beautiful spring morning. We meet for breakfast and agree there's no better way to get a feel for the city than going for a long walk. Since I've been an astronaut geek my whole life, I suggest a visit to the Yuri Gagarin museum, a memorial to the first person to fly in space. I know from something I read years ago that the museum is in the city, but I haven't a clue where.

After a filling breakfast, we approach the concierge desk and ask how to get to the Gagarin museum. The first thing the concierge does is offer to book us a limo, since the museum is some distance away. But we say no, we'd prefer to walk.

"All right," replies the concierge. "Here's how to get there."

EXPLANATION OPTION 1: THE NARRATIVE

The concierge tells us: "It's a long walk, two hours or more, but here's what you do: walk out the front door and bear to your right. Pretty soon you'll find yourself at the river—that's the Moscow River, of course—and when you reach it, turn left on the embankment. Follow the embankment for a few minutes as you pass by the Kremlin on your left. Once beyond the Kremlin, you'll see a large bridge on your right and Saint Basil's Cathedral on your left. Head toward the cathedral, but pass it on your left. Bear right, up the hill, past the many old buildings you'll see there—incidentally, those are the oldest buildings in the entire city.

"Anyway, pretty soon you'll come to a wide road split by a garden—that's Lubyanski Way—and turn left on that road, continuing uphill. Ten minutes more and you'll find yourself in front of the Lubyanka, the old KGB building. You can't miss it: it's a big yellow neoclassical building with enormous iron doors with shields emblazoned on them. Trust me, you don't want to go inside. Immediately past the Lubyanka turn right up Sretenka Street. Now comes the easy part: you'll stay on that same street all the way to the Gagarin museum, although the name of the street will change as you walk along it. First it will be Sretenka; then after you cross the Garden Ring Road it will become Prospekt Mira, or Peace Road.

"Stay on Prospekt Mira for the next three or four kilometers as it takes you toward the northern part of the city. After maybe thirty minutes you'll pass through an enormous intersection at the Rizhsky Train Station, but just keep going straight. Another forty minutes and you'll find yourself at a fork where Prospekt Mira veers right and Ostankinsky Way veers left. Stay on Prospekt Mira for just a couple of more minutes, and you'll see the Gagarin museum on your left. That's it. Enjoy the museum."

EXPLANATION OPTION 2: THE CHECKLIST

Now let's try something different. Imagine that this time the concierge picks up a sheet of paper and a pen and, after thinking for a moment, writes out the following checklist (using both English and Russian spellings of roads):

- ✓ Right on Mokhovaya Ulitsa
- ✓ Left on the Moscow River embankment, the Moskvoretskaya Naberezhnaya
- ✓ Left at Red Square (Krasnaya Ploshchad)
- ✓ Right on Ulitsa Varvarka
- ✓ Left on Lubyanskiy Proyezd
- ✓ Right on Ulitsa Sretenka
- ✓ Cross the Garden Ring Road (Sadovoye Koltso)
- ✓ Continue on Prospekt Mira
- ✓ Pass Rizhsky Voksal
- ✓ Continue on Prospekt Mira after it splits from Ostankinsky Proyezd
- ✓ Look for the museum entrance on your left

As he hands us the list, he says, "Follow those instructions and you will reach the museum in just over two hours."

EXPLANATION OPTION 3: THE MAP

Here's another possibility. The concierge picks up a map of Moscow and draws a dot near the bottom. "That's where we are now." He then draws another dot at the top of the map, and connects the two with a line. "That's the museum." He hands us the map. "It should take about two hours."

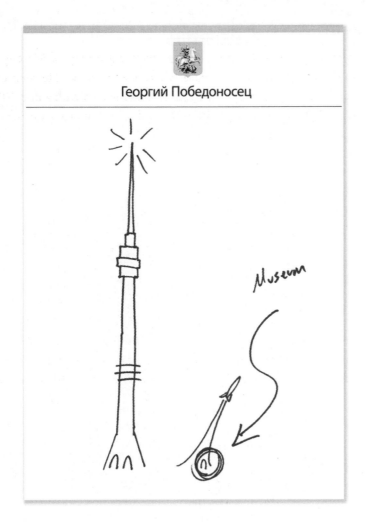

Георгий Победоносец

The hotel stationery approach.

EXPLANATION OPTION 4: THE LANDMARK

Here's our last option. The concierge picks up a pen, and on a sheet of hotel stationery draws a picture of two towers:

He says, "When you step outside, you'll see this tower far off on your left. Walk that way. The museum is there."

WHICH WAY?

All four of these sets of directions are correct. Following any one of them should in theory get us to the same place in the same amount of time. But here's my question: I'd like you to look over the four options again, really think about them for a moment, and then ask yourself this: if we actually were in Moscow, which option would you prefer?

There is no right answer, but here is my preference:

Option 1: The Narrative ▶

The narrative is fun to listen to, gives a lot of detail, and makes the trip sound interesting, but unless we've got an extraordinary memory, we will forget which way to go after the second turn. (This is like Mike's speech.)

Option 2: The Checklist ▶

The checklist is straightforward and easy to follow but doesn't give us any overall sense of where we're going. It is just a series of steps, so we really have no idea where we're headed until we get there. As long as all the steps are correct and we follow them in precise order, we should be fine. But without a broader context, if just one instruction is wrong or if we miss one step, we'll be lost without any way of getting back on course. (This is like the typical PowerPoint presentation.)

The map gives us a complete, overall view of the city (all the context in the world) and a clear path to follow through it. It contains far more detail than we need, but as long as we don't lose the map itself we should be able to find our way no matter where we are—as long as we *know* where on the map we are. (This is what I call a "where" picture, and we're going to see—and make—a lot of these.)

◀ Option 4: The Landmark Sketch

The landmark approach seems absurdly terse, but actually gives us the best view of where we're going. It leaves it entirely up to us to choose what twists and turns we make along the way, but, assuming that we're able to keep that goal in sight, also offers the best assurance that we won't get lost. (This is what we're going to call a "vision" picture, and we're going to use lots of these as well.)

Again, there is no right answer. It's how you react to the four options that gives this exercise its value. Your preference tells us a lot about yourself, about the way you like to solve problems, and about the best way for you to use this workbook.

If you liked option 1 (the narrative), this book will show you the incredible power that comes from integrating pictures with a spoken story. If you preferred option 2 (the checklist), this book will help you understand how to make your approach more compelling to and actionable for other people. If you liked options 3 and 4 (the map and the landmark), this book will help you get better at what you're already good at: seeing and explaining the world in pictures.

Now that I've been diplomatic, I want to share with you my preference. I believe without hesitation that for practical, business-oriented problem solving—when you and your team need to address something right in front of you, right now—the visual options (the map and the landmark sketch) are the way to go. The fact that we so rarely see these kinds of pictures used in business is why I wrote this book.

The rest of *Unfolding the Napkin* is about why I believe in such pictures, why it is always worth the effort to create them when approaching a problem, how to create the right picture, and how to do it quickly.

Before we start, a little prep work

WHO IS THIS BOOK FOR?

This book is for anyone who faces a business challenge of any sort, which means it's for anyone in business. It doesn't matter whether you think you can draw or not (don't worry, you can), or whether you're "visual" or not (don't worry, you are); if you're interested in improving your ability to look at problems, see patterns, imagine solutions, and show those solutions to others, this book is for you.

The visual-thinking spectrum includes everyone. (More about this spectrum on Day 1.)

WHAT ARE WE SIGNING UP FOR?
WHAT WILL WE LEARN?

Think of this as a workshop in which we'll work together to help you improve your ability to think and communicate visually. The core of this book is a universal visual-thinking, problem-solving tool kit. We'll be learning what each tool—think of them as a set of blades—is for and how to use each one, depending on the kind of problem we need to solve.

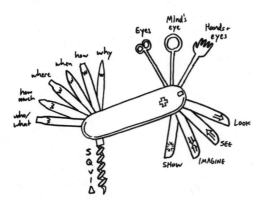

This is your visual-thinking tool kit. We'll be opening it up blade by blade.

HOW MUCH WILL WE COVER?

Lots. How much of it are you going to remember? I hope all of it. I am going to do everything possible to make sure everything makes complete sense and becomes second nature by the time we're done. I have a bad memory for long lists, processes, and sequences (in hindsight I realize that's one of the main reasons why I wrote this book). But that turns out to be true for almost everybody, so I'm confident that if I can use and remember everything in here, you can too.

WHERE SHOULD WE WORK?

Our classroom is anywhere you want it to be. All I suggest is that it be a place where you can sit quietly for a couple of hours at a time: your office, your cubicle, the library, or the kitchen table.

To help remove us from some of the distractions of our regular jobs, let's imagine that we're going to a private institute nestled among the low jungle hills of Tahiti, overlooking the turquoise South Pacific. The Visual Thinking Institute is on a lagoon, with a beach just down the hill that's close enough to see during our breaks. But this is just my own workshop-location fantasy; if you've got a better place to imagine yourself, please do.

The Visual Thinking Institute

▲

We'll meet at the the Visual Thinking Institute on Tahiti. But that's just me; you can imagine yourself anywhere you like.

WHEN DOES THE WORKSHOP HAPPEN?

If we were really working together face-to-face, this workshop would take place over four days. Since we're not, feel free to take any amount of time you need. No matter how much or little time you spend with this book, I do strongly recommend that you read through it in order, from Day 1 through Day 4. Each day's material builds directly on the previous day, and some concepts won't make nearly as much sense without understanding their predecessors.

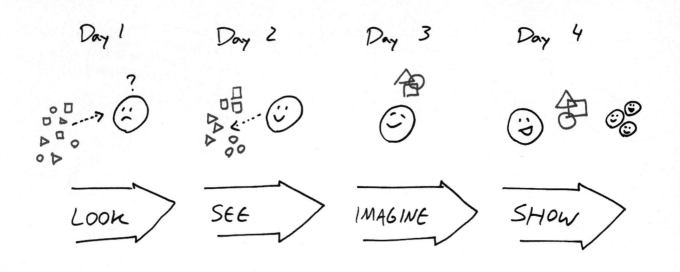

HOW DOES IT WORK?

The structure of the workshop is pretty simple: I'll introduce you to a visual-thinking idea, show you an example, work through a test sample with you, and then ask you to complete an example yourself. When we're done, you'll have solved dozens of problems with pictures—plenty to get a good sense of how pictures can be effectively used in any business situation.

▲
The four days' materials are sequential; they'll make the most sense if read in order.

▲
I'll introduce an idea then draw a sample picture. We'll review the picture, and then I'll turn it over to you to draw your own.

WHY SHOULD WE TAKE THE TIME TO GO THROUGH THIS?

Our world is becoming more information saturated and globalized, and communication is becoming more channelized, every day. Words simply are not enough anymore (they never were, but let's save that for another book). To discover truly breakthrough ideas, intuitively develop those ideas, and share those ideas effectively with others, we need pictures.

Pictures (sometimes with words)
work a lot better than just words.

WHAT YOU'LL NEED.

To complete the workshop, you'll need three things. Now is a good time to collect them.

1. **This book.** This book is your primary tool; please expect to draw in it and generally muck it up—that's what it's for.

2. **Something to draw with.** Please bring our own magic wand with you to the class. My favorites are a plain no. 2 pencil, a Sharpie, or a Pilot pen.

3. **Something to draw on.** There are three drawing surfaces we're going to talk about. Eventually we'll call them (a) "personal," (b) "participatory," and (c) "presentation," but for now we can think of them as simply S, M, and L. To get through this workbook, you're only going to need the personal, small one. That means paper or a personal whiteboard. The paper can be anything from a napkin to notebook paper. There are also places in this book where you can draw and several pages of blank scratch paper in the back. If you feel up to ordering a small personal whiteboard, I strongly recommend having one. You can buy one online or at any office supply store. They're often called "student lap boards" and cost anywhere from three dollars to twenty dollars. Any size is fine, and any brand will do.

With these items collected, we're good to go. See you at the workshop.

Welcome, and thank you for coming

want to thank you for inviting me into your work life for the next four days. I should tell you right up front that the ideas we're going to explore are not standard business fare. You won't find them taught in any business school, they're not written about in the *Economist*, and few CEOs will admit knowing anything about them. But they should.

Whatever you do for a living—whether you're a CEO yourself, or a project manager, an accountant, an engineer, a consultant, a designer, a teacher, a nurse, a postal carrier, a pilot, or a football player—the examples in this book can be applied to your work world. If you work in any organization or in any capacity where you have problems to resolve—in other words, if you're in business at all—you'll find tools in this book that will help you solve them.

In the two years since *The Back of the Napkin* was published, I've had the opportunity to share these ideas with leaders at an extraordinary range of businesses. I've talked with project managers at Boeing, scientists at Pfizer, programmers at Google, engineers at Microsoft, marketers at Wal-Mart, and policy makers in the U.S. Senate. I'll admit that in many cases I didn't know a lot about these people's work before I arrived. But in every case they saw something in visual problem solving that made sense, and they wanted to know more.

My point is this: regardless of the specifics of their individual businesses, I have a very simple proposition that I make to every one of these businesspeople, and I'd like to share that simple proposition with you. Here it is:

We can solve our problems with pictures.

That's it. That's what these next four days—and hopefully many more days throughout the rest of your career—will be about: solving our problems with pictures.

Now, I'll admit that if somebody got up in front of me and said, "Hey, we can solve our problems with pictures," I'd be dubious, especially these days when the problems we face seem so overwhelming. But if someone did say that to me, I'd like to believe I'd be on the ball enough to say, "Solving problems with pictures sounds fine, but please answer three questions: What problems are we talking about? What pictures are we talking about? And what people are we talking about—namely, who do you mean by 'we'?"

I have been asked all three, and they're good questions. So good that those three questions—what problems, what pictures, and what people—are the agenda of this workshop. Over the next four days, we're going to talk about a lot of interrelated ideas: the four unwritten rules of visual problem solving, the five focusing questions, the six ways of seeing—but we can summarize that whole workshop just by answering those three basic questions.

Before we get started answering the three questions, now is a good time to pull out your pen and drawing surface, whether whiteboard, notebook, napkin, or the back of this book. We're going to get started with writing and drawing right away. (You can also use the blank spaces in this book.)

1. What problems?

What problems can we solve with pictures? The simple answer is all of them. You name it: strategy problems, project-management problems, resource-allocation problems, political problems, financial problems—in fact any problem we can articulate at all we can articulate abundantly more clearly, *if not outright solve*, through the use of a picture.

In the space below, take three minutes to write down three business problems that have been on your mind lately. Don't put too much effort into this; it's just a warm-up drill and writing them down doesn't commit you to solving them. (Not yet, anyway.)

First, write down a small problem, one that's a low-grade bother and would be nice to solve but doesn't really impact your business one way or the other.

My small problem: I keep losing my favorite pens.

Your small problem: _____

Next, write down a medium-sized problem, one that has impact on either multiple people or multiple parts of your business but that doesn't yet threaten to explode.

My medium problem: I consistently fail to get my quarterly tax payments in on time.

Your medium problem: _____

Last, write down a big problem, one that is seriously threatening your business and that looks like it's going to take enormous effort to solve, if it can be solved at all.

My big problem: Every one of the businesses I work with is cutting back on spending. If this keeps up, my business may well run out of money within two years.

Your big problem: _____

2. What pictures?

Given that extraordinary array of problems, it only stands to reason that the pictures we'll use must be highly complex and require years of training to master, right? Wrong. The pictures we're talking about are simple. If you can draw a circle and a square, and an arrow connecting them, you can draw most of the pictures in this book. Add to that a smiley face and a stick figure, and we really do have the pieces for every problem-solving picture we'll *ever* need to create.

Can you draw me?

DRAWING DRILL: THE PICTURES WE NEED

In the space below, take a minute to draw a few of each of the shapes shown. It makes absolutely zero difference how good they look. Even if only you know what they're supposed to be, that's good enough.

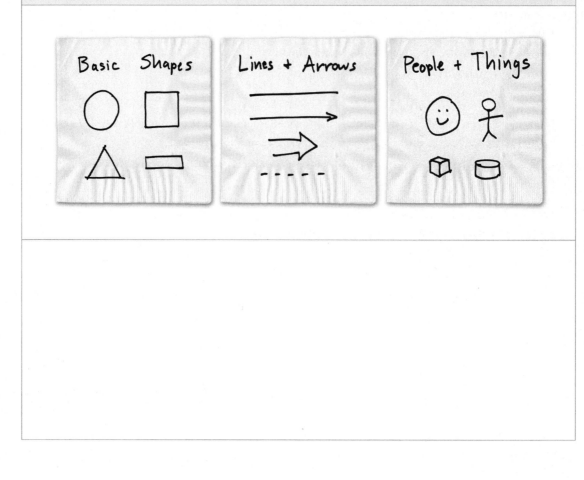

3. What people?

By drawing those simple shapes you've already answered the third question, haven't you? Who is going to create these pictures? That answer is also simple: we *all* are. Regardless of our belief in how visual we *aren't*, or regardless of how convinced we are that we *can't* draw, I guarantee that all of us can create excellent problem-solving pictures. I'm confident in saying this because all we're really talking about is doing something that we're already brilliant at: looking at the world, seeing patterns within it, imagining how to manipulate those patterns to create something different, and then showing those solutions to somebody else.

DRAWING DRILL: DRAW "ME"

Make a quick stick figure. Add something so that you know it's you: hair, glasses, a hat, clothes. We're going to use this stick figure again, so make sure it's simple enough for you to draw over again if you need to (you will).

How to spend our four days: our agenda

Our workshop agenda is based on the four simple steps in the visual-thinking process. Today we'll start by learning to look better—and we're not talking about our fashion sense. By "look better" we mean understanding how we go about visually collecting raw information about the world around us and how being aware of that process will automatically make us better visual problem solvers.

Tomorrow we'll shift to *seeing*, the process of recognizing patterns in the problems in front of us so that we can better solve them. On Day 3 we'll turn on our mind's eye in order to imagine ways to manipulate those patterns to create new outcomes, and on Day 4 we'll focus on showing our newly discovered ideas to other people.

Our four-day agenda: one day each to improve how we *look*, how we *see*, how we *imagine*, and how we *show*. ▶

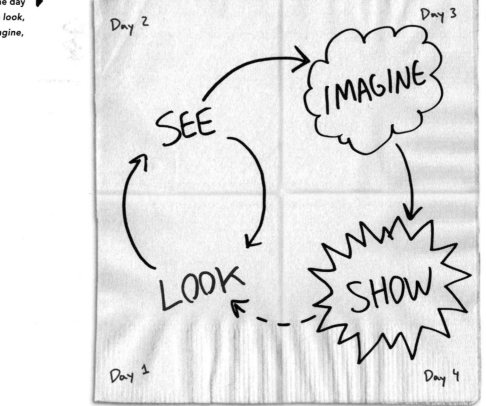

The unwritten rules of visual thinking

Each day one underlying theme will be central to everything we look at. I call these themes "the four unwritten rules of visual problem solving." I say "unwritten" for two reasons: First, because I've never seen them written down anywhere. Second, they are so important that I don't want us to simply write them down either; I want our brains to believe that we have literally picked up each one, rolled it around in our hands, looked at it, and thought about it and what it means. And I want it to be as if we physically stuck each of the rules together with the others. I want us to literally *draw* each rule.

Take another look at the problems we wrote down a few minutes ago.

How confident are you in your ability to solve them? For myself, I'm pretty confident I can find a way to solve the small one (lost pens), iffy about the medium (late taxes), and absolutely uncertain about the large (everybody's out of money). That's a marginal 50 percent success on my problem solving: not too good.

Let's look at it another way. In stating the problem (I lose pens; I'm late on my tax forms; I'm going to run out of money), I'm already alluding to a solution (no more lost pens, on-time tax forms, more money). That's good, because to "solve" something I have to know what a solution might look like.

But if I really intend to solve a problem, I have to know more about it: *What are the moving parts? Who are the players? How much time or money are we talking about? When does it need to be fixed for the fix to matter? How did it get this way to begin with?* Answering these kinds of questions—"framing" the problem so that it is solvable—takes real effort. And anything that takes effort in business takes money.

Fine: we all know that solving a business problem requires money. But how often do we think about how much it costs to just get the problem defined? That's the hard part, harder than actually solving it. Being able to map out the pieces of a problem means we understand the problem well enough to be able to solve it. It goes even further: if we can effectively map out the players, pieces, timing, and components of the problem, we've likely *already* mapped out the solution; we just need to learn to see it.

Question: in a business setting, who is going to get the money: the person who says, "I see a problem" or the person who says, "I see a problem, and it looks like *this*, and a solution might look like *that*? If I had to allocate my limited resources to solving my pen, tax, and money problems, I probably wouldn't give it to me: I haven't provided enough information to convince even myself that I know what the problems are about.

Here's Unwritten Rule 1 again, this time with its mercenary subtext:

Whoever is best able to describe the problem is the person most likely to solve it.

or

Whoever draws the best picture gets the money.

Unwritten Rule 1 is as simple as that. If you're truly serious about solving the problem—let's be blunt: *if you want to get funded*—the best way is to provide the clearest picture of what the problem looks like.

Let's look at the ultimate example.

Onward and upward, to the nation's capital

A few months before the 2008 presidential election, I was asked by Doug Steiger, the new policy director of the U.S. Senate Democratic Policy Committee, to come to Washington, D.C., to give a talk. The Democratic senatorial chiefs of staff were looking for ways to communicate complex concepts more clearly, and thought my ideas could be useful. I said yes and booked a flight to Washington.

◀ **Draw a line connecting San Francisco to Washington, D.C.***

✳

If you're wondering why I use a Southwest Airlines napkin for mapping flights, it's because Southwest—history's most successful airline—started on the back of a napkin. See *The Back of the Napkin* for the full story.

Before any talk, I always look for problem-solving pictures drawn directly from the industry I'll be addressing. In this case I had a hard time finding examples where napkin sketches played a significant political or policy role. I learned that George Washington was trained as a surveyor and loved to make maps, that JFK incessantly filled pages with doodles while making end-of-the-world decisions during the cold war, and that Ronald Reagan doodled in cabinet meetings. But I never found the great political "back of the napkin" story.

After the workshop with the staffers, Doug told me the story I'd been searching for. It turns out that back in 1974 an economist named Arthur Laffer had a meeting in a D.C. bar with two gentlemen from the GOP. When their talk turned to politics, Arthur pulled out his pen and started drawing—yes, you guessed it—on a cocktail napkin. He began by drawing a horizontal line, and as he did he said, "This axis represents the percent of citizens' income the government takes as taxes, from 0 percent to 100 percent."

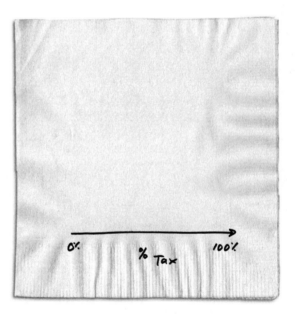

Then he drew a vertical line and said, "This axis represents the total amount of money the government collects, from none to a lot."

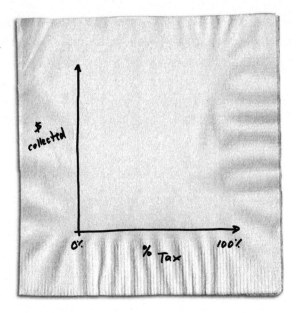

Then he drew a dot at the intersection of the two axes. "If the government takes 0 percent, it gets zero money." Drawing another dot on the horizontal line—this one way out at the far end—he continued, "And if the government takes 100 percent it *also* gets no money, because no one will work if they have to pay everything in taxes."

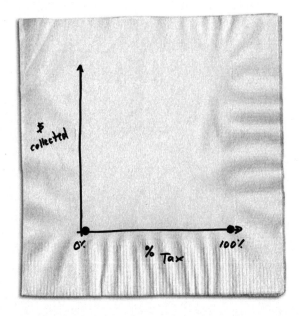

Connecting the dots, Laffer drew a line starting at the first zero point, curving up across the page—nearly reaching the top of the chart—then turning south to end back at the second zero point.

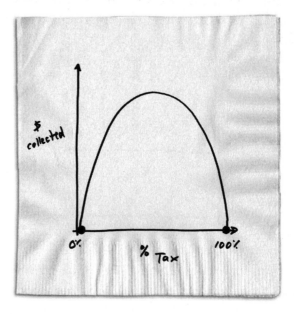

"What I think is that tax income follows a curve like this; zero at 0 percent, zero at 100 hundred percent, but up here," pointing to the apex of the curve high up on the chart, "at some point *reducing* the tax rate actually *increases* the amount the government collects."

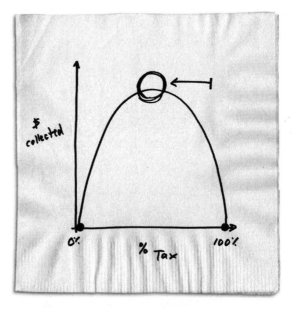

What Arthur drew became known as the Laffer curve, and it may have remained nothing more than an academic model were it not for the two men with him in that bar. They were then president Gerald Ford's chiefs of staff, Dick Cheney and Don Rumsfeld. They were so intrigued by the power of Arthur's napkin picture that they took it back to the White House and shared it with President Ford. Within a few short years, the Laffer curve became the basis of Ronald Reagan's supply-side economics, the essence of which maintains that reducing taxes—especially for the highest income earners—actually increases government revenue.

That simple napkin sketch—that little drawing, which so clearly diagramed out the *problem* of high taxation and the *solution* of supply-side economics—became the underlying image of American economic policy for the past thirty years.

And who says a napkin sketch can't be significant?

The person who draws the best picture gets the money.

Let's draw a picture.

Our first napkin sketch

For our next exercise we'll walk step-by-step through the creation of our own "back of the napkin" picture. The lessons we learn here will stay with us for every other picture we create.

On the napkin below, draw along to create your own visual problem-solving tool kit. This is the most important picture we'll draw during this entire workshop, so mark this page. Since this napkin sketch contains every visual-thinking tool in this book, we're going to refer back to it often.

Draw as we go along—and keep ▶
this page marked: we'll be back.

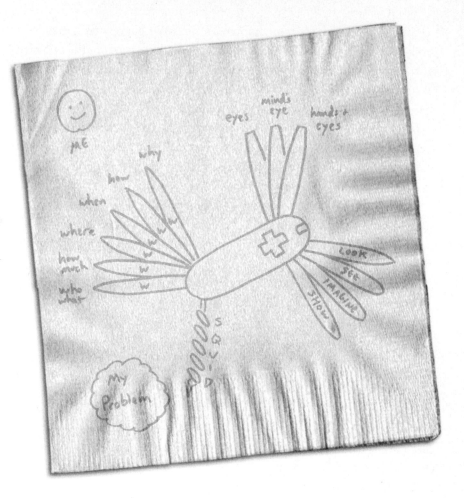

First—and this is the way we'll start every problem-solving picture—draw a circle and give it a name. In this case draw the circle in the upper left-hand corner of your napkin and call it "me." (For extra credit, make it look a little like you—here's a chance to use your stick figure from a while back.)

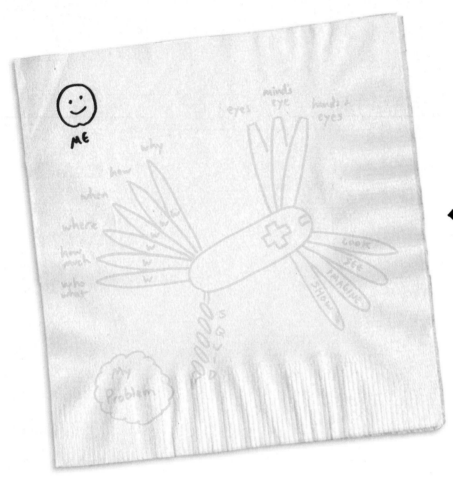

We start every picture by drawing a circle and giving it a name. In this case, call it "me."

The hardest line to draw in any picture is the first one. Looking at a blank canvas is intimidating—even if the canvas is just a napkin. By drawing a circle and giving it a name ("me," "you," "us," "the competition," "today," "tomorrow," "profit," "loss," "our product"—whatever comes to mind), we don't give ourselves a chance to get stuck. With our first circle in place, we've taken a shortcut past the usual "a picture is too hard to draw" roadblock.

Now draw another circle in the lower left corner. Make it a little bigger and kind of cloudy in shape. Call this one "my problem."

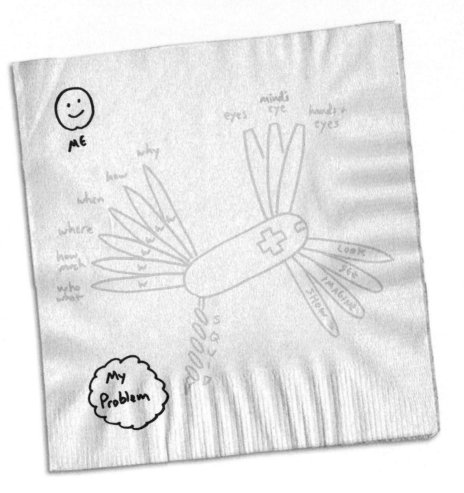

Draw a second circle—a lumpy one—and call it "my problem."

Believe it or not, with just those two circles drawn, our mind is already jumping. *What's next? What's the connection? Where are we going?* Our brain is firing off questions left and right—it can't help it; that's how it's hardwired to respond to visual input. After ten seconds of work, we are quite literally drawn into our own picture, and our mind is excitedly trying to imagine what's next.

To keep things interesting, let's now throw our brain a curve. Rather than connecting the two circles—which is what our mind really wants to do— we're going to add a third circle. Only this time make it elongated, kind of like a hot dog, and place it front and center on the napkin. This time, let's *not* give it a name.

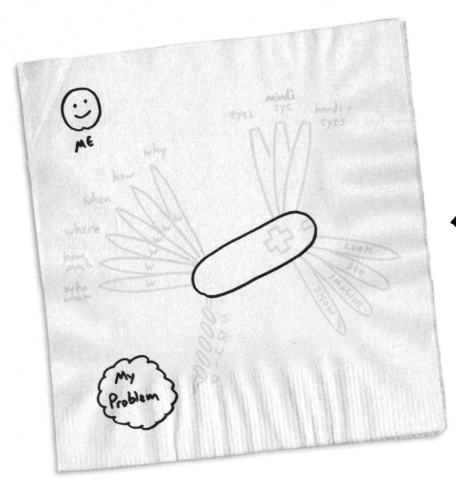

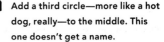
Add a third circle—more like a hot dog, really—to the middle. This one doesn't get a name.

Before we go on, here's the story on what we're drawing. When I started out as a consultant, it took me a long time to figure out what a consultant really does. After many years, I finally realized that a consultant's role is to be an on-demand problem solver: you're called into a business meeting, presented some data and questions, and expected to start solving the problem right then, whatever it might be. Hopefully you've got general familiarity with the problem *type*, but the specifics are almost always new.

I realized that what I really needed was a universal problem-solving tool kit, something I could take with me anywhere, so I could walk into a meeting, listen to what was being said, and then confidently select the right tool to begin the problem-solving process. That hot dog we just drew is our tool kit.

But rather than write all that, there's a better visual way to label our tool kit: let's just draw a small cross on it. You got it: the tool kit we're drawing is a virtual Swiss Army knife.

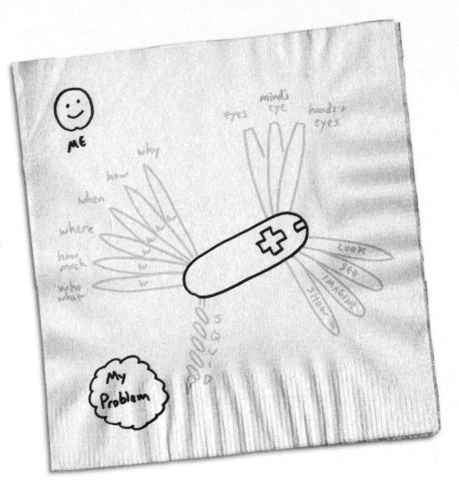

Aha! Our problem-solving tool kit is a virtual Swiss Army knife. ▶

If you're not familiar with the Swiss Army knife, it is a compact pocket knife that contains many blades, each slightly different and each tailored for a specific task—be it cutting a rope, sawing wood, scaling a fish, or opening a bottle of wine. For decades the Swiss Army knife has been the symbol of the take-anywhere, do-anything tool. Lore tells us that if you have a Swiss Army knife, you can build a log cabin, fight off a grizzly, and then relax and clean your fingernails. Heck, with a Swiss Army knife you can repair your airplane while still in flight—if only the TSA would let you take it aboard.

Point being, I wanted *that* tool—only I wanted mine to be equipped with the "blades" needed to approach a problem from a visual perspective. Carrying a pocket knife into a meeting obviously wouldn't do me any good; this had to be a mental tool kit, which meant it had to be comprehensive, memorable, and simple. The blades in our tool kit are therefore ordered in the unforgettable numeric sequence of three, four, five, six, with each numbered set representing a unique aspect of visual problem solving. Let's start with the first set of three.

The first three blades: our "built-in" tools

On the upper right side of the knife (the oblong), draw our first set of three blades. These represent the visual-thinking tools we are born with and which enable us to do all the sophisticated visual problem solving that follows. They are our eyes, our mind's eye, and our hand-eye coordination.

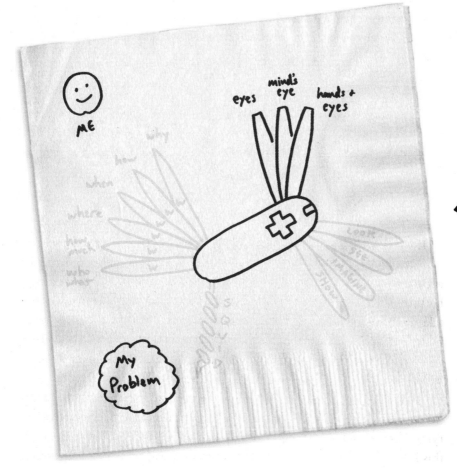

◄ Add the first three blades: our "built-in" visual-thinking tools.

We're not going to spend much time talking about these tools, except to say that we can all get a lot better at using them.

Think about this: nearly 75 percent of the neurons in our brain that process sensory information—smell, taste, touch, hearing, sight—are dedicated to vision. Maybe 75 percent sounds like a lot, but it turns out that human brains are notoriously bad at understanding percentages when they are spoken as words. So rather than just thinking about that number, let's *look* at it.

DRAWING DRILL: HOW MUCH IS 75 PERCENT, REALLY?

Imagine that these four people represent our entire mental capacity for processing the information coming in through our senses. Fill in how many of them are fully occupied only with what we *see*.

How many are left for everything else?

Here's another way of drawing this so that we can really see it. Fill in each of the squares below with one of the five icons. Fill them in according to the correct proportion of visual neurons to other sensory neurons.

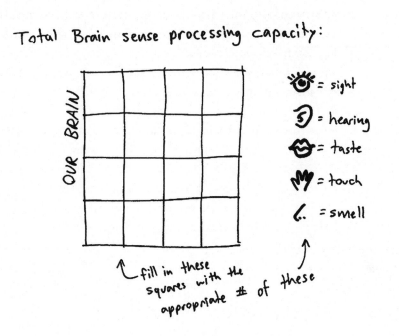

Total Brain sense processing capacity:

OUR BRAIN

👁 = sight
🖐 = hearing
👄 = taste
✋ = touch
👃 = smell

← fill in these squares with the appropriate # of these

You should end up with a chart like this:

Here's how much we've got:

👁 = sight
🖐 = hearing
👄 = taste
✋ = touch
👃 = smell

Which do you mostly use in your meetings?

Now look at that chart and ask yourself this: if that's how our mind is set up to process incoming information, how much of that "vision" do we usually take advantage of in our meetings?

The next time you or someone you know says, "I'm not visual," think about the chart you just drew. We are, all of us, visual—profoundly so. These first three blades remind us of what makes us that way: we've got eyes to bring visual information in, we've got a mind's eye in which to roll it all around and see if we can make something interesting with it, and we've got enough hand-eye coordination to be able to convey (even roughly) what we've come up with. These three blades remind us to use what we've already got: the magnificent visual-thinking engine that we were born with.

I set the bar for visual thinking really low: if you're visual enough to walk into a room and, without falling down, find a place to sit down, you are visual enough to understand everything else that we're going to talk about.

That's not to say we all process visual information exactly the same way, rely on vision the same way, or even think the same way; far from it. We all have our own talents and abilities, and we all look at the world in slightly different ways. What we're looking for here are the ways in which our unique approaches overlap.

Black, yellow, or red: which color is your pen?

In hundreds of business meetings, I've conducted a survey of how people approach visual problem solving. I've learned that these approaches fall into a distinct spectrum, from those of us who draw everything to those of us who hate to pick up a pen.

When it comes to visual problem solving, we all fall somewhere along this spectrum. ▶

1. The first group I call the Black Pen people. These are the people who can't wait to jump to the whiteboard and start drawing in heavy black pen two minutes after the meeting starts. They enjoy using visual metaphors and analogies to express ideas, and show great confidence in drawing simple images, both to summarize their ideas and then to help work through those ideas.

2. The second group I call the Yellow Pen people. These are the people who are happy to watch Black Pens working at the whiteboard but who require a little encouragement to go up and draw themselves—and they do need to go to the board because they see connections in the drawing the Black Pens often miss. That's why they are Yellow Pens: they're highlighters, adding to and riffing off the most compelling parts of someone else's starting sketch. Yellow Pen people always begin by saying, "I can't draw, but . . . ," but once they're going, they invariably uncover intriguing ideas and hidden connections.

3. The last group I call the Red Pen people. These are the quiet ones sitting in the back: the people becoming increasingly agitated as the Black Pens and Yellow Pens tear up the whiteboard. Careful, though: Red Pens aren't quiet because they don't get it; they're quiet because they think what they're seeing is a lot of crap. They're frustrated because the pictures emerging are so superficial that they're actually making the problem worse. The Red Pen is the type with the greatest grasp of the details and facts, so it's difficult for them to take simple drawings seriously—and they're often right: a lot of what's up on the board probably is crap. But it's visible, and that makes all the difference.

To create a true problem-solving picture, we need the participation of all three colors: the Black Pen gets the process started by putting something—however superficial—up for all to see. Then the Yellow Pen adds connections and insights, perhaps taking the entire picture in a new direction. Then—oops—we grind to a halt: how do we get the Red Pen's critical facts and details up on the board when the Red Pen is averse to simple pictures? There is a way: the Black Pen and Yellow Pen must get the Red Pen so pissed off that he or she finally bursts from the chair, erases half the picture, and then creates a new sketch from the ashes: one that likely comes the closest to really nailing *what's what*.

As you think about this, what color do you think your pen might be?

Let's find out.

WHICH COLOR IS YOUR PEN?

Select the single best answer for each of the questions below.

A. I'm in a brainstorming session in a conference room that has a big whiteboard. I want to
   1. Go to the board and start drawing circles and boxes.
   2. Go to the board and start writing categorized lists.
   3. Add something to clarify what's already up there.
   4. Forget the whiteboard—we've got work to do!
   5. I hate brainstorming sessions.

B. Someone hands me a pen and asks me to sketch out a particular idea. I:
   1. Ask for more pens—in at least three colors.
   2. Just start sketching and see what emerges.
   3. Say, "I can't draw, but . . . " and make something ugly.
   4. Write a few words then put boxes around them.
   5. Put the pen on the table and start talking.

C. Someone hands me a complex, multipage spreadsheet printout. I first:
   1. Glaze over and hope it will go away.
   2. Flip through and see if anything interesting pops out.
   3. Read across the column headers to identify categories.
   4. Look for common data results across multiple cells.
   5. Notice that OPEX variance to budget is down 2nd Qtr.

D. On my way home from a conference, I run into a colleague at the airport bar, and he or she asks me what I do. I:
   1. Grab a napkin and ask the waiter for a pen.
   2. Build an org chart with packs of sugar.
   3. Pull a PowerPoint page out of my carry-on.
   4. Say, "Better buy another round—this takes a while."
   5. Shift the conversation to something more interesting.

e. If I were an astronaut floating in space, the *first* thing I would do is
1. Take a deep breath and take in the whole view.
2. Pull out my camera.
3. Start describing what I see.
4. Close my eyes.
5. Find a way to get back into my spacecraft.

Now add up your total score to rate yourself.

Score	Calculated Pen Preference
5–9	Hand me the pen! (Black Pen)
10–14	I can't draw, but . . . (Yellow Pen)
15 +	I'm not visual. (Red Pen)

Where did you come in? Is it where you expected or wildly off? If wildly off, why do you think that might be? I've given this assessment hundreds of times, and the distribution almost always follows a typical bell curve. Roughly a quarter of any meeting population identifies itself as Black Pen, half identifies itself as Yellow Pen, and the remaining quarter sees itself as Red Pen. Something like this:

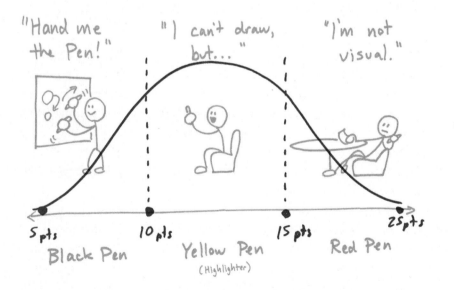

In most any meeting, the distribution follows a bell curve. Where do you sit?

I like this self-assessment exercise for many reasons: First, it gets us to think about our own natural problem-solving approach in a way we normally don't. Second, it shows us that there isn't a single way—even visually—to approach a given problem. Third, it reminds us of the breadth of possible ways there are to think about what we see and how we communicate it. Given this breadth of possibilities, why is it that 90 percent of business presentations look like this?

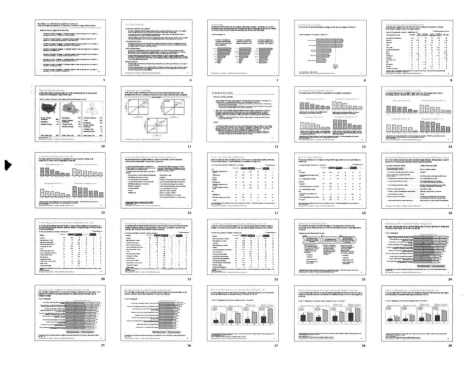

Given our extraordinary range of problem-solving approaches, why do most business presentations look like this?

Over the past three years, I've worked on a number of projects at Microsoft. Being mostly an Apple guy since 1984, I've found Redmond, Washington, to be nothing like the evil empire I'd expected: I've been surprised by how much I like the people and the processes there. That said—and at the risk of biting the hand that occasionally feeds me—I'm going to bash Power-Point now. No, let me rephrase that: I'm not going to bash the software; I'm going to bash all of us that use it.

There's nothing fundamentally wrong with PowerPoint; like any other piece of software, it is just a tool.* In the same way that we don't blame the hammer when the house falls down, we shouldn't blame PowerPoint when our communications fail. The problem is this: PowerPoint makes it too easy for us to become lazy. Because we can quickly plow through the creation of what might have once taken various modes of work (writing, typing,

✳

Unlike many in the anti-PowerPoint movement, I use the program all the time and find that it works well for me in creating simple, clean presentations. In fact, in Day 4 I'm going to share with you what I think is the greatest "live" drawing program ever. Want to guess what it is? PowerPoint.

sketching, outlines, index cards, Post-its, flip charts, etc.), we've come to expect that we ought to be able to bang out meaningful presentations in a couple of hours.

Guess what? We can't.

Well, we can, but the result is that we stop thinking along the way: we stop thinking about what we're really trying to say because it's so easy to say so much; we stop thinking about what is really important because it's so easy to throw in "just a couple more pages"; and, most dangerously, we stop thinking about what it's like to be on the other side of the presentation.

Every single time I go to a business conference or meeting, somebody fires up their PowerPoint bullet-list bonanza and starts their reading-from-the-screen drill, and everybody in the audience cringes. And yet—and this is what's scariest of all—when the next person from that freshly tortured audience gets up to give their talk, *they do exactly the same thing*. No wonder business problem solving and communication are out of whack: we know from our own direct experience that this approach doesn't work, and yet we go up and do the same thing ourselves when it's our turn. That's remarkably close to Einstein's definition of insanity: "Doing the same thing over and over again and expecting different results." We need another process for thinking, testing, and presenting ideas.

Luckily, we've got one: *the picture process*.

◀ At the midpoint of each day's session, we'll take a lunch break. This is a sign to you that we're about to make a fundamental shift in content—and that it's a good time to go back over anything that didn't make sense so far. This is also a sign to us that it's time to check e-mail, Facebook, and Twitter and to make sure we get something to eat.

Back from lunch:
we need a picture process

As visual thinking becomes a core part of our problem-solving and communicating approach, we need to change how we think about pictures. Those of us who are Black Pens can no longer rely on sudden inspiration each time we need to call up our visual-thinking engine; those of us who are Yellow Pens can no longer rely on someone else to get the picture started; those of us who are Red Pens can no longer sit in the back of the room and dismiss other people's too-simple sketches. What we need is a process that we can rely on to make visual thinking happen easily, effectively, and consistently.

Let's go back to our Swiss Army knife and draw the next four blades. They are called "look," "see," "imagine," and "show." Those four steps are our visual-thinking process.

Draw your next four blades ▶ and label them: "look," "see," "imagine," and "show." That's our process.

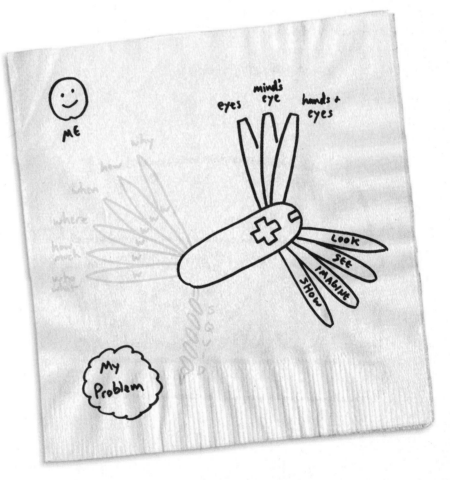

A quick hand of poker

In *The Back of the Napkin* I use the example of playing a hand of poker to introduce the steps in the visual-thinking process.

Here's why: when we play a game of cards, the first thing we have to do is *look* at the cards we've been dealt. Looking is the semi-passive process of scanning what's in front of us; after all, if we don't know what cards we have, we can't begin the game.

First, we have to *look* at our cards.

Turning our cards over and looking at them gets us started but isn't enough; we then have to be able to *see* the patterns contained within them. Seeing means actively recognizing what cards we have, what sets they represent, and whether we can see patterns emerging; in poker that means what numbers or faces appear on our cards, what suits they contain, and whether we have the beginnings of a winning combination.

Next, we have to *see* the ▶ patterns the cards contain.

Yet even seeing still isn't enough. Once we know what we have in our hand, we have to use our mind's eye to *imagine* what additional cards we'll need to complete our winning combination, imagine the chances of getting those cards in the remaining deals, and even try to imagine—based on what we can see—what's hidden in the other players' hands.

Third, we have to use our mind's ▶ eye to *imagine* what combos we can make.

Last, we have to *show*. Unless we're an incredible bluffer, the only way we can win the game is to show our combination of cards to everyone else still playing the game.

◀ Last, we have to *show* the pattern we've created in order to win the game.

I like this poker example for many reasons: it's a process that most people are somewhat familiar with, it's easy to imagine playing the game even without a deck of cards in front of us, and it makes the point that there are important differences between the steps, and that they need to take place in a specific order. There is a step that our eyes do without any conscious effort from us (looking), a step that requires our undivided attention to pattern and detail (seeing), a step that requires us to actively engage our mind's eye (imagining), and a final step that requires a bit of showmanship (showing).

As a linear progression, the visual thinking process looks like this:

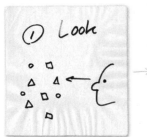 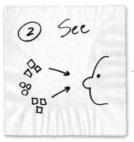 

What is out there?

What am I looking at?

What are the limits?

What do I see? Have I seen this before?

What patterns emerge?

What stands out? Is anything missing?

How can I manipulate these patterns?

Can I fill in the gaps?

Have I seen enough – or do I need to go back and look at more?

This is what I saw, and this is what I think it means.

Is this what I expected... or not?

When you look at this, do you see the same things?

▲

"Look," "see," "imagine," and "show": the process of visual thinking in four simple steps.

The beauty of this process is that it applies to almost everything we do that requires coordination of sight and action.

 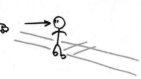  

LOOK SEE IMAGINE SHOW

▲

The four-step process applies to how we cross a street.

The four-step process applies to how we create a business document. ▶

LOOK SEE IMAGINE SHOW

The four-step process applies to how we explain a set of complex data. ▶

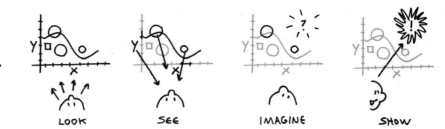

LOOK SEE IMAGINE SHOW

By making the steps distinct, we're able to think about each step, one at a time. That means we can take a process that appears mysterious—how is it that our eyes help us understand the world?—and get to know it well enough to practice, improve, and gain confidence in our ability to rely on it every time we face a problem.

Relying on this "look, see, imagine, show" process helps us take business problems apart in a consistent and repeatable way. It's almost as if it gives us a default script to run the next time something nasty looms ahead: (1) let me look at the problem; (2) aha! I see what's missing; (3) I can imagine what it will take to fix it; and (4) here, let me show you a solution.

It might not solve the problem right then, every time, but it gives us a starting point, which at the beginning is all we need.

Active looking

Once we get good at something (we've played poker a few times, learned to cross the street, etc.) we don't spend much time thinking about *how* we do it; we just do it. Since we've been using our eyes to look at things for our entire life, we don't think much about *how* we look. (Actually, we spend way too much time thinking about how we look, but that's not what I'm talking about here.)

◀ No, that's not the kind of "good looking" we're talking about.

 I don't think we are very good at looking; nowhere near as good as we could be, anyway. I spend a lot of pages in *The Back of the Napkin* explaining "how we look" because I believe we can look a whole lot better by understanding what's happening and then taking charge of the process. "Active looking" means hijacking our innate looking process in order to push it beyond our default passive mode. In the next examples we're going to put active looking into practice; we're going to seize a normally unconscious process and make it work for us on demand.

◀ Active looking is what we're aiming to improve.

THE STEPS OF ACTIVE LOOKING

Here are the essential steps in active looking:*

If you're interested in learning more about where these steps come from and why they're important, please refer to *The Back of the Napkin*, chapter 4. Here we're only going to show how to use them.

1. Collect all the data you can.
2. Lay it all out where you can really look at it.
3. Establish the underlying coordinates.
4. Map the data.
5. Draw a conclusion.

To practice active looking, we're going to use examples of data visualization. Before we begin I want to interject that solving problems with pictures (as we'll see in the following days) goes far beyond the synthesis and presentation of data. But raw data analysis is a good place to start, since that is essentially what our eyes do every time we look at the world around us. Think of these next exercises as warm-up drills, launching pads that will propel us to much higher levels of visual thinking in the coming days.

DATA DRILL: ACTIVE LOOKING, EXERCISE 1

Here is a set of data. Take sixty seconds to look it over, and as you do, try to note what you look at first, where your eyes shift, where they pause, and where they notice something interesting. Go ahead and scribble notes directly on the data if anything catches your eye.

Here is some data to look at:

Item	Unit	1978	1990	2007	growth
College Tuition: Public	Year	$688.00	$1,908.00	$6,185.00	9.0
College Tuition: Private	Year	$2,958.00	$9,340.00	$23,712.00	8.0
Prescription Drugs	Month	$11.37	$33.59	$68.26	6.0
New Single-Family Home	Home	$55,700.00	$122,900.00	$247,900.00	4.5
New Vehicle	Vehicle	$6,470.00	$15,900.00	$28,800.00	4.5
Unleaded gasoline	Gallon	$0.67	$1.16	$2.80	4.2
CPI (Urban: all items)	CPI-U	$65.20	$130.60	$207.30	3.2
Movie Ticket	Ticket	$2.34	$4.22	$6.88	2.9
First-Class Postage	Stamp	$0.15	$0.25	$0.42	2.8
Whole Milk	Gallon	$1.05	$2.27	$3.76	2.5
Grade-A Large Eggs	Dozen	$0.82	$1.01	$1.68	2.0
Air Travel: International	Mile	$7.49	$10.83	$12.71	1.7
Air Travel: Domestic	Mile	$8.49	$13.43	$12.98	1.5

Okay, now stop.

Before we start with the specific steps of active looking, what do you think we're looking at here? What do you think this data represents? Does any "problem" jump to mind that it might help solve? If not, don't worry: flat data like this is hard for most people to quickly "get"; after all, that's the point of this book. That's why we're going to make a picture of this data, so that we can *see* what it's all about.

Step 1: Collect all the data you can

In this case I've already collected the data for you. (Actually, it was collected by a national association whose name I'm not going to mention until we're done; part of what makes this exercise enlightening is figuring out which association.) If this were your own example, you'd be collecting data because there was a problem you were trying to solve or an insight you were hoping to see. For now, all we know is that I've dumped a bunch of data in front of you, and it's only by *actively looking* that we're going to be able to make much sense of it.

Step 2: Lay it all out where you can really look at it

I know from experience that many people—especially the most confident Black Pens—find it odd that our first full visual-thinking exercise starts with a spreadsheet. Good grief! What could be *less* visual than that? If that's what you're thinking, here's your scary answer:

As visual problem solvers, we must submit to our destiny: the spreadsheet is our friend. Not because it is a good presentation device (it's not: a spreadsheet sucks as a way to convey data in real time), and not because it is easy to use (it's not: the only people good at making data dance in spreadsheets are people who practice every day), but because a spreadsheet gives us a *single place* to lay everything out and look at it. When it comes to looking at information delivered in the form of data, the spreadsheet *is* our level playing field.

When we look at data it is easy for the good stuff to hide, and we can't look for connections and see patterns if we can't look at everything side by side. Think of the "garage sale" principle: the only guaranteed way to find our missing lamp shade is to sell everything in our garage. It's only when we get all our stuff out of boxes and closets and into the light of day that we're certain to find what we were looking for. The same holds true for data.

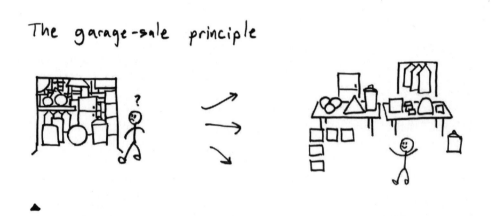

▲

The "garage sale" principle: the only way to see what we've got is to lay it all out in the sun: no more data hiding over here in Fig. 16b and other data cowering over there in appendix XIV. Lay it all flat out in the same spreadsheet, and only then can we look at what we really have.

Step 3: Establish the underlying coordinates

There it is: our table full of data. It's what we do with it now—how we look at it—that begins to give our data shape and meaning. Wait a minute: *give shape to data?* What the heck does that mean?

Every problem-solving picture is created from the raw materials found in a well-phrased question or a half-glimpsed idea, and most often that raw material arrives in the form of data. Giving shape to our data means the same as giving shape to any raw material: we need to first build a framework to hold it all together. That framework is our "underlying coordinate system."

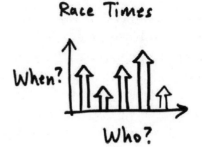

▲

Every picture has an underlying coordinate system to give it shape and structure. In a chart or map, that coordinate system is often the most prominent part of the entire picture.

Every picture has an underlying coordinate structure. In a chart or map, it is the north–south and east–west axes, usually the most prominent feature of the chart. In other types of pictures, it may be less visible, but it is always there, whether clearly labeled or not.

Looking back at our data table, a few coordinate systems seem like they could work. In most charts the x and y axes reflect an item and a quantity.* We have items, and we have several quantities to map them to: prices, years, and something called "growth," which appears to be a result of comparing the change in prices over those years.

✳

Make a note: if we think of "item" as "what" and "quantity" as "how much," this is our first overt mention of what we'll come to know as the 6×6 rule—the most important framework in this book.

Coordinates?

dates

Item	Unit	1978	1990	2007	growth
College Tuition: Public	Year	$888.00	$1,900.00	$6,185.00	9.0
College Tuition: Private	Year	$2,958.00	$9,340.00	$23,712.00	8.0
Prescription Drugs	Month	$11.37	$33.59	$68.26	6.0
New Single-Family Home	Home	$55,700.00	$122,900.00	$247,900.00	4.5
New Vehicle	Vehicle	$6,470.00	$15,900.00	$28,800.00	4.5
Unleaded gasoline	Gallon	$0.67	$1.16	$2.80	4.2
CPI (Urban: all items)	CPI-U	$65.20	$130.60	$207.30	3.2
Movie Ticket	Ticket	$2.34	$4.22	$6.88	2.9
First-Class Postage	Stamp	$0.15	$0.25	$0.42	2.8
Whole Milk	Gallon	$1.05	$2.27	$3.76	2.5
Grade-A Large Eggs	Dozen	$0.82	$1.01	$1.68	2.0
Air Travel: International	Mile	$7.49	$10.83	$12.71	1.7
Air Travel: Domestic	Mile	$8.49	$13.43	$12.98	1.5

Items

prices

result?

▲

Our data contains several possible coordinate options.

When looking at an unfamiliar set of data, the best way to identify a viable coordinate system is to simply wing it: pick a couple of possible coordinates and make a quick sketch of them. If they look like they might work, great; if not, just sketch up another.

Let's test a coordinate system mapping "item" to "year" to "price growth."

"Item" to "year" to "price growth" could be good model, except we'd have to make fourteen different charts to cover all the items. ▶

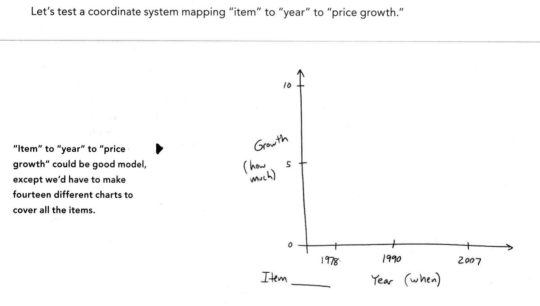

That looks like it might work as a way to contain all our data. Let's keep going. Now we have to think about how we'd map the items. Oops! Looking at this sketch, we see a problem: this coordinate system would support comparing the growth in price over time to one item, but we've got *fourteen* items. Using this coordinate system, we'd have to make fourteen different charts, and then somehow superimpose them. That doesn't look right, so let's try something else.

How about forgetting years as a coordinate element? After all, they're accounted for in the growth number already, since we see that that number has been calculated by comparing the 1978 price to the 2007 price for each item.

Item	Unit	1978	1990	2007	growth
College Tuition: Public	Year	$688.00	$1,908.00	$6,185.00	9.0
College Tuition: Private	Year	$2,958.00	$9,340.00	$23,712.00	8.0
Prescription Drugs	Month	$11.37	$33.59	$68.26	6.0
New Single-Family Home	Home	$55,700.00	$122,900.00	$247,900.00	4.5
New Vehicle	Vehicle	$6,470.00	$15,900.00	$28,800.00	4.5
Unleaded gasoline	Gallon	$0.67	$1.16	$2.80	4.2
CPI (Urban: all items)	CPI-U	$65.20	$130.60	$207.30	3.2
Movie Ticket	Ticket	$2.34	$4.22	$6.88	2.9
First-Class Postage	Stamp	$0.15	$0.25	$0.42	2.8
Whole Milk	Gallon	$1.05	$2.27	$3.76	2.5
Grade-A Large Eggs	Dozen	$0.82	$1.01	$1.68	2.0
Air Travel: International	Mile	$7.49	$10.83	$12.71	1.7
Air Travel: Domestic	Mile	$8.49	$13.43	$12.98	1.5

Maybe it's better to use these "normalized" numbers

▲

This last column of numbers looks interesting: it "normalizes" the prices to a standard scale while effectively accounting for the "year" data.

That leaves us with a coordinate system mapping just the items (but all of them) to their change in price over those years. In other words, let's keep growth on the vertical axis (growth seems like a vertical sort of measure, doesn't it? Growth = up) and list our items along the bottom.

Mapping all "items" to their "price growth" looks like a solid and workable coordinate system. ▶

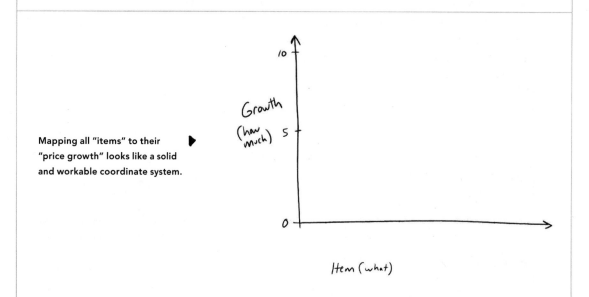

There, now we've got an underlying coordinate system in place that makes sense, accounts for the most important aspects of the data, and has a scale we can manage. It took trial and error to get here, but the good news is that the process forced us to actively look at the data and try to see what it was telling us. With a workable coordinate system in place, we no longer need to rely on the data to *tell* us anything; now we can get it to *show* us.

Step 4: Map in the data

The hard part is over. Now all we have to do is map in the data. Let's start by adding our items.

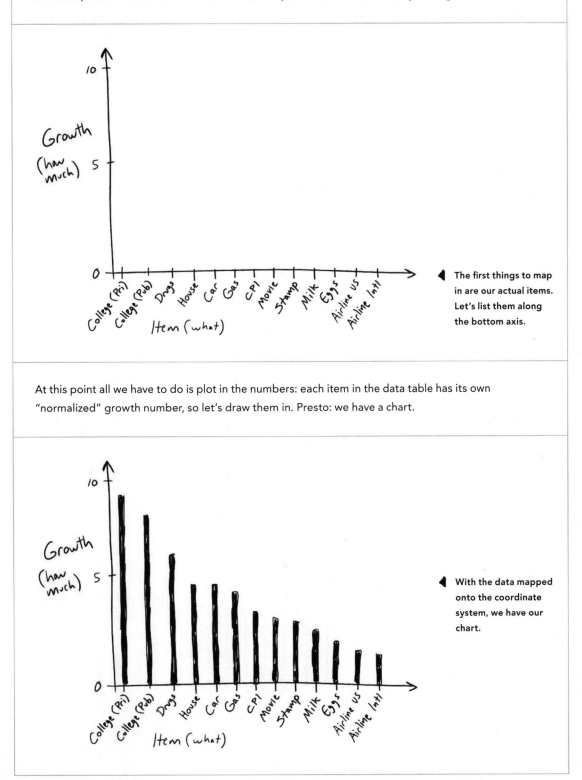

The first things to map in are our actual items. Let's list them along the bottom axis.

At this point all we have to do is plot in the numbers: each item in the data table has its own "normalized" growth number, so let's draw them in. Presto: we have a chart.

With the data mapped onto the coordinate system, we have our chart.

We're no longer scouring around the spreadsheet, trying to glean meaning from it; now we've got a chart that *shows* us the meaning. Now we can see what that data is all about and can even give our chart a title without anyone giving us a key; we figured that out just by actively looking at it.

Aha! This chart *shows* ▶ the relative increases in prices of a range of consumer items from 1978 to 2007. Just by looking at the finished table, we know exactly what the original data was all about. We don't have to ask anybody what to call our chart; the picture tells us.

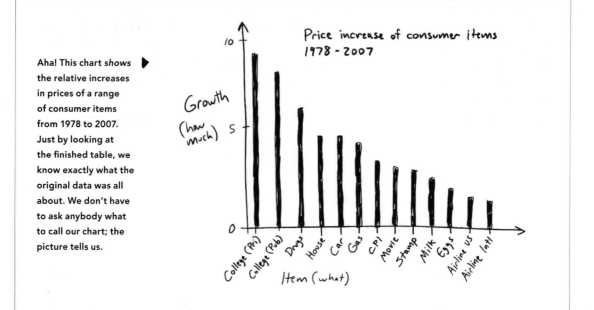

Step 5: Draw a conclusion

But wait: there's more. Now that we can see the data, can you guess who might have collected it?

Want to guess who col- ▶ **lected this data? What do you think they were trying to show?**

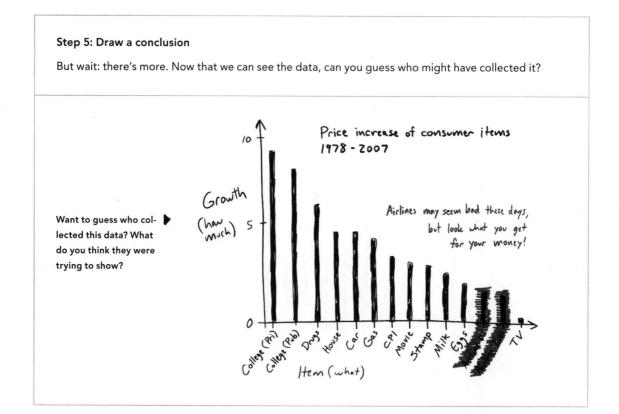

This data set comes from the Air Transport Association (ATA), America's largest airline trade association.* Since we started this morning with a Southwest napkin, I thought it made sense to look at airlines again.

If you've flown much during the last few years, I think you'll agree that airline travel has lost the romance it once had. I suspect that the ATA collected this data to support the case that, unpleasant as it may seem, airline travel is extraordinarily inexpensive compared to most other items we buy. Since 1978 the price of a college education has gone up almost ten times, the cost of a house five times, and postage stamps have almost tripled. Meanwhile, an airline flight (in the fastest, safest, and arguably most comfortable seat in history) hasn't even doubled.

Thanks active looking (and ATA), I find that a fascinating insight. Next time I'll be nicer to the flight attendant!

✻

Unless I indicate otherwise, all data sets in this book reflect actual numbers pulled from publically available and verified sources.

Look, Mom, no Excel!

I'm pretty sure this wasn't the first time you've made a chart, but I'm willing to bet it's the first time you've made one without turning on a computer.* Yes, we started with a spreadsheet produced on a PC, but we didn't use any spreadsheet charting tools to help us. Why not? Because letting the machine make the decisions about creating the coordinate system—the most critical part of creating a meaningful chart—denies us the ability to engage in active looking.

Yes, Excel and other spreadsheet applications have great chart-making functions, allowing us to generate and modify extensive tables accurately and quickly. But I hope you see from this exercise that the actual plotting of the data isn't the hard part. Sure we need the computers to make things line up nicely and to do calculations, but the hard part of making an insightful picture is figuring out what our data *might* be able to tell us if we compare the right coordinates. That is a trial-and-error process that demands active, and *intelligent*, looking. That is something no software can do; only we can.

✻

I've designed this entire book so that you can learn and do everything in it without any technology other than pen and paper. That's fully intentional, and I'll explain why, in detail, on our last day.

COMPARE:

Here is some data to look at:

Item	Unit	1978	1990	2007	growth
College Tuition: Public	Year	$688.00	$1,908.00	$6,185.00	9.0
College Tuition: Private	Year	$2,958.00	$9,340.00	$23,712.00	8.0
Prescription Drugs	Month	$11.37	$33.59	$68.26	6.0
New Single-Family Home	Home	$55,700.00	$122,900.00	$247,900.00	4.5
New Vehicle	Vehicle	$6,470.00	$15,900.00	$28,800.00	4.5
Unleaded gasoline	Gallon	$0.67	$1.16	$2.80	4.2
CPI (Urban: all items)	CPI-U	$65.20	$130.60	$207.30	3.2
Movie Ticket	Ticket	$2.34	$4.22	$6.88	2.9
First-Class Postage	Stamp	$0.15	$0.25	$0.42	2.8
Whole Milk	Gallon	$1.05	$2.27	$3.76	2.5
Grade-A Large Eggs	Dozen	$0.82	$1.01	$1.68	2.0
Air Travel: International	Mile	$7.49	$10.83	$12.71	1.7
Air Travel: Domestic	Mile	$8.49	$13.43	$12.98	1.5
Television	Unit	$101.80	$74.60	$16.90	0.2

▲
Active looking turns this . . .
. . . into this. I know which one I'd
rather have an analyst put in front
of me.

▶

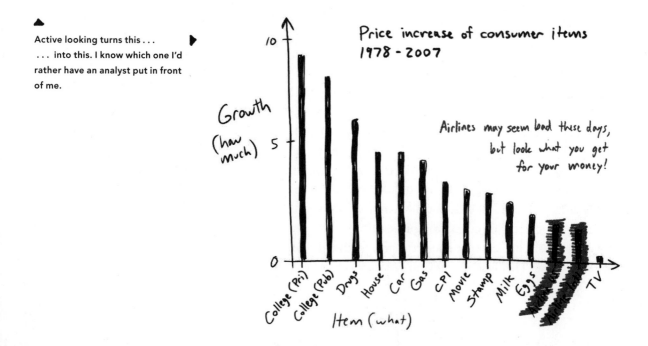

Price increase of consumer items
1978 – 2007

Airlines may seem bad these days,
but look what you get
for your money!

Growth (how much)

Item (what)

DATA DRILL: ACTIVE LOOKING, EXERCISE 2 (YOUR TURN)

I've walked you through an example of using active looking as a way to make a picture that makes sense of a pile of data. Now it's your turn. Run through the exact same drill we just did but using the data dump below. I'll provide you with lots of blank graph paper on the following pages, so feel free to try as many views as you like.

		Refrigeration	Heating	Vehicles	Electricity	Total CO2 output (Tonnes)
Argentina	CO2 output (Tonnes)	na	na	na	15,182	15,182
Brazil	CO2 output (Tonnes)	151,204	na	270	47,442	198,917
Canada	CO2 output (Tonnes)	25,732	42,300	4,721	100,661	173,414
China	CO2 output (Tonnes)	na	333,299	na	261,592	594,891
Costa Rica	CO2 output (Tonnes)	8,128	308	532	27,595	36,563
El Salvador	CO2 output (Tonnes)	3,639	27	113	19,212	22,990
Germany	CO2 output (Tonnes)	35,798	22,617	1,234	101,739	161,387
Guatemala	CO2 output (Tonnes)	4,225	601	na	31,951	36,777
Honduras	CO2 output (Tonnes)	3,639	95	143	6,141	10,018
Japan	CO2 output (Tonnes)	44,184	50,585	75	322,128	416,972
Mexico	CO2 output (Tonnes)	130,030	120,770	na	631,884	882,684
Nicaragua	CO2 output (Tonnes)	365	33	na	4,614	5,012
Puerto Rico	CO2 output (Tonnes)	86,341	1,051	953	86,823	175,168
United Kingdom	CO2 output (Tonnes)	285,095	132,755	na	624,900	1,042,750
United States	CO2 output (Tonnes)	1,553,698	828,478	1,391,152	11,590,829	15,364,157
	Total CO2 Output (Tonnes)	2,332,078	1,532,919	1,399,193	13,872,692	19,136,882

Shading signifies data which are either 1) not applicable, 2) outside of the defined boundary conditions of this inventory, or 3) unavailable.

Remember, your active looking steps are

1. Collect all the data you can (I've done this for you).
2. Lay it out where you can really look at it (I've done this too).
3. Establish the underlying coordinates.
4. Map the data.
5. Draw a conclusion.

Refer back to our previous drill as often as you need. Your goal here is to make sense of the data by making a picture.

- What do you think this data is about?
- Who do you think might have collected this data?
- Why might it be meaningful to them?
- Are there any conclusions you can make about what you looked at?

I'm not leaving you completely on your own on this one: I made my visual version of this data already; if you really get stuck, you'll find mine in the appendix, page 271.

This is our last exercise of the day. When you're done, we're going to take a step back and look one more time at the big picture, then head to the beach.

The dawning of the age of the napkin sketch

So far today we've seen examples of powerfully simple sketches expressing powerful ideas; we've created our own "back of the napkin" sketches; we've looked at data, seen patterns, imagined possibilities, and shown solutions; and we've only started. As we close out our first day, let's take a step back and look at the bigger picture; namely, why this all matters.

I believe we've reached a point in history where our ability to create and express ideas though simple pictures will soon be one of our most important business assets. To understand why, we're going to need to look both inside (inside our own minds and into cognitive science and neurobiology) and outside (outside our own businesses and into emerging social and global communities). That's a big spread, but we can do it in just a few minutes.

To see the power of pictures, we need to look inward and outward.

1. Pictures help us think

We know that we have many more neurons in our brains dedicated to vision than to any of our other senses, but the cognitive importance of pictures goes much deeper than that. Just scratching the surface of visual processing reveals an amazing array of ways that pictures help us think.

Because of the way our brains are wired, we do most of our verbal and analytic processing in the left hemisphere of our neocortex and most of our spatial and synthetic processing in the right hemisphere. This "split-brain" structure impacts how we think about and react to the world. When we talk and think in words, we generate ideas that are generally sequential, linear, and time based. When we draw and think in pictures, we generate ideas that are generally nonsequential (connected in multiple ways), spatial, and place based.

What's interesting is that while the left brain appears to be the sole domain of verbal processing, visual processing takes place all over the brain—right side and left, top and bottom, reptilian brain and neocortex. This means that thinking in pictures triggers more centers throughout our brain—and makes more connections across our brain—than thinking in words alone. Thinking simultaneously in words *and* pictures activates our whole brain—something that simply does not happen when we rely only on words alone.

Even the still dubious among us—the "I'm not visual" people—will probably admit that by drawing even a crude pictorial representation of our concepts while we verbally describe them, we, if nothing else, at least make our ideas available in more forms. From that perspective, including simple pictures in our verbal narrative adds much and diminishes nothing. You can rightly think of drawing as the definition of a "value-added" service.

2. Pictures make our brains happy

Our brains want to enjoy what they're doing. They want to learn, they want to see new things, they want to better understand old things, and above all they really, really want to figure stuff out. Pictures are pure excitement for our minds—especially when we see them drawn right in front of us. When we see the pieces of a picture come together, our brain starts to play mental fetch: it so much wants to "get" whatever we're being shown that it starts making connections, guessing, and anticipating what is likely to come next.

This is how we learned about the world as infants, long before any of our verbal processing capability was formed, and we're extremely good at it. Simple pictures actually encourage our brains to work the way they are hardwired to work, and so our brains get happy.

If you really want someone to get what you mean, remember it, and then *do* it: draw them a picture.

THE MACRO: EXTERNAL REASONS WHY WE NEED MORE PICTURES

We're just at the beginning of enormous and inevitable shifts that are going to take over business operations and communications. My belief in the emerging power of pictures is due to three megatrends evolving in the world of business: globalization, information overload, and staggering increases in the availability and speed of communications.

Staying on today's theme of airlines, I recently read an eye-opening article about Boeing's next-generation 787 airliner and how it is being built literally around the world. I can't think of a better illustration of total globalization: here you have arguably the most complex machine ever created, being assembled to tolerances of a millionth of an inch (and fractions of a penny) on thousands of assembly lines, in multiple countries, by people speaking dozens of languages. All this is possible only because the whole thing (the plane, the processes, the project) is mapped out and shared in countless pictures.

While we ourselves might not work on building airplanes, the fact is that we never know anymore what the native language of the members of our project teams might be; we may be working directly with people who don't speak our language at all.

As globalized supply chains and emerging markets flatten the world, as information overload becomes the status quo, and as communication channels proliferate, the complexity of business problems is only going to increase. There's more data out there, in more forms and languages, than ever before, and there's a greater need for businesspeople to make good decisions quickly and communicate their thinking to others.

As businesspeople, becoming comfortable with and confident in our visual abilities—improving our ability to look at complex information, see important patterns emerge, imagine new possibilities, and clearly show those discoveries to others—is going to become our most valuable asset.

Looking just a short time into the future, I believe we will see visual thinking significantly alter how business gets done in three ways. It will:

1. Help us make better decisions faster

I fully expect that within the next few years we will see most business analysis done in immersive graphic formats that allow for simultaneous manipulation of individual numbers and the visualization of complex interactions and outcomes. There are many companies out there now—like Tableau and BusinessObjects—building these tools, and even plain-Jane Excel has enormous potential given the graphics-processing capabilities of even the most basic business PCs.

2. Help us communicate our decisions (and visions) more effectively

As more businesspeople become more aware of the power of pictures as a communications tool, more and more tools (both software based and "real life") will become available to help create meaningful charts, diagrams, time lines, maps, flowcharts, etc., both alone and as teams. The great issue here is to first understand what we want to show and what our audience is willing to see, and only then to boot up the machines.

3. Help our teams execute those decisions more efficiently

Project managers have always known the power of a visual time line to ensure that everybody knows what they're supposed to be doing and when. The problem is that the PMs were usually the only ones who knew how to understand the charts they created: to their teams they looked like a wall of hieroglyphics. Several companies are now working on interactive, team-created time-line tools of incredible scalability. Such tools will allow for globally distributed groups to be in instant visual contact with their project and each other, monitoring whatever needs to be happening at the level of detail that matters most at that moment.

No matter how we look at our world and where it is going, pictures are going to matter more and more. Being better able to *look* is our starting point.

DAY 2:
SEEING

Welcome to Day 2

oday we're going to focus on improving the way we *see* the world around us, and that's a big step. Luckily, there is only one tool we need, and it's so powerful that once we understand it everything else in this book will fall into place.

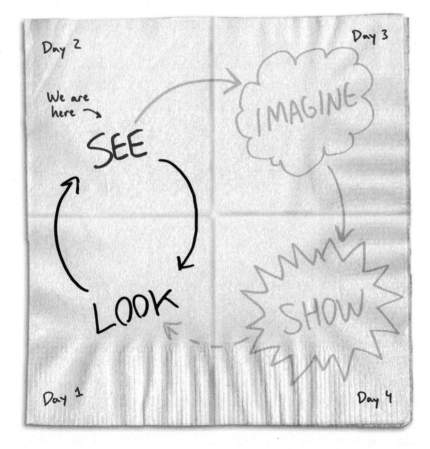

◀ Today we're going to focus on improving how we *see* the world around us.

UNWRITTEN RULE 2

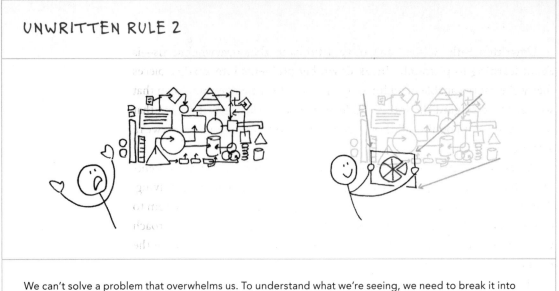

We can't solve a problem that overwhelms us. To understand what we're seeing, we need to break it into bite-size pieces.

✷

We get better at visually parsing complex systems once we become familiar with them. That's because the more times we see something, the more we learn about how to look at it and quickly find the elements that matter most.

†

Humans are the masters of pattern recognition. We have yet to come close to building a machine that can detect visual patterns as well as we can; perhaps that's because we really have no idea what makes our internal system so good at it.

Too much, too new, too fast = ▶
deer in the headlights.

Most of us are not very good at understanding big problems, especially complex problems with lots of moving parts.* As good as humans are at recognizing patterns,† it's hard for us to detect meaningful patterns when there are too many new, different, or unexpected things dancing in front of our eyes. It's that "deer in the headlights" look: all of a sudden something big and nasty is barreling right at us, and our brain seizes up. "Gee . . . ," we might say to ourselves, "what an interesting car." *Bam!*

To compensate for the visual complexity of the world around us, our vision system has evolved to help rapidly detect the most important parts of whatever we see. It does this by constantly divvying up whatever is in our field of view into sets of discrete elements. We address these elements individually before mentally putting them together and tackling the whole monster. The system fails when it can't quickly identify those individual elements.

Unwritten Rule 2—we can't solve a problem that overwhelms us—is about learning to pictorially break down big problems into smaller pieces that we're more capable of addressing quickly. This rule does not mean that we need to disregard the forest and focus solely on the trees: it means that only when we recognize all those green things *are* trees do we know we're looking at a forest.

Yesterday's exercise in active looking showed us how to hijack elements of our built-in scanning system and use them for conscious problem solving. Today's tools show us how to use our built-in pattern recognition system to help us pictorially break up problems into bite-sized pieces. This approach works so well because it aligns directly with how we're hardwired see the world.

Here's Unwritten Rule 2 again, this time with its tactical subtext:

We can't solve a problem that overwhelms us. To understand what we're seeing, we need to break it into bite-size pieces.

or

There are only six kinds of problems out there, and they all share the same six pieces; identify those and your problem is half solved.

Unwritten Rule 2 is that simple: if you want to solve a big, nasty problem (or even a small, innocent one) let your internal "seeing" system go to work on it. Our eyes love to find patterns on their own; with a little conscious guidance we can help *them* help *us* make sense of anything we see.

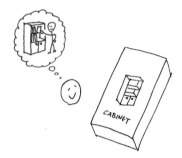

Let's look at examples.

McKinsey and the Lego blocks: the power of "what"

If you ever find yourself sitting around a campfire with a bunch of consultants—a scary enough concept itself—here's a scary story you can tell to give them nightmares at bedtime.

In the world of on-demand problem solving, there are consultants and then there are consultants, and then there is McKinsey & Company. When golfers think golf, they think Tiger Woods;* when serious drivers think cars, they think Ferrari. When consultants think consulting, they think McKinsey.

McKinsey consultants think the same thing, which makes them arrogant, intolerant, and very, very good at what they do. In other words, nothing is more terrifying to a non-McKinsey consultant than to have to pitch to McKinsey.

A few years ago, I was working at a consulting company (not McKinsey) when Shane, our director of sales, received a "Request for Proposal" from McKinsey, asking *us* to pitch *it* about building an Internet system. Shane and I suspected that we'd received the RFP by mistake, because it was inconceivable that McKinsey would hire us to do anything.

Shane called and established that, indeed, McKinsey really did want us to respond. The director of IT had heard that we were experts at "knowledge management portals" and wanted us to make a pitch to the firm about what we had to offer.

Our company had built many such systems—in those days everything was called a "portal"—so we knew that everyone had a different idea of what "portal" meant. We also knew that it was so hard to get people to agree on the meaning of "portal" that we'd spend forty-five minutes of our one-hour pitch just establishing with McKinsey *what* a portal was—leaving only fifteen minutes to sell our approach.

One evening, a couple of days before the McKinsey meeting, I was playing with Lego blocks with my daughter. Since we were building things with the little plastic bricks, she asked me what I built at work. I said, "Portals" and proceeded to explain the concept using the colored bricks, which turned out to be easier than any other way I'd ever tried to explain a portal to anyone. That's when it occurred to me that we could do the same at McKinsey: use a drawing of Lego to explain our portal concept.

◀ What if we explained a portal using Lego bricks?

I told Shane about the idea, and we agreed that since we were probably going to lose the McKinsey pitch no matter what we did, we might as well try something different.

 Corporate Communications

 Business Applications

 Information Aggregation

Knowledge Management

 Collaboration Tools

 Business Dashboards

◀ Was this really a good idea? After all, this is McKinsey we're talking about.

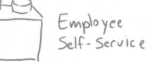 Employee Self-Service

Community Development

The morning of the pitch, I awoke terrified. "What are we doing?" I thought. "Are we actually going into a meeting with the senior leadership of McKinsey with pictures of Lego?" But it was too late: Shane and I agreed that the show must go on, so we headed up to the McKinsey HQ, our drawings of Lego bricks prominently displayed throughout our PowerPoint presentation.

It turned out that we didn't need to worry. Ten minutes into the meeting the senior technical officer from McKinsey said, "That's the best description of a portal I've ever seen. You've won the project. Let's talk about the details."

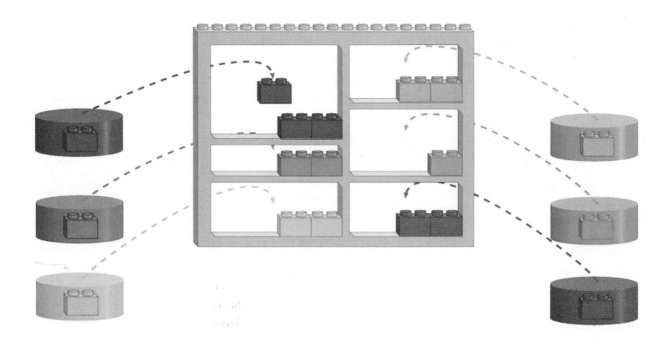

▲

A portal does make sense represented with toy bricks though.

I've since realized what happened in the McKinsey conference room: when we used toy bricks to demonstrate what a portal was, we visually broke the "problem" down into nothing more than a simple "what." We didn't talk about how much content it could contain, or when consultants might use it, or how it would technically work, or even why McKinsey might need it. We started the meeting with a simple visual that explained exactly *what* we were talking about, and everyone got it—and we got the job.

How can we see a problem?

If we're going to use our innate "seeing" system in order to make sense of the world we see, we need to understand a little bit about how vision works, especially how our vision system guides us through the real world.

Because we live in a three-dimensional, physical world, our vision system has evolved to become really good at understanding three-dimensional space. It does this by breaking our environment down into a three-dimensional coordinate system of length, height, and depth.

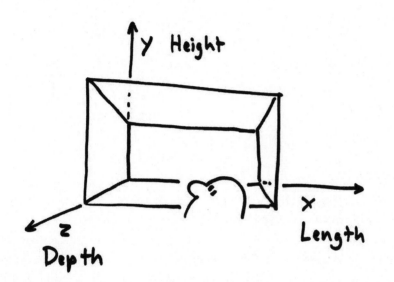

◀ We live in a three-dimensional world.

We understand most of the physical world around us by relying on our vision system to build *inside our heads* a mental model of the world *out there*. We navigate a room by using the three-dimensional model our eyes have created.

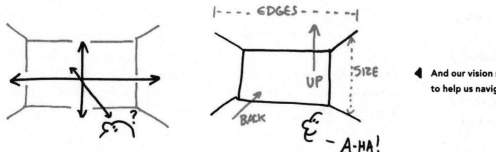

◀ And our vision system has evolved to help us navigate it.

But the business problems we face today aren't about getting around in space: they're about seeing lots of moving pieces—sometimes physical things like people, money, or products, but more often abstract things like concepts, ideas, language, or rules—and then building a mental model of them so we can understand the connections between the pieces.

In order to see problems as readily as we see the world around us, we need a coordinate system that can account for more than just the physical dimensions and position of concrete things.

What kind of coordinate system helps us see a problem? ▶

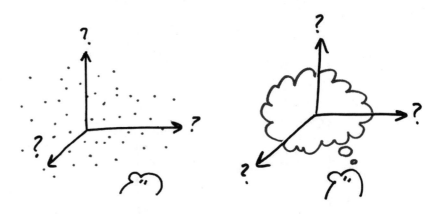

The good news is that we already have the coordinate system we need—and we're already as comfortable with it as we are with length, height, and depth. In fact, the coordinate system we're going to use for "seeing" problems is as innate as the three-dimensional model our brain uses for seeing space; it just happens to have a few more dimensions—six, in fact. But don't worry if that seems like a lot: again, we all already know them: "who and what," "how much," "where," "when," "how," and "why."

The 6-W coordinate system: this is how we're going to train ourselves to see problems. ▶

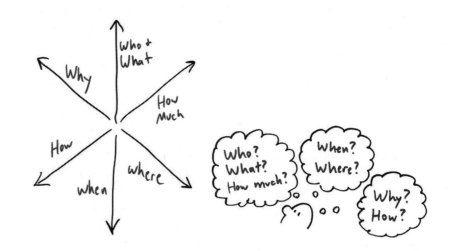

Our next six blades

Before we go into detail about this "six-dimensional model" of seeing, let's nail down the six coordinates in our problem-solving tool kit. Pull out the Swiss Army knife from yesterday and draw these as the next six blades. (We're going to save the corkscrew for tomorrow.) Label them as follows:

W#1: "who and what"
W#2: "how much"
W#3: "where"
W#4: "when"
W#5: "how"
W#6: "why"

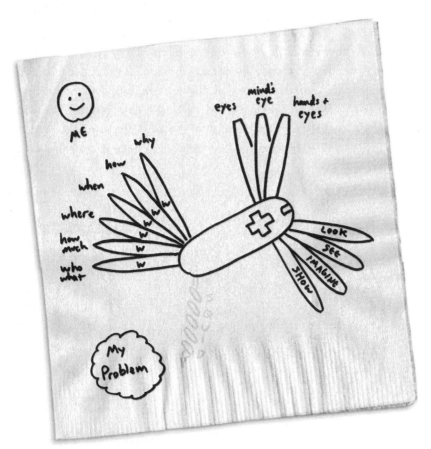

◀ Add the 6-W blade: "who and what," "how much," "where," "when," "how," and "why."

Heads or tails? Either way, we win

Our Good Luck coin:

This rule is like a lucky "don't ▶
panic" coin: no matter how
we flip it, we win.

Think of Unwritten Rule 2 as a good-luck coin. The two sides of the coin represent two different ways to understand the rule. The first side tells us that there are only six kinds of business problems: if we can identify the kind of problem we're facing, we'll be in a great position to see solutions. The second side reminds us that every problem is composed of the same six elemental pieces: if we can identify them, we'll already have our problem half solved.

Six problems, six pieces: both ▶
sides remind us how easy it is
to *see* our problem in a way
that immediately helps us
begin to solve it.

Heads

Only so many
problems.

Tails

Only so many
pieces.

Heads: what kind of problem do we see?

"Wait a minute," you might say, "the whole world in just six problems? That's not the business world I live in: I can think of a lot more than six problems I have to deal with."

Of course there are an infinite number of problems out there, just like there are an infinite number of solutions. But we don't have infinite mental processing capabilities to account for them all. To make sense of the world and manage our way through the tough parts, our brain creates simple working models to guide us, and that's what we're talking about here: a simple underlying framework for managing big-picture problem solving. It's not a perfect model, but as we'll see, it works.

Heads

Only so many problems.

◀ Heads: there are only six kinds of problems out there. (You'll have to trust me on this for the moment.)

Here are the six types of business problems we're likely to encounter.

The six problem types

1. **"Who and what" problems.** Challenges that relate to things, people and roles, such as:

   - Who are all the players in this problem, and what do they do?
   - What makes this thing different from that one? Which do I prefer?
   - Who is in charge and who else is involved? Where does responsibility lie?

	2. **"How much" problems.** Challenges that involve measuring and counting:
	• Do we have enough of X to last as long as we need?
	• How much do we need to keep going? If we increase this, can we decrease that?
	3. **"When" problems.** Challenges that relate to scheduling and timing, like:
	• What comes first, and what comes next?
	• What do we need to do, and when, to get everything done on time?
	4. **"Where" problems.** Challenges that relate to how things fit together and work together:
	• Where do all these pieces fit? What's most important and what matters less?
	• Where are we going now? Are we headed in the right direction, or should we be moving elsewhere?
	5. **"How" problems.** Challenges that relate to how things influence one another:
	• What will happen if we do this? What about that?
	• Can we alter the outcomes of a situation by altering our actions?
	6. **"Why" problems.** Challenges that relate to seeing the big picture:
	• What are we really doing and why? Is it the right thing, or should we be doing something different?
	• If we need to change, what are our options? How can we decide which of those options are best?

PROBLEM IDENTIFICATION DRILL:
WHERE DO I WHEN, AND HOW DO I WHAT?

Look over the following statements and see which of the six problem types best describes each. As we'll see later, all problems are combinations of the six to varying degrees, so our goal here is to find the best possible starting point.

A. I'm a project manager, and I have to make sure we launch our new product this quarter.

☐ who/what ☐ how much ☐ where ☐ when ☐ how ☐ why

B. I'm on the business-strategy team, and we're struggling to determine the best direction for our company.

☐ who/what ☐ how much ☐ where ☐ when ☐ how ☐ why

C. I'm on the marketing team, and we think we've identified the best market segment for our new service but aren't entirely sure.

☐ who/what ☐ how much ☐ where ☐ when ☐ how ☐ why

D. I'm a software programmer, and I can't nail down what these two interface buttons are supposed to do.

☐ who/what ☐ how much ☐ where ☐ when ☐ how ☐ why

E. I'm in HR and have been told to plan for layoffs, but I don't know what to tell people.

☐ who/what ☐ how much ☐ where ☐ when ☐ how ☐ why

F. I'm a financial analyst, and I need to justify my cost-cutting recommendations.

☐ who/what ☐ how much ☐ where ☐ when ☐ how ☐ why

G. I'm a consultant, and my client wants to know what it can do to increase market share.

☐ who/what ☐ how much ☐ where ☐ when ☐ how ☐ why

H. I'm the CEO, and I want to let everyone know about some big changes we're going to make around here.

☐ who/what ☐ how much ☐ where ☐ when ☐ how ☐ why

Again, there are no "absolutely right" answers here, only good starting points, which, as we'll see later this afternoon, is all we really need.

Why do some pictures work and others fail?

For years, when I was first helping people solve problems with pictures, I wondered why it was that certain types of pictures seemed to make everything clearer while others seemed to make everything worse. It didn't come from the quality of the picture: just because the people in Diagram A were drawn more accurately than the stick figures in Diagram B didn't make A work any better. Nor did it have to do with complexity: I saw exceedingly simple sketches that confused people more than complicated diagrams, and vice versa.

I wondered if there might be something in the way pictures are drawn that either aligns them with the way our brains work or causes a mashing of mental gears. In a combination of vision-science textbooks and conference-room experiences, I found an answer that made it all click.

I call it the 6×6 model, and here it is.

There are six ways we *see* a problem, and there are six ways we *show* it.

The six ways of seeing

Recent findings in neurobiology and vision science tell us that as we look at the world around us, our vision system divides everything up into discrete types of visual information. These are processed via different "vision pathways," including (among others) the "where" pathway, the "what" pathway, and the "how" pathway. Those simple names are good descriptions for what each does: the "where" pathway tells us where everything is, the "what" pathway identifies all the objects we see, and the "how" pathway helps us understand the interactions of objects (and ourselves) through changes in their quality, number, or position.

While vision is so extraordinarily subtle and complex that we are only beginning to understand the most basic elements of how it works, these pathways give clues as to how the pieces fit together. The picture that is emerging looks like this:

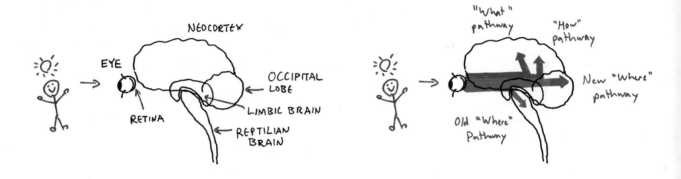

As the world enters our eyes, in the form of light striking our retinas and triggering electrical signals, we separate the signals into distinct pathways for initial processing, and then stitch all the results together to create the big picture we see in our mind's eye. Let me show you what I mean.

▲

The visual signal enters through our eyes and gets broken up into different "pathways" for different kinds of processing.

DRAWING DRILL: THE BIRD-DOG EXERCISE

Take a few minutes to look at these two pictures; then answer the questions that follow.

A:

B:

Do you see any differences between the two pictures? List two or three.

How are these pictures related?

How much time do you think has passed between A and B?

According to these pictures, which travels faster: a plane, a boat, or a baby buggy?

How do you know that? What in the picture tells you that?

Some of the characters in both pictures are identical, some are the same but have moved, and some look different. Do you think it is the same dog in both pictures?

Now look at this picture and compare it to the previous two (flip back and forth several times and note whatever differences you see).

C:

Several more things have changed. Can you spot two to three additional differences?

Something dramatic is taking place; do you see it?

Why do you think it is happening?

What do you think is going to happen next? Why?

Look at this last picture.

D:

What is the relationship of this picture to the previous one?

Does it take place before or after? What makes you think so?

Here's the rationale for what we just did: with just a few simple sketches, we've created an accurate model of how we see the world. This isn't just a model for how we see black-and-white sketches of simple stick figures; it's how we see every time we open our eyes.

DRAWING DRILL: THE 6x6 PROBLEM-SOLVING NAPKIN

To summarize what's going on, let's create another napkin sketch, just like we've been doing with our Swiss Army drawing. Only this time, instead of showing the whole knife we're only going to focus on the set of 6-W blades.

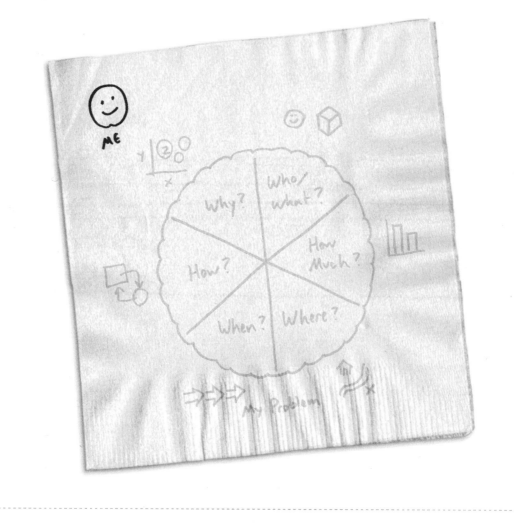

We start just like we do with every problem-solving picture: draw a circle (upper left, as before) and give it a name ("me", as before). We're going to draw our second circle again and even give it the same name ("my problem"), but this time put it in the center and make it big enough to fill most of the napkin. We can think of this big circle as a pizza: my problem pizza.

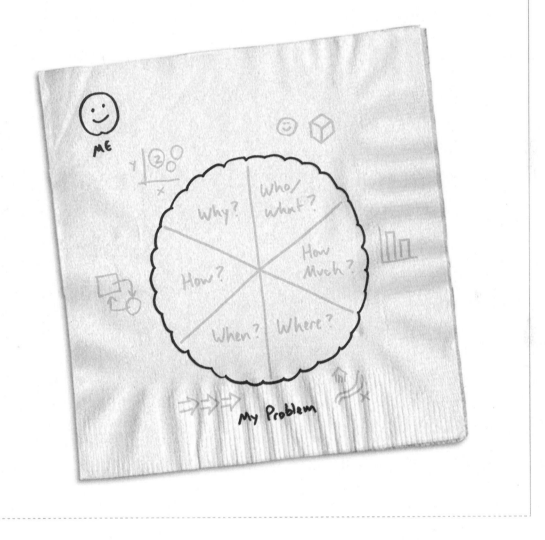

Now we've got a big problem in front of us. We don't want to be overwhelmed, so let's divide it up into six slices and label them one by one as we look at them.

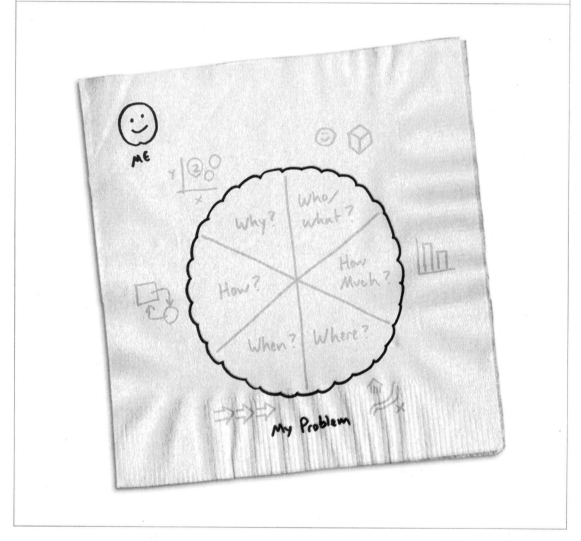

Slice 1: "who and what"

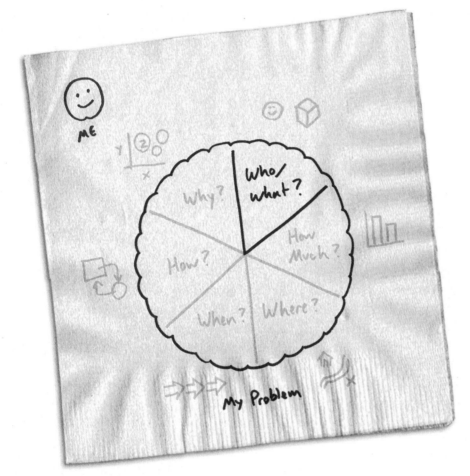

Let's start with the "who and what" slice. In our built-in vision system, the "who and what" pathway is responsible for singling out the people and objects we see, comparing them to known objects in our mental database, recognizing them, identifying them, and classifying them.

▲
Our "who and what" pathway
sees birds, a plane, people at a
table, a girl with a dog—all the
physical objects that make up the
world in front of us.

The "who and what" pathway does this by processing those parts of the incoming signal that contain identity information: shape (determined by edges, forms, and shadows), size and proportion (to distinguish one thing from another), color, texture, and the millions of other minute identification marks that make all the people and things we know unique.

The "who and what" pathway is so busy just figuring out who is who and what is what that is doesn't care how many people or objects there are or where they're located; it just keeps barreling along picking out stuff and figuring out what it is.*

✸
As we'll see when we start
making pictures using this
6×6 model, "who and what"
are going to be the basic
building blocks of every
picture. In fact, we've already
seen this in action: when we
start a picture by drawing a
circle and giving it a name
(which should be every time),
all we're doing is giving our
brain the first "who and what"
to play with.

Slice 2: "how much"

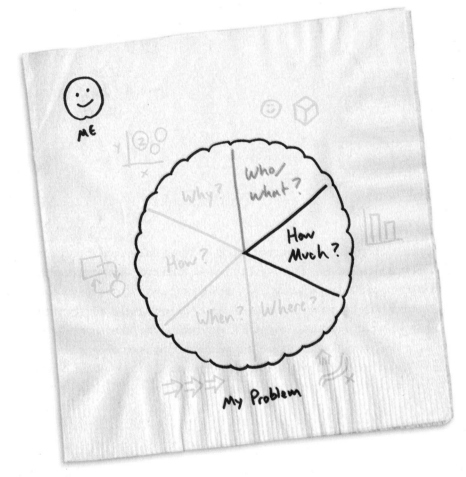

Meanwhile, over in Slice 2 something entirely different is happening. As Slice 1 identifies what things are, "how much" is measuring quantities: How many of these things, how many of those? Are there more of these or less of those? That looks like a few; that looks like a lot.

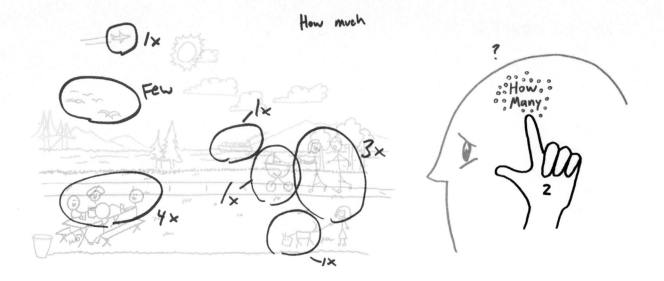

▲

Our "how much" slice detects the numbers of objects we see: four of those, three of these, a lot of the others.

Usually, Slice 2 is so busy quantifying everything that it's really only accurate for instant measures of up to five things. Beyond five, "how much" either just wings it and makes a best guess (several, lots, zillions), or it slows down to count, which it would rather not do since that brings the whole process grinding to a halt and puts "how much" way behind the other slices.

As before, Slice 2 couldn't care less *what* anything is or *where* it is; "how much" has its hands full just running the numbers.

Slice 3: "where"

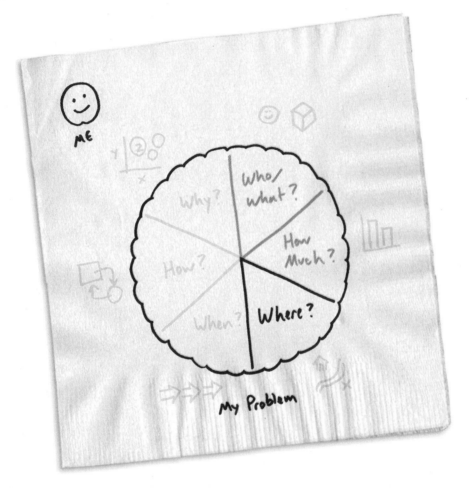

While Slices 1 and 2 are busy identifying and counting, Slice 3, the "where" pathway, is noticing and keeping track of *where* everything is, both in relation to everything else that we can see and in relation to us.* Slice 3 does this by processing those parts of the incoming visual signal that contain clues about location, such as relative size (for determining distance), light and shadow (for determining orientation), and edge overlap (for deducing what is in front of what.)

✱

Slice 3 is the great-grandma of vision. While Slice 1 got started identifying "who and what" about 30 million years ago, the old "where" pathway has been around closer to 300 million years. Needless to say, we're extremely good at seeing where things are, which helps out the next slice a lot.

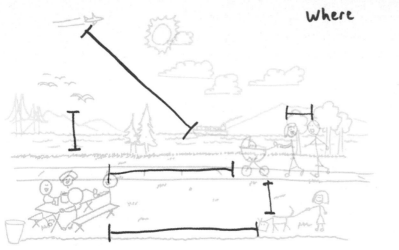

Where

? Where

3

▲
Our "where" pathway sees that some of the objects are far from others, some are above, some are almost on top of each other. It doesn't know what any of those things are, but it knows our position relative to them.

Slice 4: "when"

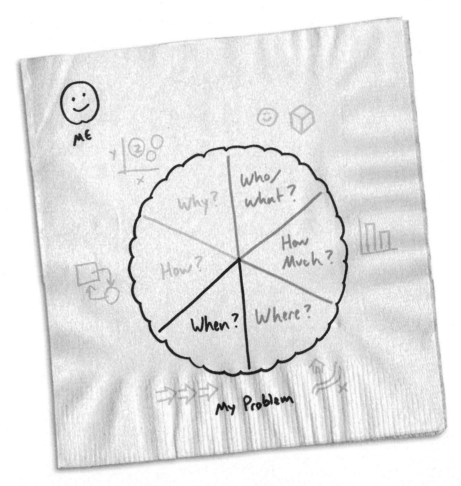

While "who and what," "how much," and "where" plug along on their own, operating in physically separated parts of the brain, "when," Slice 4, is different. In fact, without the input from the first three slices, "when" would have no idea what to do. That's because the job of Slice 4 is to see *when* things are happening.

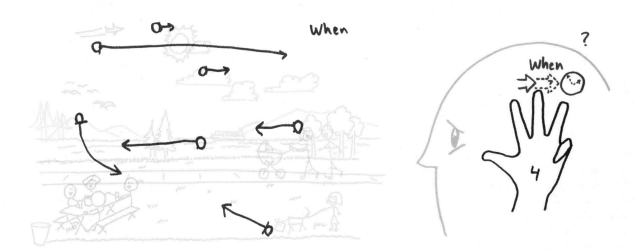

In order to do that, there has to first be something to see, which is what Slice 1 provides. When we then see some kind of change—either in quality (Slice 1 reports a change in color or shape), quantity (Slice 2 reports an increase or decrease in number), or position (Slice 3 reports that something moved)—we literally see time passing by. In all cases, we see the "when" by noticing things change in position, quality, or quantity over time.★

▲

We see "when" when we notice a change in the "where" of the "who and what" we identified earlier; in other words, we recognize that time is passing when we see things move.

✳

It turns out that one of the fastest ways for us to lose our sense of time is to close our eyes. In the absence of seeing the change in quality, quantity, or position of the objects around us, our ability to keep track of the passage of time rapidly becomes murky. Animators know this better than anyone: want to throw off the audience's timing immediately? Just stop moving things on the screen; audiences will swear that time has stopped.

Slice 5: "how"

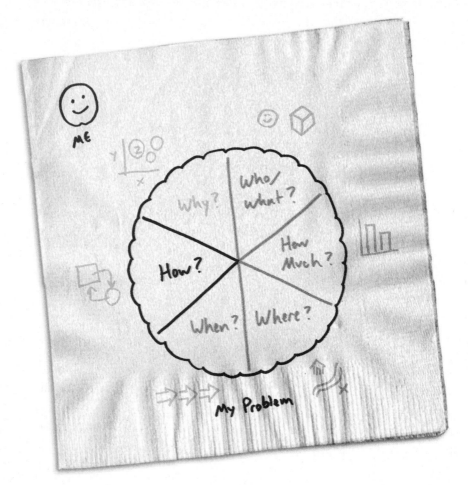

Slice 5 is where our mind's eye stitches together everything we've seen thus far and begins to discern cause and effect. After we've seen lots of "who and what" interacting over time, we build models of causality: we see *how* the world works.

When we're infants or when we see something truly new, our "how" slice takes time to make its deductions. We learn how the world works by watching similar scenes play out over and over again. The first time we see something, we don't yet know how it's going to end, so we have no models of cause and effect related to it yet. But after we've watched enough objects interact enough times, in similar ways, we gradually come to believe that we know how the things we see are likely to play out.

The "how" slice adds everything together so that we can see cause and effect: if a dog sees birds, it will chase them—and if the dog intersects with a baby carriage, parental panic will ensue.

Slice 6: "why"

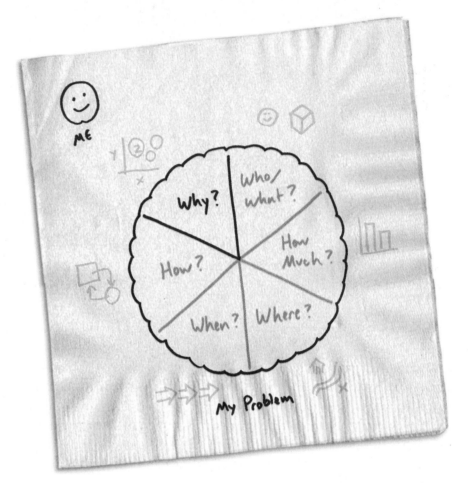

Our minds aren't happy knowing only what is out there, how many there are, where they are, when they happen, and how they interact. Cause and effect is great, but what our mind really wants to know is *why*. Why does this happen and not that? Why does that occur but not this? And why does it happen over and over again, or not at all?

The "why" slice isn't really a visual pathway at all; it is the summation of all the other slices repeated time and again until our mind feels confident drawing conclusions—based on all that we have seen—about why the world around us works the way it does.

▲ Aha! Why did this happen? Clearly, it's because dogs love birds, but birds do not love dogs. Our "why" slice adds everything we've seen together and draws conclusions about why the world is the way it is.

Every problem has its own pizza

We now have our 6×6 problem-solving napkin sliced up and labeled. What we first saw as a big problem we can know see is really nothing more than a pizza: we can digest the whole thing easiest if we first slice it up.

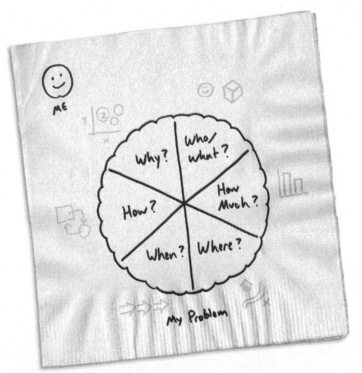

◀ Any problem is a pizza: hard to digest all in one go, far easier to tackle if we first slice it up.

Six ways of seeing? So what?

That's a lot of theory we've just covered. Since we started today, we've already introduced a new underlying coordinate system for looking at problems, added six new blades to our visual-thinking tool kit, taken a quick tour through our brain, and ended up with a pizza. To make all of this real—and to show how it all applies in the world of business problem solving—let's shift to a case study in which everything we just discussed will come into play.

What do these pictures have in common?

To get started, we're going to look at two pictures side by side. The first is a drawing from the exercise we just completed. The second is a picture of several pages pulled from a typical business presentation.

▲

What do these two pictures have in common?

As we can see, these two pictures look nothing alike. Seen side by side like this, it's silly to even put them on the same page. But you know what? It turns out that as far as our eyes are concerned, they are identical, and understanding how we see the first gives us great insight into how to look at the second.

Here is what I mean: while at first glance we may consciously think that these two pictures have little in common, our vision system would disagree. Look again at the pictures. They are the same size, the same color; they have the same density of dark lines and white spaces; they're even causing the same light-sensing neurons in our eyes and lower-level visual processing areas to fire in the same order. The point is, from a visual-processing point of view, our eyes don't know (and don't care) that one is a picture of a Sunday at the beach and the other a picture from a meeting we really don't want to attend.

The second thing these two pictures have in common is that they are composed of exactly the same visual information. But because of the way that information is presented, one is easy for us to look at and see as meaningful, while the other is like looking at a brick wall: there's nothing there for our eyes to grab on to. But we're going to use what we've already learned about visually slicing up problems to slice up the second picture so we can see more clearly what it is showing us.

In other words, we're going to use the six new blades in our tool kit to make an invisible problem visible.

The Thomson Corporation and the multimillion-dollar chart

In late 2001 the consulting company I was working for received a request from what was then the world's largest publisher of business information. The Thomson Corporation, one of Canada's largest companies, was going to be listed on the New York Stock Exchange and wanted help planning a brand strategy that would ensure global audiences were familiar with the company.*

Thomson had grown enormously over the preceding years by acquiring dozens of financial, legal, educational, and health-care information publishers, and its corporate management wanted to make sure that investors knew the size and global reach of the company. The issue for management was twofold: first, to understand what businesspeople around the world knew about Thomson—indeed, to determine whether businesspeople knew of the company at all—and second, to find a cost-effective way to make sure investors knew that Thomson, previously a nearly invisible company, was big and powerful; in other words, an excellent company to invest in.

When Thomson came to us, it had just completed a six-month brand survey, during which it had collected data from hundreds of interviews with business leaders around the world on issues from brand recognition (have you ever heard of Thomson?) to perceptions of product quality (which company do you think offers the better product?) to financial information (do you know how big company X is?).

*

If you've read *The Back of the Napkin*, you might recognize this as "Daphne's Information Overload," the example I used to make a quick point about visual problem solving in a business setting. Here's the rest of the story.

At the conclusion of the survey, all the data was collated and sliced and diced into hundreds of lists, tables, and charts, all of which were in turn pasted together into several lengthy presentation documents. From those, a single "greatest hits" executive summary was boiled down, and it looked like this:

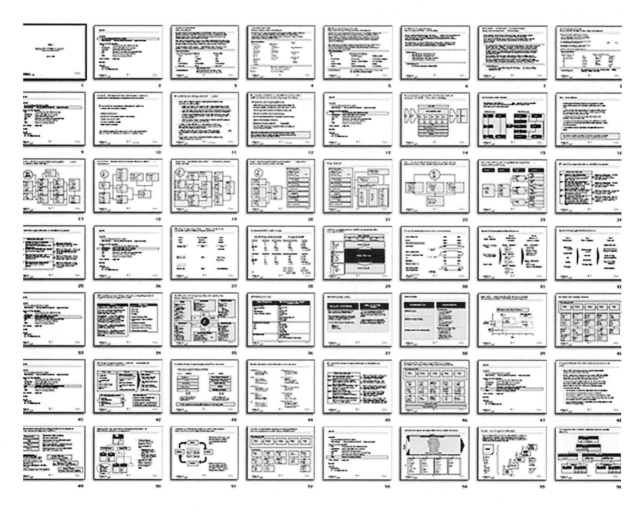

▲

Talk about "deer in the headlights": how are we even supposed to start with this barreling toward us?

The report certainly looked comprehensive, but unfortunately for management it was as if they'd bought their presentation by the pound. While it was an impressive document to behold, it was an impossible document to look at. It contained so much information, in so many different forms, that the initial reaction of anyone who looked at it was classic "deer in the headlights": You want me to understand *this*? Better give me a couple of months.

Let's be clear: there was nothing wrong with the data collected. It was a rigorous study, and Thomson's management was sure that what they needed to know was in their somewhere. But they also knew they didn't have months to try to find it. That's when they called us in.

Based on the collected data, Thomson's communications team was expected to come up with a brand-positioning strategy that would inform the design and creation of advertisements, marketing materials, Web sites, and investor packages—everything that would lay the marketing groundwork for the stock exchange listing. The task was clear. But ask yourself this: if you had just been handed more than four hundred pages that looked like the picture above, how would you go about coming up with a communications strategy?

It's scary to contemplate, and yet it is a reality that businesspeople face constantly: how do we take more information than we can even look at today and turn it into a coherent plan to share with someone else tomorrow? The answer is the 6×6 rule.

STEP 1: FIND THE "WHO AND WHAT"

When our consulting team received the mountains of data, the first thing we did was to scour through it to identify the cast of players; namely, the competitors reflected in the data. We identified seven companies whose names consistently appeared throughout the study. Three of them we had all heard of: Bloomberg, Reuters, and McGraw-Hill. The other four were unknown to us: Reed Elsevier, Pearson, Wolters Kluwer, and, last but not least, Thomson. Knowing *who* we were going to be looking at gave us our starting point.

◀ Identifying the seven competitors gave us the starting point: "who" we would be looking at.

Next we looked for "what," as in "what each company does." Since the report told us they were all publishers, it made sense to look for what they published. We saw that together the seven companies published information in four main categories: financial, learning, legal and regulatory, and science and health care.

What did they publish? Information in four main categories. ▶

| Financial | Learning | Legal & Reg | Scientific & Health |

STEP 2: FIND THE "HOW MUCH"

Once we'd identified the players and what they did, we went back through the documents to find quantitative data about each: something to measure the "how much" of each. In the piles of data, we decided that the first "how much" we'd look at was simply the size of each company as measured by annual revenue. When we mapped the seven together, we were able to rank them according to size of revenue.

Here's how the seven stacked up in 2001 revenue (in billions of dollars): Thomson on top, along with the other "unknowns." ▶

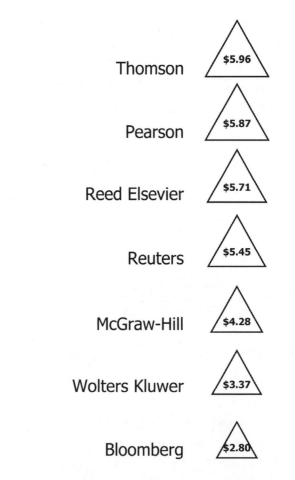

Thomson $5.96
Pearson $5.87
Reed Elsevier $5.71
Reuters $5.45
McGraw-Hill $4.28
Wolters Kluwer $3.37
Bloomberg $2.80

Right away we saw something interesting: not only was Thomson the biggest of the companies, the top three were all companies we'd never heard of. That was surprising.

But we also saw that just mapping the companies by total revenue wasn't particularly meaningful: we remembered from identifying the "who and what" that they were all active in a range of industries. So we decided to map out how much revenue each generated from the different industry segments.

Then we mapped how much revenue was generated by each company in each industry. What do you know? Thomson, although biggest, didn't dominate in any one industry. (Look at Reuters in finance, for example.)
▼

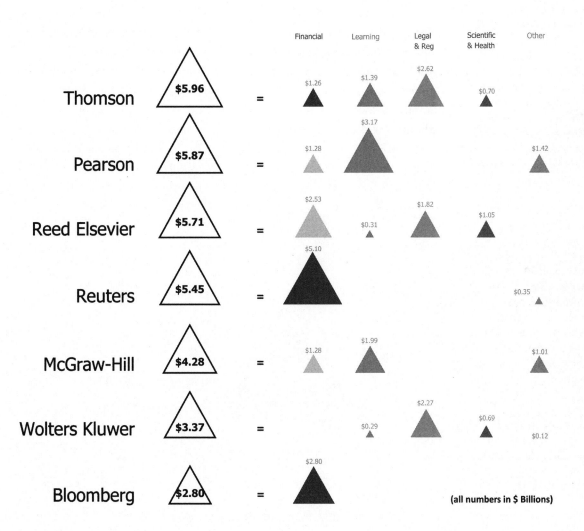

(all numbers in $ Billions)

Look at that: while Thomson was the biggest company overall, it was overshadowed in individual industries by smaller companies. In fact, we saw that the only industry where Thomson was biggest was legal, and even there not by much.

Just by looking at the "who and what" and the "how much," we'd already learned several things about the professional information publishing industry. But what did we really know?★

STEP 3: FIND THE "WHERE"

We now had interesting data laid out so that we could look at it side by side. But just knowing who was bigger in what industry wasn't all that compelling. What we really wanted to see was *where* these businesses overlapped, and *where* they operated alone, and *where* within their revenues was "brand equity." What we needed was some way to map them all together.

For each company, we created a pyramid chart. The idea of the "brand pyramid" is that every company is branded at many levels: at the top of the pyramid is the parent corporation (Thomson, for example). Each company is then broken into industry or market groups (financial, legal and regulatory, etc.), then each of those groups is broken into products or services (First Call, Westlaw, PDR, etc.).†

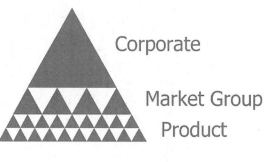

The "where" that we were after was twofold: First, we wanted to see where the survey data indicated there was name recognition within each brand pyramid (Have you heard of Thomson? Have you heard of First Call?). Second, we wanted to see where the seven competitors were positioned in terms of customer familiarity with them at all.

As with any good map, what we needed first was to create a key to define the types of data included.

size of pyramid =
relative revenue

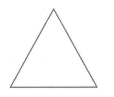

placement within pyramid =
level of brand awareness

Corporate

Market Group

Product

color of pyramid =
market group

Financial

Learning

Legal & Reg

Scientific & Health

Other

intensity of color =
level of brand awareness

High awareness

Some awareness

Low awareness

The key to our map included "revenue," "industry segment," and a brand pyramid for each competitor, reflecting measured "name recognition." In other words, this was all the "who and what" and "how much" data we had.

In order to create the map, we first had to come up with a coordinate system. (Remember yesterday's airline chart exercise? Same drill.) After playing around with the data categories, we elected to map (1) the number of industries each company published for versus (2) total measured brand recognition. As before, we didn't know what would appear until we'd laid out the actual data, but it seemed like as good a coordinate system as any.

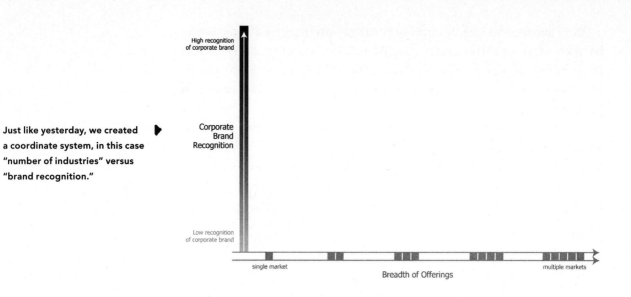

Just like yesterday, we created a coordinate system, in this case "number of industries" versus "brand recognition." ▶

Our coordinate system in place, we then mapped the data for each of the competitors. The picture that emerged showed how seven different types of information overlaid one another:

1. Company
2. Industry offerings
3. Revenue
4. Brand pyramid with corporate-industry-product recognition
5. Number of industry offerings
6. Overall relative brand recognition
7. Relative market position

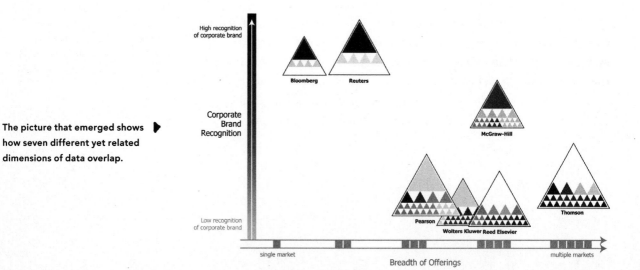

The picture that emerged shows how seven different yet related dimensions of data overlap. ▶

In all fairness this isn't the simplest of maps. Then again, it doesn't need to be: with a little verbal narration, it's still far clearer and more accessible than the hundreds of pages of data it replaces, and it delivers immediate insight. In addition it is simple enough to be visually inviting yet elaborate enough to be compelling.

Let's take a tour of the map; I'll point out the landmarks. First, we see that Thomson is the biggest pyramid (most revenue, but not by much; Pearson is a close second) and the furthest out along the "number of industries" horizontal axis, indicating that Thomson represents four industries, as opposed to Bloomberg's one, for example.

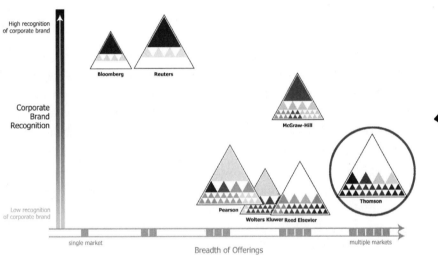

◀ **Thomson is the biggest company and operates in the most industries.**

But we also see that Thomson is near the bottom of the vertical axis, indicating that it scored low on corporate-brand awareness among the surveyed audience. For comparison, we see that Reuters is way up at the top, indicating that everyone surveyed was familiar with the Reuters brand.

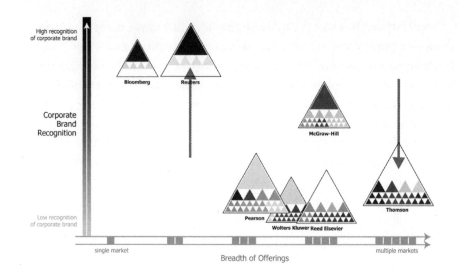

Thomson has low corporate-brand recognition, while everyone has heard of Reuters. ▶

Next we see that where the brand pyramids of Bloomberg, Reuters, and McGraw-Hill are filled in on the top (high corporate-brand recognition), the Thomson and Reed Elsevier pyramids are completely blank at the top (meaning no one had heard of these corporations). Conversely, the bottom of Reuters's and Bloomberg's pyramids are empty, while the bottom of Thomson's and Reed Elsevier's are full, showing us that in spite of never having heard of Thomson, everyone was familiar with its product brands. (Using the tortilla chip example from note 9, that's the equivalent of saying that few chip eaters are aware of PepsiCo, but they all know Doritos.)

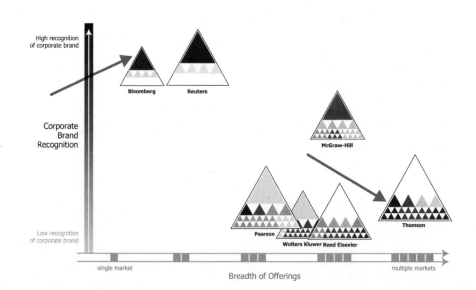

Thomson has lots of "name recognition," but it is all at the product level. Bloomberg, on the other hand, has a well-known brand, but nobody can identify any of that company's products (or maybe they're just called Bloomberg too). ▶

Lastly, there is an overall descending line of brand recognition from those companies that serve only one industry to those that serve many. In other words, the map shows us that as of 2001—with the exception of McGraw-Hill—no one had heard of any of the companies serving multiple industries, even though those were the biggest companies. Hmm, that's interesting. What could it mean?

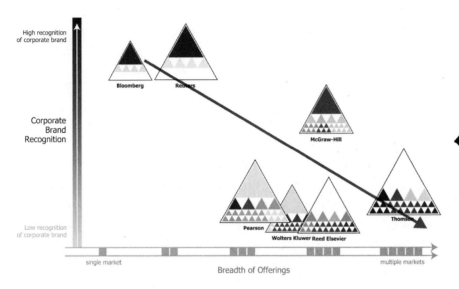

Brand recognition diminishes as companies serve more industries.

Before going there, it's worth noting that everything I've just pointed out is derived directly from the collected data. The picture simply made these insights easier to see than when they were in the original tables. The picture didn't alter the data: it just made it clear. That's important to think about because of what is about to happen: we're going to use these now clearly visible facts to draw a conclusion.

After mapping together all the data we have, here's what we can conclude: there is a gaping hole in the professional-information publishing industry; as of 2001 no publisher had achieved high brand recognition while serving multiple industries.

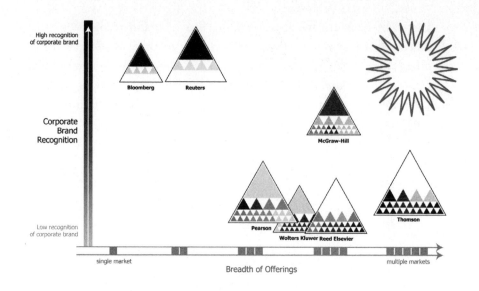

The map does not tell us *why* this is so. It could be any number of things; perhaps there is some underlying business force that makes it difficult to be known for doing many things, or perhaps no company had yet focused on occupying that space. We don't know the reason, but at least now we can see the hole.

Something we know about business is that open niches tend not to stay open very long once they've been spotted, and as you're about to see, this chart provided the rallying cry that Thomson had been looking for.

STEP 4: FIND THE "WHEN"

The map we created showed one point in time: the year 2001, which was when the survey was conducted. We had a snapshot of one date that essentially said, "Look: here's how the professional-information publishing industry looks today." But remember the whole point of this exercise: the goal was to prepare Thomson to list on the New York Stock Exchange in 2003, two years after we took our snapshot. So we were really interested in two "whens": *today* and *two years from today*.

That's where this chart started to sing. By plotting hundreds of points of data on the same map, using the same coordinate system, we found ourselves finally able to see what was going on. And here's what we saw: that in two years Thomson should occupy that open space on the map.

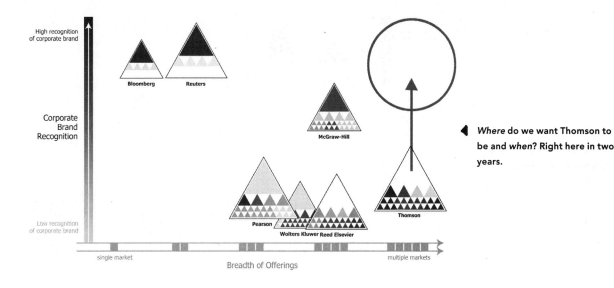

◀ **Where** do we want Thomson to be and **when**? Right here in two years.

STEP 5: FIND THE "HOW"

Now we knew where we wanted Thomson to go (up into the open quadrant) and when (within two years). That really left only one question to discuss: *How could Thomson move its pyramid up?* Looking at the chart, we saw one way. Let me show it to you the same way we showed it to Dick Harrington, then the CEO of Thomson, since his reaction to this picture is the best part of the whole story.

STEP 6: THE MULTIMILLION-DOLLAR MEETING

We were so energized by the clarity and simplicity of the chart that we couldn't wait to get back to Thomson to present our findings. Apparently Thomson felt the same way: when we arrived to present to the communications team, Dick Harrington unexpectedly asked if he could join the meeting. We had a wall-sized printout of our chart, and we were confident it showed something intriguing, so we were pleased that the CEO himself wanted to see it.

We taped the chart to the wall and walked the executives through it just as I have done on the previous pages, which took only a couple of minutes. And just as we were about to explain the gaping hole, Harrington—who had been sitting quietly but attentively—stood and asked for my pen.

As he approached the chart, he said, "I see something here that I find fascinating. I've been with this company for twenty years, but I've never seen it represented this way." He then drew a big circle in the upper-right quadrant (our gaping hole) and continued, "Here's what I want us to do: I want Thomson to occupy this high ground." As he handed back the pen, he asked, "Since you're the folks who made the chart, do you have any thoughts on how we could do that?"

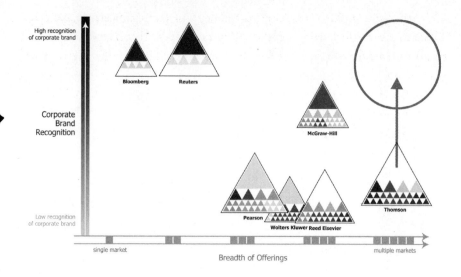

Look familiar? Thomson's CEO Dick Harrington looked at the same picture we had and saw the same space open for opportunity. ▶

We did. In fact, two thoughts were uppermost in my mind. First, thanks to the willingness of the CEO of the world's largest information publisher to look for strategic insight in a picture, I now had validation that visual problem solving had a place in the boardroom. Second, I was glad we'd rehearsed the "how" in advance.

Taking the pen back from Harrington, I drew a new pyramid in the upper quadrant and filled it in, saying, "We recommend taking advantage of the name recognition you have with your products to drive the Thomson name upward. That would involve the relatively simple and cost-effective rebranding your individual products to include the Thomson name. This approach would do nothing to minimize your existing products' brand recognition but would immediately let everyone know who Thomson is."

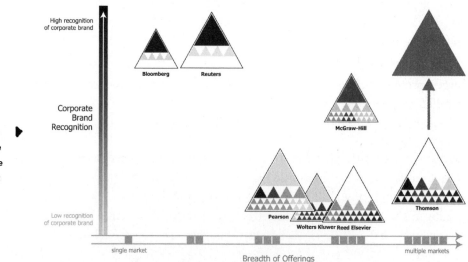

I drew a filled-in pyramid in the upper right, proposing that the name Thomson be added to the company's well-known product brands. ▶

Harrington nodded. Looking to his head of communications, he said, "That makes perfect sense. Let's see if we can't make that happen." Then he stood and said to the whole room, "Excellent work. Thank you for letting me participate." As we stood to thank him, he asked for the pen one more time.

On his way out of the room, he stopped again at the chart. "You know," he said, "there is another way we could move up to this quadrant."

He paused, then put a big circle around the Reuters pyramid in the upper left of the chart. "We could just buy them."

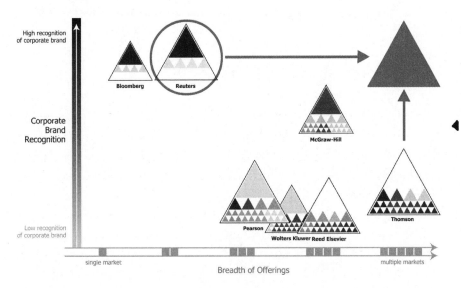

As he left the room, Harrington drew a circle around **Reuters** and jokingly added, "We could just buy them." Joke, indeed.

Then we winked and left the room. Looking at the relative sizes of Thomson's and Reuters's pyramids, it was obviously a joke. We all politely laughed.

FIVE YEARS LATER

In 2007 the Thomson Corporation bought Reuters, far and away the world's largest provider of financial information, for $17.2 billion. The new company is called Thomson Reuters.

Again, who says a picture isn't a powerful business tool?

Perhaps our chart was worth $17.2 billion?

On that note, it's time for lunch. ▶
When we come back, we'll flip
the coin and start drawing.

Tails: the six ways of showing

All morning we've been studying the "heads" side of the coin, learning to
look at big problems without becoming overwhelmed. For the rest of the
day, we're going to flip the coin and look at how we can clarify any type of
problem by drawing just six simple pictures.

Tails

Only so many
pieces.

Tails: Each problem is composed ▶
of the same six pieces. Identify
those six and you're already close
to the solution.

The theory behind the 6x6 rule

Rather than trying to describe an entire problem at once by drawing an elaborate picture, what would happen if we created a series of six simple pictures: one
to appeal directly to each of the visual pathways in our vision systems? Couldn't
we then easily draw the slices of any problem and simultaneously ensure that
anybody else looking at our pictures would also "get it" right away?

With this premise in mind, I sketched out the 6×6 rule.

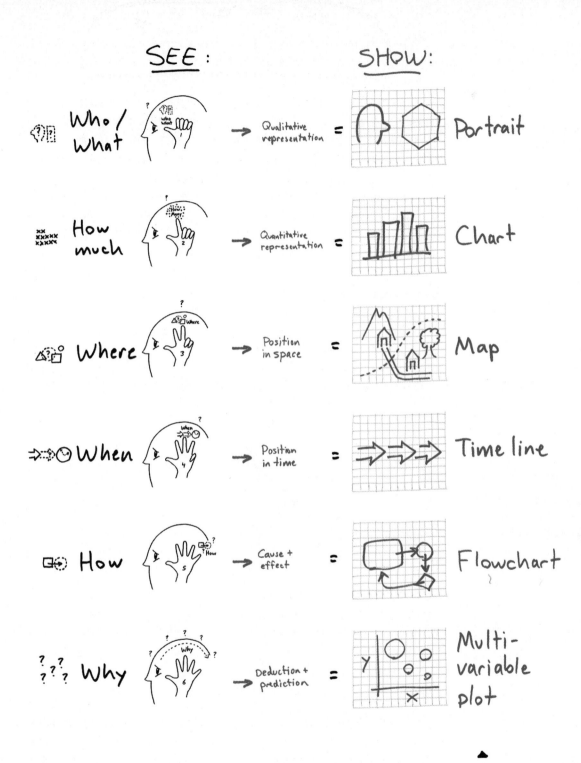

SEE:

SHOW:

Who / what → Qualitative representation = Portrait

How much → Quantitative representation = Chart

Where → Position in space = Map

When → Position in time = Time line

How → Cause + effect = Flowchart

Why → Deduction + prediction = Multi-variable plot

▲

The 6×6 rule tells us that for each of the six ways we *see*, there is one corresponding picture we can use to *show*.

The 6×6 rule tells us that for each of the six ways we see a problem, there is one picture we need to draw in order to illustrate that aspect of the problem. In the same way that our vision system stitches together a complete picture of our world by breaking the visual signal into different elements, we can simply reverse the process to create the appropriate picture of any problem.

For example, if we were a project manager who needed to launch a new product by the end of the quarter, we might say that we primarily faced a "when" problem, as in *when does everything need to happen in order to meet the deadline?* To visually clarify "when"—to see what it really means to get everything done on time—we would rely on our mind's ability to see the passage of time and would create a picture that reflects that. Maybe we wouldn't need to draw the entire problem—all the "who and what," "how much," "where," and "how"—to see what we were looking for in this specific case. Maybe all we'd need is a single picture of "when."

Hey, Mr. Project Manager: *when* ▶
are you going to get that all done?

If that's true, then I have some good news for anyone willing to try visual problem solving: we can create pictures to represent *any* problem. And if that's true, the even better news is that we can do it with only six simple pictures. And if that's true, the really great news is that anyone who can learn to draw six simple pictures (which is everyone) can learn to draw any problem.

I believe all these are true. Let's prove it.

What six pictures?

From this morning, we already know the six slices of any problem: "who and what," "how much," "where," "when," "how," and "why." To test out the 6×6 rule, all we need to do is identify the best simple picture to represent each slice. Let's go back to our "problem pizza" napkin and work our way around it once again, only this time instead of thinking about what to call each slice, let's figure out what to draw for each.

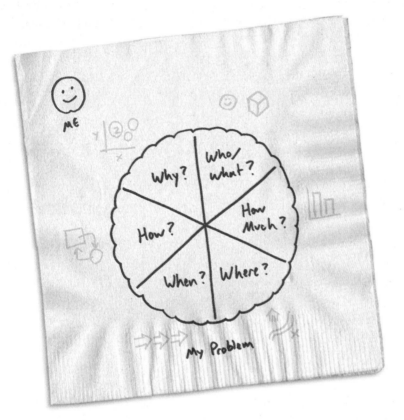

Time to pick up our "problem pizza" napkin; now we're going to draw our six pictures on it.

PICTURE 1: "WHO AND WHAT" = A PORTRAIT

"Who and what" problems relate to the *objects* in the world around us—the stuff picked up and processed by our "who and what" pathway: the people, the things, the concrete ideas, the machines, etc. Here are examples of "who and what" problems:

- I'm on the marketing team, and we think we've identified the best market segment for our new service but aren't entirely sure. *Who is our segment? What makes them distinct from the people in another segment?*

- I'm a pilot flying a plane, and I can't remember which lever to pull to slow down. *What distinguishes one lever from another? What is each lever there to do?*

- I'm studying comparative religions, and I can't keep track of who believes in what. *What are the tenets of each religion? What makes them alike? What makes them different?*

What's common about each of these problems is that they're looking for the qualities that make one thing the same or different from another. The way our "who and what" pathway handles that is by making millions of tiny measurements of the thing we're looking at and comparing them to something else, either in front of us or stored away in our visual memory banks.

For example, take a look at this sketch:

Our first problem-solving portrait: Tom is not like Dick but has a lot in common with Harry. ▶

I see that Tom is not the same as Dick because he is taller. I also see that Tom is a lot like Harry because, not only are they the same height, but they also have the same color hair. For good or for bad, my mind's eye has profiled Tom, Dick, and Harry and made decisions about them.

To figure out which picture we'd use to draw such a "who and what" problem, all we have to do is turn around the process we've just been through. Since we know Tom from Dick and Harry by measuring them, all we need to draw to differentiate them is a simple portrait that shows those measurements, like the sketch above.

There are lots of different kinds of portraits we can draw easily just by noticing the differences between objects, then capturing those differences on paper. In the end, all these portraits work the same way: they show the visual elements of one thing that make it distinct from another.

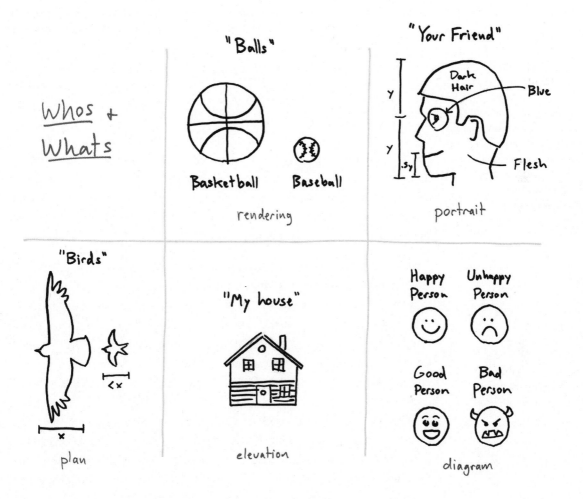

Our goal in creating a portrait is not to prove our artistic abilities and talents; it is to make sure that we have visually *identified* and *recognized* the things that make up our problem. Regardless of how realistic it looks, we know we've created a good portrait when we feel comfortable that it tells us something about the things that make up our problem and that anyone else who sees our portrait will feel the same way.

▲
The simplest picture that distinguishes one thing from another is all the "portrait" we need.

To get a better feel for the kinds of portraits we're talking about, let's look at a couple of examples. Then we'll draw a few of our own.

How does it feel?

From emergency rooms to airplane seat-back safety cards to IKEA instructions, simple portraits can immediately convey a spectrum of information that transcends spoken language. If we want someone to know exactly how we're feeling, or what we want them to feel, nothing is more powerful than a portrait visually representing a universal emotion.

An enormous amount of our visual processing capacity is focused on the subtleties of the human face. When we want to immediately convey a feeling, it takes only the most basic of pictures to guarantee a response.

How do I slow this thing down? (part 1)

Before jets, back when every airplane in the sky had a propeller, pilots were forever mistakenly turning their engines off in flight when all they really wanted to do was slow down. This was because every airplane had two different engine controls: the "throttle," which determined the speed at which the engine ran (push forward = more power; pull back = less power); and the "mixture," which determined the ratio of fuel to air being fed to the engine (push forward = more fuel in the mix; pull back = cut off fuel = kill engine).

The problem was that both levers looked the same and were located in the same part of the cockpit. If a pilot was in a rush, or didn't look before pulling a lever, it was highly likely that he or she would pull the wrong one. This was eventually fixed by coding them according to a standardized set of visual cues: (1) different colors: the throttle is always black and mixture is always red; (2) different shapes: the throttle is smooth and the mixture has teeth.

Throttle

Mixture

◀ Visual cues (color and shape) are used to distinguish the throttle from the mixture. Lives are saved.

How do I slow this thing down? (part 2)

We don't have to look to airplanes for this kind of engine-control "portrait." Look at these two simple side-by-side portraits, and see if you can't guess what they differentiate. (Here's a hint: this is a big part of the *second* most important financial decision most people make in their lives.)

◀ Can you guess what these two portraits differentiate?

Automatic

Manual

◀ Now, which one would you buy?

What do you believe?

Few areas of human endeavor are as rife with both small and big distinctions as religion, and few have such enormous consequences when those distinctions are overstated, understated, or just misstated. Look at these exceedingly simple portraits, and you will see (and feel) the power of a "differentiating" picture.

See how few words we need to generate a strong response? ▶

A couple of lines on a sheet of paper—again, who says a simple picture doesn't carry meaning? To further prove the point, here's a variation on the theme.

Even small differences within the same picture trigger big reactions. ▶

When we're creating our problem-solving portraits, it's often the little things that make the biggest difference.

YOUR TURN TO DRAW A PORTRAIT

Look over the following three portrait exercises and pick any one to complete. (If you're on a roll, do all three: there's extra paper in the back of the book for precisely that purpose.)

PORTRAIT OPTION 1: AUDIENCE SEGMENTATION

In the space below, draw a portrait visually describing the difference between these customer segments.

   (Hint: start with faces or stick figures and see if you can't conjure up one or two visual distinctions between each.)

- Yuppie
- Tween
- Young adult
- Soccer mom/dad
- Retiree
- Anyone else?

PORTRAIT OPTION 2: ARE WE THERE YET?

In the space below, see how little you need to draw to show how different these modes of transportation really are..

- Bus
- Ship
- Airplane
- Car
- Submarine
- How do you get work?

PORTRAIT OPTION 3: WHERE SHOULD WE VACATION?

In the space below, draw what comes to mind for each of these places:

- Hawaii
- NYC
- Paris
- Montana
- The moon
- Your favorite vacation spot

Visual lists stick better than word lists

You might notice something about these examples: in all cases they make visual comparisons between lists of things. That's where portraits really shine: rather than asking our minds to use words alone to distinguish and remember differences between items, it's far more effective to let our extraordinarily well-developed vision centers into the game as well.

When we really want to notice and remember multiple items, visual lists stick better than word lists because we're giving our brain far more differentiating data to work with. Comparing apples and oranges using pictures—even exceedingly simple ones—is abundantly more stimulating to our brain than using words alone. Let's face it: since our visual processing system is always working anyway, we may as well use it. Let me give you one more example.

What to keep, what to chuck

Let's say that we're a brand manager at a major consumer packaged goods manufacturer. We're conducting a product assessment with an eye toward streamlining our sales lineup. Our goal is to divide everything we sell into three clumps to help us decide what to do with it: what's selling really well and deserves continued support, what's selling well enough to warrant investments to improve, and what's selling so poorly we should quit making it.

First we're going to assign each of our products to a performance category based on customer, marketing, and sales feedback. The categories are: stellar, best in class, on par, middling, lousy, and unsold.

Okay, that's the setup. Now here's the question: our minds have just read twelve different categories in three different hierarchies (sales performance, what to do financially, product quality). That's a lot of words and structure for our mind to keep track of, not to mention the fact that each of the twelve categories means something qualitatively different.

For most people, even keeping that relatively simple list clear is difficult. Once we start assigning products, it will become nearly impossible. That's why we have spreadsheets. Here's what many of us would probably create to keep track of everything:

Action	Sales status	Ranking	products:				
support	selling really well	stellar					
		best in class					
invest	selling okay	on par					
		middling					
drop	selling badly	lousy					
		unsold					

This is a fine tool for us to begin making our assessments and filling in the data. But I think there's an even better way. Why not activate our mind's eye to help us keep the distinctions we're making visceral?

Imagine how we'd feel about what we were doing if we could *see* it at the same time:

Action	Sales status	Ranking	products:				
support	selling really well	stellar					
		best in class					
invest	selling okay	on par					
		middling					
drop	selling badly	lousy					
		unsold					

The point is that if we really want to remember something within a long list, it's not enough to just assign words; giving our visual-processing centers a role adds an entirely new level of mental participation.

YOUR NEXT PORTRAIT: MAKE A LIST AND CHECK IT TWICE

In the space below, you will notice there are both "categories" and "items" listed. Your job is to create a simple visual list (like the one above) that accounts for both. To help your mind with the categorizing, make everything *visceral*; make the various terms actually mean something by showing what they look and feel like. (Hint: the goal here is to get your visual-processing centers involved in your decision making.) For my solution, see the appendix, page 272.

The categories are

1. No worries: doing just fine
2. Worth whatever it takes to save it
3. Let it die

The items are

- General Motors
- Washington, D.C.
- Whole Foods
- My local bank
- Wall Street
- Google

That's enough portraits for now. Don't worry though: they're going to come back again and again as we make our way through the rest of our problem-solving napkin. Before we move on, let's record on our "problem pizza" a simple sketch that reminds us that when we face a "who and what" problem all we need to draw is a portrait.

On our "problem pizza" napkin, ▶
let's draw a portrait to show
"who and what."

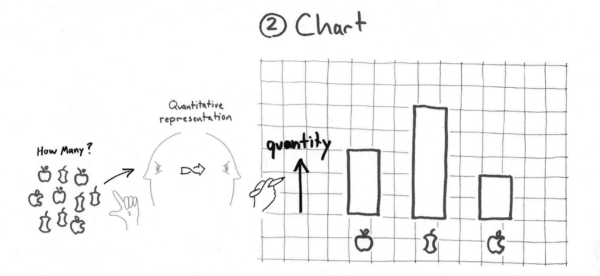

"How much" problems are all about the numbers. How many did we sell? Do we have enough money to get through the quarter? What's happening on the stock market? These are the kinds of questions that occupy our visual "how much" pathway, the part of our vision system that is always counting (or trying to, anyway) the stuff around us.

Here are examples of "how much" problems:

- I'm a financial analyst, and I need to justify my cost-cutting recommendations. *How much are we presently spending? What is our return on investment (ROI) for this initiative?*

- I'm a manager thinking about hiring new staff and want to be sure we can afford more people. *How much will it cost to employ them? How much will they contribute to our bottom line?*

- I'm a fruit buyer for a major food chain, and I want to know if I can save money by sourcing new banana suppliers. *How much will I save on a product that costs less to buy but requires longer transport? Can I bundle the shipping with other products for efficiency?*

What these problems have in common is that they're solely focused on the numbers. "How many" and "how much" are literally what our "how much" vision pathway takes notice of. It's true that to know "how many of *what*," we have to know *who* and *what* we're measuring, but our "how much" pathway doesn't care at all about those squishy "qualitative" differences; what our "how much" pathway obsesses over are quantities.

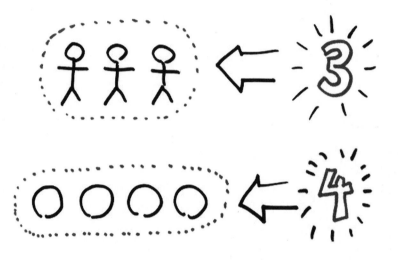

I don't care *who* they are or *what* they are, but I see three and four of them! ▶

✷

There are also more books about charts than about any other kind of picture, so we're not going to spend a lot of time covering charts in detail. There are just a couple of aspects of charts that I think are most important to understand in order to make good decisions about which to use, and those are what we're going to focus on.

For example, I may look up and see that I've got three people in front of me (remember Tom, Dick, and Harry?) and then look down and see that I've got four apples in my hands. "How much" doesn't care about differences in height or anything like that; it just sees three and then four—and realizes that I've got an extra apple for myself.

There are more types of charts seen in business than any other kind of picture.* That makes sense in a world where business success and failure is judged entirely by measuring quantifiable "how much" numbers: market cap, stock price, P/E ratio, profit and loss, market share. You name a criteria by which the people behind the money decide whether to support a business or not, and you'll come up with a quantifiable measure.

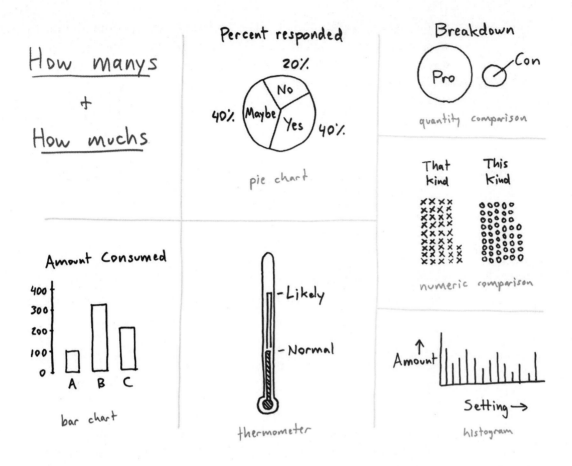

How manys + How muchs

Percent responded

20%

40% | Maybe | No | 40%
Yes

pie chart

Breakdown

Pro Con

quantity comparison

That kind | This kind

xxxx / ooooo
xxxx / ooooo
xxxx / ooooo
xxxx / ooooo
xxxx / ooooo
xxxxx / ooooo
xxxxx / ooooo

numeric comparison

Amount Consumed

400
300
200
100
0
A B C

bar chart

— Likely

— Normal

thermometer

Amount ↑ histogram

Setting →

histogram

Since there are so many aspects of business that can be measured, and so many things we can learn from seeing how those measures stack up, we have lots of different kinds of charts available to us: bar charts, pie charts, histograms, time series, bubble charts, radar charts—it's a long list. For those of us who like to see things in pictures, it's nice to have so much choice. Then again, that much choice makes picking the right chart a challenge in itself: here we are, all ready to create a great data picture, and we're once again the deer in the headlights—this time trying to figure out which chart to use.

Let's not let all these chart options, or the software that feeds them to us, fool us. We need to remember that at the end of the day there is only one fundamental thing that any of these charts is going to help us show: "how much." And there are really only two ways any chart is going to show that: either by showing actual numbers or by comparing relative amounts.

▲
How much of this do I have? And how much compared to that? Although they look different, every "how much" chart is simply a visual representation of quantity.

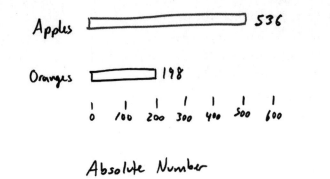
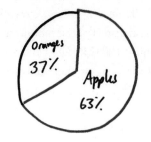

Absolute Number   Comparative Amount

If you can decide what aspect of your "how much" matters most—and whether it matters most in absolute numbers or relative to another number—you've got a far easier choice of which chart to use. Let's use a couple of simple pictures to help answer those questions.

Absolute quantities versus comparative amounts

Absolute quantities are the "pure" way to show how much of something we have. How many apples do I have? Four. That's pretty clear—no visualization needed there. We like to know exactly how many of something we have because it gives us a sense of certainty and ability to be precise, both of which are critical for us to confidently make important decisions like how many apples to give to Tom.

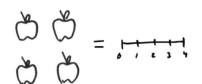

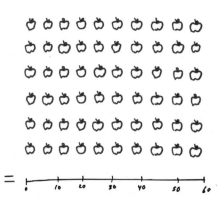

But absolute quantities have some problems. First, it turns out that we humans are pretty miserable at really "getting" big numbers. For most people, the biggest quantity we can instantly recognize without conscious effort is five. (Think about that the next time someone starts throwing "billions" around.) That's not to say we can't picture much larger numbers; we can, but the important word is "picture." Since most of us can't really comprehend bigger numbers, seeing a visual comparison of one quantity to another helps us understand how many we're talking about.

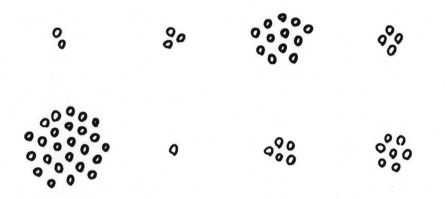

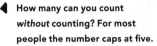 How many can you count *without* counting? For most people the number caps at five.

For example, with four people (Tom, Dick, Harry, and me) and four apples, it's easy to see how they compare. But what if I had thirty-nine apples, or seventy-two thousand? Long division is one way to come up with the absolute answer, but a comparative-amount picture also does the trick, especially if we're interested in making a quick estimation.

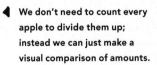 We don't need to count every apple to divide them up; instead we can just make a visual comparison of amounts.

The most simple, obvious, and frequent comparative amount we use is one hundred. Doing so gives us a percentage, which we all know is a magnificent way to quantitatively compare parts to wholes or to compare one number to another.

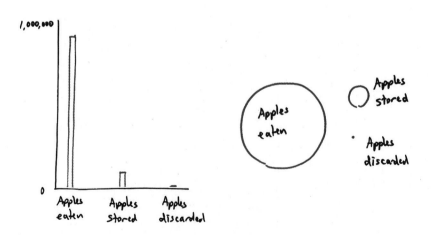

Using a comparative standard also helps alleviate the second problem with absolute quantities: once they get really big (or really small), absolute quantities become hard to manage on any kind of chart, especially when we trying to show a big quantity next to a small one.* Shifting to comparative numbers often gives us more flexibility in coming up with a way to make our numbers visible.

Let's look at examples.

An apple a day

When someone says "apple," for most of us one of two images comes to mind: a fruit or a computer. As we know from the previous 6×6 slice, there's a very easy and effective way for us to visually draw distinctions between the two: a simple portrait.

Which kind of apple? A portrait helps differentiate.

But if that person then says, "I mean the fruit. What does it mean when we say, 'an apple a day keeps the doctor away?' " We're going to need a very different image. Why *does* an apple a day keep the doctor away? Is it because an apple is red? Not likely. Is it because the apple is round? No. Is it because the apple tastes good? Perhaps, but knowing what we do about how much doctors love to *measure* health—they take our temperature, read our blood pressure, weigh us, count our cholesterol, etc.—we can assume that there must be something *measurable* about an apple that makes it a good doctor repellent.

How can we measure what it is about an apple that makes it healthy? How about the vitamins it contains?

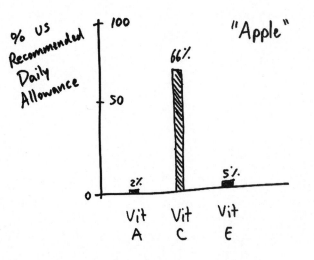

A chart shows the measurements that make an apple an effective doctor repellent.

The price of bananas

Speaking of fruit, let's go back to our banana buyer for a moment. Remember what we were interested in? We wondered if it made financial sense to buy our bananas from a source that sells them at a cheaper price but is located further away. We're not worried about what makes a banana a banana; we're solely concerned about costs. To see those, we're going to need a chart.*

This chart shows the wholesale price of bananas in several (fictitious) banana growing countries: Burola, Howloo, Westango, and our present supplier, Quixos:

✱
The numbers and locations in this exercise are complete fabrications. Please don't become a banana buyer based on anything you see here.

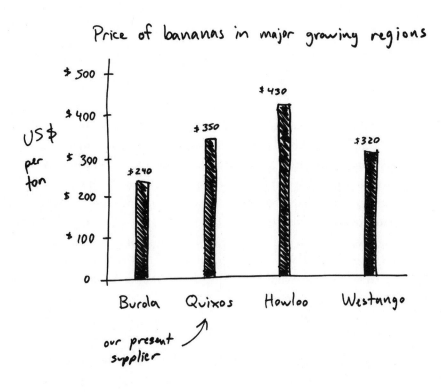

We can see that Burola bananas ▶
are much cheaper than those
from our present supplier,
Quixos.

This chart shows the cost of transport from those four countries to us:

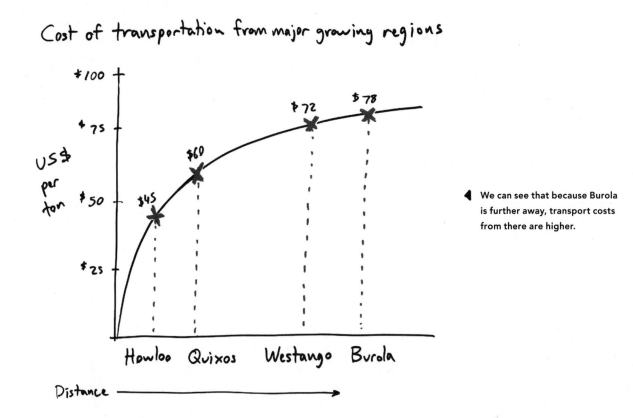

Cost of transportation from major growing regions

We can see that because Burola is further away, transport costs from there are higher.

Looked at solely from the perspective of "how much," and combining two simple charts, the quantitative answer becomes clear: we should stop buying from Quixos and start buying from Burola:

Total Banana cost per ton

Even with the greater transport costs, Burola bananas are a lot cheaper than what we buy now. ▶

$500

$400

USS per ton

$300

$200

$100

$318

$392

$410

$475

Burola
↑ our new supplier!

Westango

Quixos

Howloo

We're a big banana buyer in Quixos, and bananas represent almost two-thirds of its economy. What might happen if we stop buying its bananas?

▼

Nation of Quixos

other

Bicycles

Coffee

Bananas

Exports as % of
Gross Domestic Product

Of course, the problem with only looking at the "how much" slice is that we might be missing something. Remember, we've been a big buyer of Quixos bananas for years. What will happen in that country if we stop buying its bananas? Charts can't tell us that, but they can show us that any reduction in banana sales will seriously hurt Quixos's economy:

From a strict "how much" perspective, that's not our problem. But perhaps one day might it become our problem. Maybe we could negotiate a lower price? Maybe we should walk away and leave Quixos to find another buyer or another way to make money? Who knows? The charts certainly don't show us the answers to these questions. The lesson here is that we always need to be aware of what we are measuring and what we are not. The "how much" answer (the first picture a businessperson reaches for) is always missing critical information from the other slices, the other ways we see.

YOUR TURN TO DRAW A CHART

Look over the following chart exercises and pick one to complete. (Again, if you're in the mood for "how much," go ahead and do both.) For my solution, see the appendix, page 272.

CHART OPTION 1: WHO SEES HOW?

Yesterday we talked about the "spectrum" of visual problem solvers and how each of us falls into one of the following categories:

- Black Pen
- Yellow Pen
- Red Pen

Part I

In hundreds of meetings, I've asked people by a show of hands to identify which of these catergories comes closest to describing them. In most cases, hands go up in the following numbers: slightly more than one-quarter of the attendees raises their hands for the first category, about half for the second, slightly less than one-quarter for the third, and one or two don't raise their hand at all. What does that look like?

Part II

In a meeting attended by about one hundred people from the nation's largest teachers' organization, I asked exactly the same question, based on the same spectrum. I had a result that was uniquely different from any other group: just a couple of hands were raised for the first category, four for the second, and every other hand—well over one hundred—for the third. No hands remained unraised. What does that look like, especially compared to Part I?*

❋

This is true, and it was a shock to me: the biggest skew I've ever seen in the results of this (granted) highly nonscientific survey was when I gave it to one hundred-plus people from the National Education Association; they almost all identified themselves as Red Pens! We could read a lot into this to bolster our lack of confidence in solving problems with pictures, but probably most of it is wrong. To figure out what, if anything, this means, someone with a lot better statistical background than mine needs to conduct a more valid set of tests. We might learn something interesting about our teachers, our educational system, our understanding of intelligence, or a whole lot of other things. Any PhD students looking for a dissertation?

Seeing beyond the numbers

To see just how important charts are in business, look at all the charting capabilities built right into to most business software packages, from spreadsheets to word processing. It's great that these programs can so readily help us see "how much," but wouldn't it be equally great if they contained built-in portrait- and map-making tools?

As we've discussed, charts are a really big deal in business.* Since businesses measure success and failure almost entirely (and exclusively) by numbers, it's not surprising that when a business presentation contains any pictures at all, they're charts. There's nothing wrong with that: the more pictures of any sort, the better. But what is wrong is that our reliance on charts alone to explain business eventually skews what "business" means and severely limits, if not outright warps, our ability to see the bigger picture.

We spent our entire morning showing that there are six ways we see the world, and that they combine in various ways to give us the big picture. If the only pictures we see in business are charts, that's telling us that the only *way we see* that means anything in business is "how much." Yes, numbers represent money, and money is important, but there's a whole lot more going on in business than how much money is changing hands—like *where* the money is coming from, for example. To see that, we need an entirely new kind of picture: we need a map.

Before we go there, let's close this slice with a note on our "problem pizza" napkin: when we face a "how much" problem, the picture we draw is a chart.

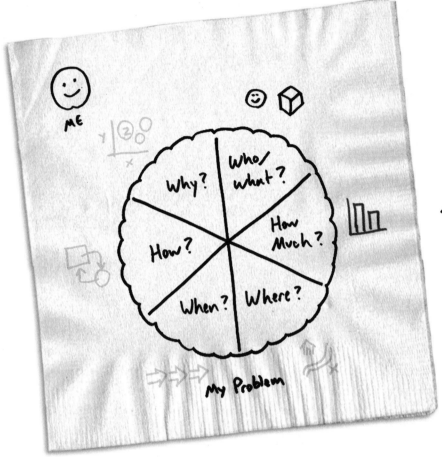

On our "problem pizza" napkin, let's add a simple chart to the "how much" slice.

EXTRA-CREDIT CHART: YOUR "HOW MUCH" PROBLEM

Can you think of any challenge you or your business faces that could be considered a "how much" problem? To help clarify it, what chart could you draw?

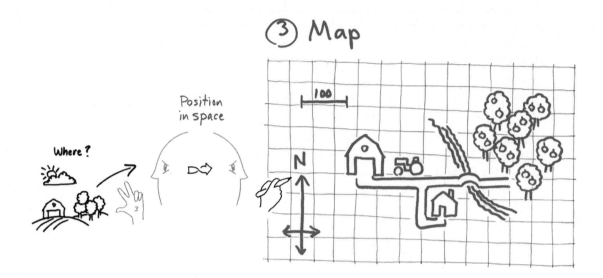

Our "where" pathway sees where everything is and keeps track of the spatial relationships between it all. It does this by instantly creating maps of the relative positions of everything we see around us. Sometimes those maps put us at the center of the action (something is approaching us right now!), and other times those maps might not contain us at all (the location of the refrigerator in my kitchen). Either way, neither of these maps care *what* any of that stuff is—that's handled by the other pathways.

For example, it's our "where" pathway that detects that we're being approached from ahead by potential danger. If, like a crocodile, all we had was this pathway, we'd already be taking "fight or flight" action without even knowing what was approaching. Being mammals, though, we have the ability for our "what" pathway to recognize that it's only Tom and gang coming for their apples, and since we've got an apple for everyone, we're probably safe.

Our "where" pathway only tells us that something is coming. We need our "who and what" pathway to know who or what it is.

OOOhh! Something is coming!

Oh: it's just the guys.

Here are some examples of "where" problems:

- I'm on the business-strategy team, and we're struggling to determine the best direction for our company. *Where are we now relative to our competitors? Are there unexplored places in our market space? Where do our unique offerings, cost structure, and capabilities all intersect?*

- I'm an architect, and I want to determine the best place to locate the septic tank and the terrace. *Where is the best place to locate one item relative to the next? Are there relative positions that are better for each piece?*

- I'm a wedding planner, and I want to know where I should put the guests during dinner. *Where should I concentrate the main players of the wedding party? How far out can I spread the difficult relatives to minimize damage?*

Of all the pictures we're going to look at, maps are the most flexible. That's because there are so many different ways to detect and measure the relative positions of things, regardless of what those things are.

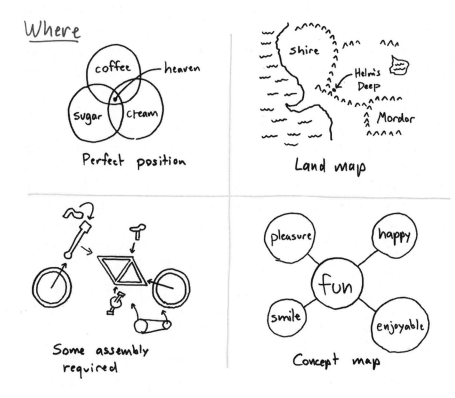

◄ Regardless of how varied they may look, all maps show the same thing: the spatial relationship of one item to another. Those items could be anything from bicycle components to abstract concepts; if our concern is how they fit together or overlap, a map is the picture we need.

Our goal in creating a map is to mimic the actions of our "where" pathway: to indicate the spatial relationship of one item to another. As far as our map is concerned, it makes no difference *what* those items are—they could be houses, business-plan components, or marketing concepts—what matters is where they fit together, where they overlap, and where they may be in spatial conflict.

Let's look at three map examples.

Map 1: where's my data?

In the business world, one of the places where we see a lot of maps is in technology, particularly technical architecture. As the name indicates, technical architecture means figuring out where all the various measuring devices, computers, servers, software, and data fit together so the "system" collects useful data and we (the "users") can get access to it. In a "where" situation like this, it makes sense to draw a map.

In the old days (like last week), technical-architecture maps looked like the following: we see a whole bunch of different systems feeding a whole lot of different information to a harried "user" who tries to figure out what it all means.

In the typical "old-school" technical-architecture map, many disconnected systems collected their own data and fed it all to a harried "user," who had to figure out how it all fit together. ▶

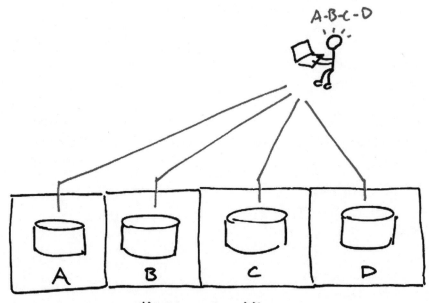

Now let's compare that map to a new emerging standard of technical architecture called the "services" model. In this map, we can see that something has changed. While the different systems remain different, a new "services bus" or "services layer" has been added between the systems and us. That "bus" uses a bunch of predefined business rules to figure out how to fit the data together so that, rather than being delivered a data overload, we get useful insight.

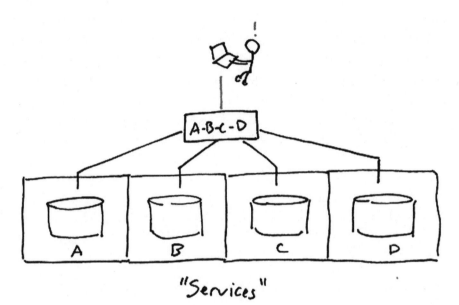

In the new "services" model, a "services bus" puts together the disparate data according to predefined rules, so that we can focus on insight rather than data overload.

"Services"

As we'll see tomorrow, being able to compare "before" and "after" maps side by side helps us immediately spot the differences. Let's quickly look at those two maps again. Now we can see why technical architects are so excited about "services-oriented architecture," or SOA: it makes it easier for the user to get what they need without demanding that the entire system be rebuilt.

See the difference? In the second map, life is made easier for the "user" without having to rebuild the entire system. This is why SOA (services-oriented architecture) is a favorite model among technical architects.

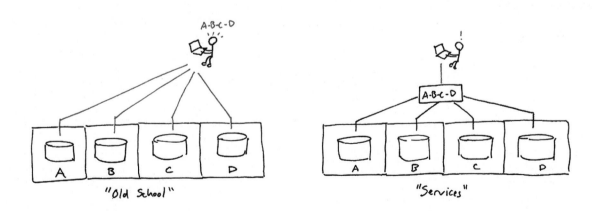

"Old School"   "Services"

Map 2: where's the money?

A few years ago a bank asked me to help it map out which customers were making it a lot of money and which were losing it money. The bank was concerned because its branch managers were putting a lot of effort into clients that were using only high-cost, low-profit services, distracting those managers from focusing on developing relationships with more lucrative clients. The bank wanted to know if there was a way we could plot all this out on a simple map to help their managers see where they should be spending their time.

Based on criteria identified by the bank managers, we created the following map. It included four "zones" whose borders were defined by a coordinate system* mapping the amount of maintenance the client required against the profitability of that client.

✳

Remember from yesterday that one of the first things we need to do to create a chart is to define a "coordinate system"? The same holds true for maps, and indeed for almost every picture we'll ever draw.

▶ We first defined our map's coordinate system (remember yesterday's airline chart?) using "profitability" versus "required maintenance."

†

This, by the way, is called a 2×2, or quad, map and is the most frequently used "where" picture in strategy consulting. Because it is such a clear way to map multiple points of view (good versus bad and rich versus poor; growing versus shrinking and profitable versus costly, etc.), strategy consultants love it as a way to see where competitors sit or where there may be unclaimed market territory. If you're involved in strategic planning, the 2×2 is an extremely useful map to draw.

▶ The four zones represent how fertile the "land" is relative to the amount of maintenance it requires. "Prime land" yields a lot of profit with little effort, while "desert" can suck up all our energy and never bloom.

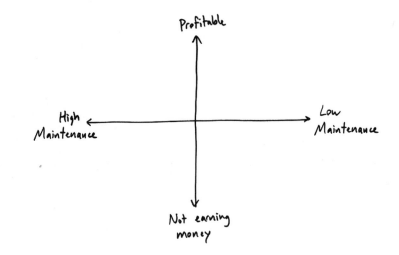

With the coordinates established, we mapped the four zones like this:†

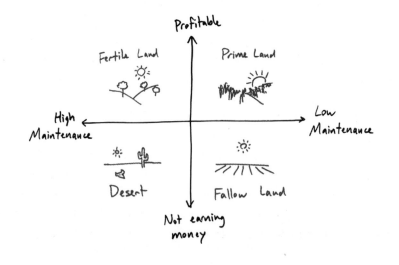

Looking at this map, it became clear to the bank managers that not all their "land" was the same: prime land was great to cultivate, because it yielded high profits with little maintenance required, while desert was a challenge because even with high maintenance it was never going to earn much money.

With this simple map in hand, the question posed to the bank managers was how they would map their clients. Would a new client with great earning potential warrant being placed in the same zone as a long-standing client who had long ago become unprofitable?

As a way of seeing where to direct their business, this simple map became the basis for many heated discussions among the branch and bank managers, as well as the basis for plotting their client calls.

Map 3: saving America (or tilting at windmills?)

I'm writing this book at a time when the United States economy has hit the most difficult circumstances since the Great Depression, and the rest of the world's economy is suffering alongside. During the time I've been writing, there has been an unprecedented amount of activity around the country focused on fixing the economy and an equally unprecedented amount of talk.

As both an active participant in the economy and a deadly interested bystander, I'm frustrated by our leaders' inability to use pictures to explain what happened and what they're doing about it. There's no shortage of words, theories, laws, and stimulus packages being debated in D.C., but how are any of us expected to make informed choices about which plans to support when our leaders themselves appear unable to clarify them?

Listen up, Washington: add pictures to your words and perhaps we'll begin to see a way out of this. How? Let's start with a map.

In the past few months, an enormous array of economic problems has appeared. Some, like the bust in housing prices and the related drop in consumer spending, were long anticipated. Others, like the nearly overnight collapse of Wall Street and General Motors, came seemingly out of nowhere. In an apparent panic, our government began throwing money at each problem, one by one, with a bailout for Wall Street, another for Detroit, and another for consumers. Maybe that's the right approach, but, lacking a "big picture" vision behind it, how would we know?

Imagine, instead, what would happen if one of our leaders picked up a pen and sketched out the following "problem map." She starts by identifying the three biggest challenges of the day: the collapse of Wall Street, the collapse of Detroit, and the approaching depletion of global petroleum.*

*

A year ago, with gas prices above four dollars a gallon, all anyone could talk about was the need to economize on energy use. Today, with gas prices down, we seem to have forgotten that problem. No worries: it will come back.

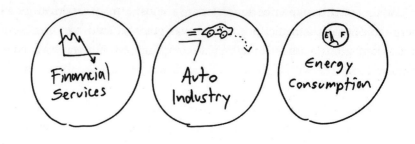

Three of our biggest problems: Wall Street has crashed, Detroit has driven off a cliff, and we're running out of gas. Ouch! ▶

✳

This is of course a Venn diagram, named after English logician John Venn (1834–1923), which uses circles to represent logical relationships.

Then she says, "Rather than looking at these three independently, let's see where they overlap." She then redraws the three as intersecting circles, their overlapping areas creating a whole new set of shapes.✳

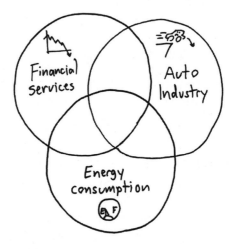

Let's look at those areas of overlap. ▶

She continues, "Where financial services and the auto industry intersect is credit: auto companies need loans in order to invest in creating better cars, and consumers need loans to buy them. So let's inject billions into Wall Street, but let's make it contingent on banks reopening credit to the auto manufacturers and consumers.

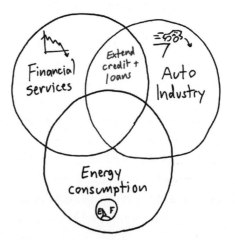

Money injected into Wall Street is contingent on banks reopening credit to auto businesses and consumers. ▶

"Where the auto industry and energy consumption intersect is in energy technology and efficiency. So let's make those loans to the auto companies contingent on their investing in creating more efficient and more desirable cars.

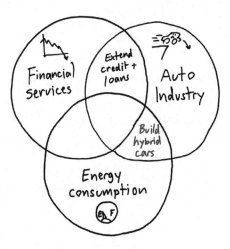

The credit money guaranteed to Detroit is contingent on automakers building more fuel-efficient and desirable cars.

"Energy consumption and financial services intersect in investing in more sustainable business practices overall. So let's encourage consumers and investors to support businesses that contribute to a greener economy.

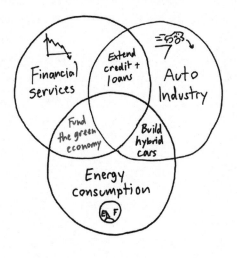

Meanwhile, money injected into the economy helps to support green technologies and build greener businesses.

"Now we're not looking at three separate problems with three separate and costly solutions; we see that we've actually got a cycle going where improvements to one problem automatically lead to improvements in the others. And here in the center, we create an entirely new American manufacturing base by retooling existing factories to mass-produce alternative energy systems.

"After all, if American auto companies could retool from building cars to building planes during WWII, why can't they do it again in this time of economic need?"

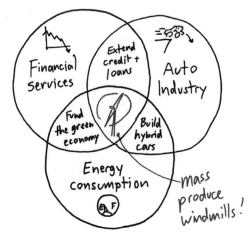

A nationwide project to ▶ manufacture windmills: it keeps assembly lines running, keeps money flowing, reduces petroleum reliance, and reduces carbon emissions. What's not to like?

Here we've got a single vision that addresses three of our major problems simply by showing *where* they overlap. It shows a potential way to keep Detroit's assembly lines working and Wall Street going while reducing energy consumption and supporting the growth of a sustainable economy. It took about three minutes to draw. And if we hadn't drawn it, those ideas wouldn't have become visible at all.

I don't know who the leader might be who would draw a map like this, but I know I'd vote for her. Not only do I literally see the "big picture," I feel assured that somebody really does know what's going on.

YOUR TURN TO DRAW MAPS

This time, complete two of the following exercises by drawing maps to show where things fit.

MAP OPTION 1: SAVING TIME

Fix this watch by drawing all its pieces back in place.

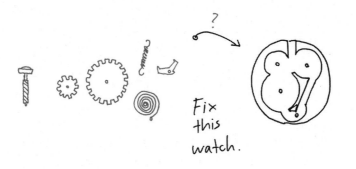

Fix this watch.

MAP OPTION 2: WHAT TO KEEP, WHAT TO CHUCK (REVISITED)

Remember this consumer packaged goods list of "who and what"? You'll notice that this time I've filled in several made-up products. Use a map to create a more visual way to see where they all fit together. (Hint: create a 2×2 coordinate system like in the banking example above, and then plot the individual products.) For my solution, see the appendix, page 273.

For extra credit, draw where some of these "products" might be consumed.

Action	Sales status	Ranking	products:				
support	selling really well	stellar	Starchips	Crumpetz	Purple Hays		
		best in class	Doreos	Heehaws			
invest	selling okay	on par	Blastpops	Blewpers			
		middling	Wingz				
drop	selling badly	lousy	Slingies	Orange-os			
		unsold	Snodoze	Lemon Plops			

MAP OPTION 3: YOU WANT IT VENN?

Below are five concepts. Create a Venn diagram (like the saving America circles) that shows how at least three overlap. Then identify a new concept that emerges from that overlap.

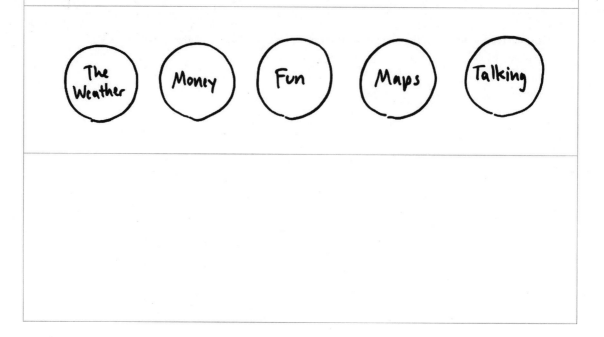

Time to mark our "problem pizza": ▶
when we face a "where" problem,
we draw a map.

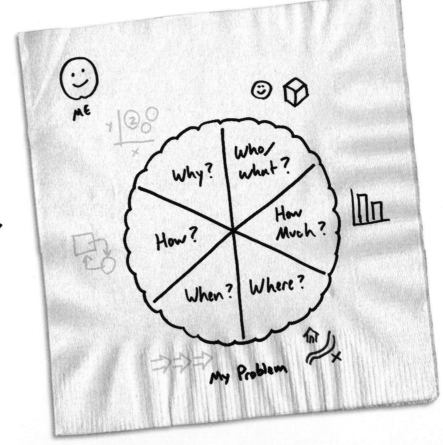

PICTURE 4: "WHEN" = A TIME LINE

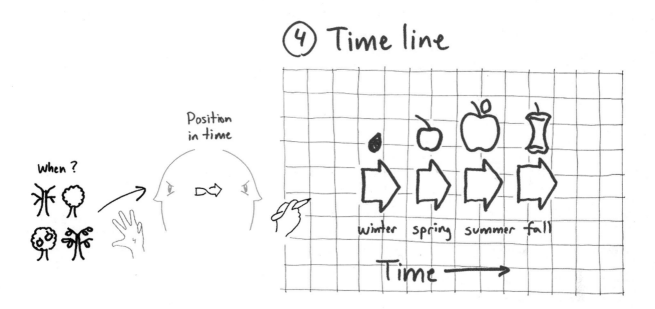

Did you know that there's an entire part of our vision system responsible for tracking whether it's dark or light out?* It uses that information to tell us when we're supposed to go to sleep. If you travel a lot by plane, you know how easy it is for jet lag to mess that system up.

It shouldn't be surprising that our sleep patterns are driven by light; it turns out that one of the most important ways we track the passage of time is by what we see. Remember how we see "when"? By noticing the change in quality, quantity, or position of a "who and what" object, we literally see time passing before our eyes. The picture we draw to show that phenomenon—the picture we draw to show the passage of time—is a series of steps reflecting change. In other words, we draw a time line.

＊
The suprachiasmatic nucleus measures the change in light detected by our eyes and feeds that information to the hypothalamus, which (among many other things) monitors our biological clock.

A Time line

As we discussed, the "when" slice is different from the three we've seen so far ("who and what," "how much," and "where") because while those three operate simultaneously, and more or less independently, "when" depends on their input in order to work at all: we can't see something change until we see the something to begin with.

In other words, it takes some time to see time, which may explain why we always feel we're behind it.

Examples of "when" problems include:

- I'm a project manager, and I have to make sure we launch our new product this quarter. *When does everything need to happen in order to meet our deadline? What is the best order of events?*

- I'm a traffic cop trying to piece together what happened at the stoplight, and I've got four witnesses who "saw it all." *What was the sequence of events that lead up to the accident? What did you hear just before the crash? Did the driver enter the bar before or after the pileup?*

- I've got a plane to catch later this morning but have about a thousand things to do before I can leave for the airport. Will I make the flight? *Do I have enough time to get everything done? Is there a particular order to do everything that will buy me some time? Are there things I'm simply not going to get done?*

The term "time line" is a one of those lucky examples of a name that perfectly describes the thing it stand for. When we draw a time line, we're going to represent time as a line (usually running from left to right*), along which we'll place marks to indicate that, as time passes, things change.

✳

Like many aspects of any language, the "visual grammar" of time flowing from left to right is probably culturally based. Most of the languages of the Western world read from left to right, and since English has come to dominate business communications, it stands to reason that most Americans tend to see time flowing in that direction. In other cultures time lines may flow in different directions.

When

Time line

Process map (linear)

(round)

Lifecycle

Swim lanes

Linear Progression

Gantt Chart

Time lines have fewer variations than the other five pictures we're looking at. In all cases the line representing time serves as a kind of backbone from which the changing events and details are suspended. Whether time lines are called life cycles, Gantt charts, swim lanes, or linear progressions, they all begin with a starting point and flow in one direction toward an endpoint. In many cases they may start over again once they've reached the end, but what sets off a time line from other "flow" pictures (e.g., the "how" flowcharts we'll see in the next section) is that time lines always move inexorably forward.

Let's look at an example of using a time line to help us clarify a "when" problem.

Breakthrough "when" example: Thomson again

Earlier this morning, we left the CEO of Thomson Corporation excited by the brand possibilities he had seen in our chart. When he left the room, we knew generally what we had to do, so the next question was, "Okay, when do we have to do it?"

Enter the project manager. In our case that meant Keith. Keith's favorite quote was, "If they weren't important, they wouldn't call them 'deadlines.' " To Keith, it was all a question of "when." We knew there was a lot to get done; Keith was the one who had to figure out the order; the timing; and, above all, the deadlines.

There would be a lot of people involved in this project, a lot of different things to do, a lot of dependencies, and a lot of meetings, and Keith knew it was up to him to make sure all the rest of us understood our roles. So Keith made a timetable using a spreadsheet program. But Keith knew from experience that none of us were going to look at his detailed spreadsheet, so he decided to create a simple time line he could draw anywhere.

Keith started out the way every time line begins: he drew "today."* Then he drew our deadline, March 13. Then he divided the space between into the number of weeks we had left.

✳

Remember: we can start all problem-solving pictures by first drawing a circle and giving it a name. In this case the name is "today."

Keith's time line started out as all time lines do: with "today" and "deadline" and a bunch of tick marks between them. ▶

Today
●
| | | | | | | | | | | | | | | |
March 13
○
|

Then Keith added in all the major steps he knew we would have to take in order to deliver the project on time: first, we'd have to get everyone the project would impact to buy in; second, we'd have to make detailed plans covering every detail and contingency; third, we'd do the actual rebranding; and then, finally, we'd have an all-hands check-in to make sure everything was ready before the launch.

Keith then added the major steps and milestones. ▶

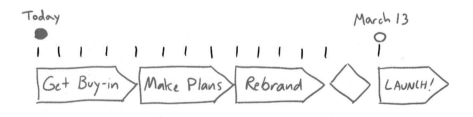

Using the time line as a backbone, Keith then laid in all the teams that would be working on the project and shorthand descriptions of what each needed to do and when.

The hand-drawn timeline shows:

Today ● ——— (timeline with tick marks) ——— **March 13** ⚲

Teams:

Phase →	Get Buy-in >	Make Plans >	Rebrand >	◇	LAUNCH! >
○ Design	collect materials	prep mockups	Design logos		
△ Content	Collect copy	write samples	write copy		
□ Technology	determine existing technologies	Design tech. arch.	Build platform		
▷ Project Mgt	Create teams	Create project plan	Coordinate reviews		Support →

CHECKPOINT!

With that basic time line, we could all see what we needed to be doing and when we needed to do it. Since it was simple and clear, we could all see where we fit into the project.

▲

Keith completed his time line by adding the project teams and when each needed to complete its tasks.

TIME LINE DRILL: LET'S GO FOR A SWIM

In recent years the term "swim lane" has entered the language of project managers, and it has nothing to do with keeping fit in a pool and everything to do with keeping the members of a project team on track and on time. What a swim-lane picture does is show *who* is supposed to get *what* done *when*, and compare it to others working in parallel at the same time.

For example, if Tom, Dick, and Harry are all taking a lunch break at the same time, the swim lane of their lunch hour would look like this:

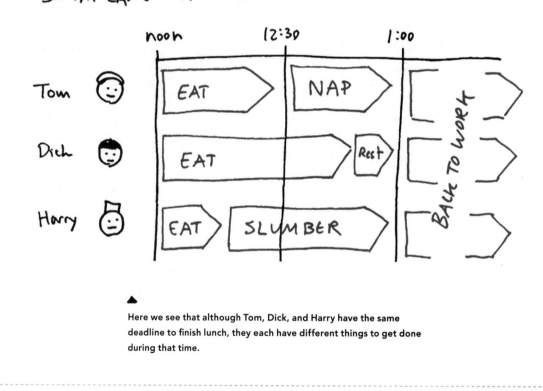

▲

Here we see that although Tom, Dick, and Harry have the same deadline to finish lunch, they each have different things to get done during that time.

Your exercise: using the time line provided below, create a simple swim-lane combination showing how the following characters' actions map out in parallel.

character	task	timing
Suzie (secretary)	answer phone	1:00–1:05
	check mail	1:05–1:30
	put out fires	1:30–3:00
Mitch (tech guy)	read blogs	1:00–1:30
	hear "crash" in boss's office	1:30–1:31
	fix Maud's laptop	1:35–3:00
Maud (the boss)	take client call	1:02–1:29
	freak out	1:29–1:30
	calm down	1:30–2:00
	Pilates	2:10–3:00

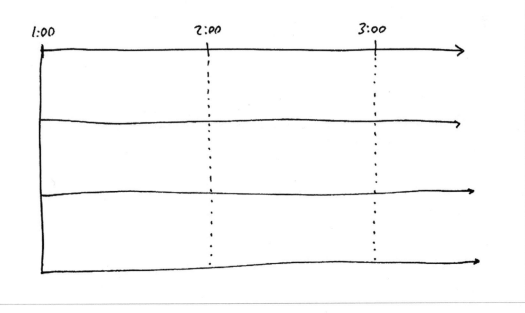

Let's add the picture to our "problem pizza" napkin: when we face a "when" problem, we draw a time line.

The picture we draw to show "when" is a time line. ▶

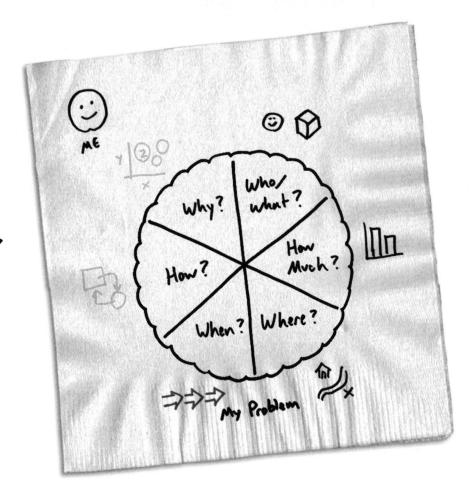

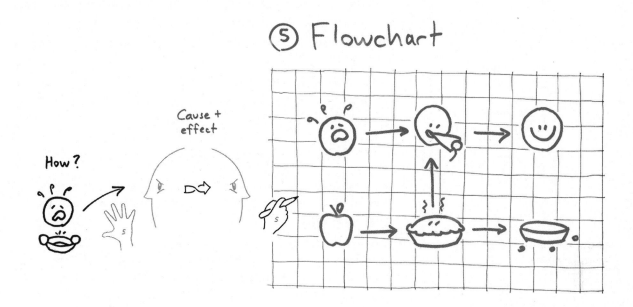

⑤ Flowchart

Cause + effect

How?

Our brain likes to build models of the world around us. The world is a complicated place, and having mental models of how it works helps us navigate it. In fact, the only way we get through the day at all is by relying on simple instinctive models (I need to eat to live) combined with models our minds developed as infants (if I touch something hot, I get burned) and fine-tuned as we grow (if I do a good job, I get rewarded).

We rely on both instinctive and deduced mental models to make our way through the world. ▼

By the time we're adults, we've built so many models that we've got at least a couple ready to go for just about any circumstance we can imagine. These models are the guidebooks we call upon every time we make a decision or take an action; without them we're literally babes in the woods.

Where do these models come from? It's been debated since the beginning of time whether we are born with them or learn them as we go, and we can be sure that debate will continue to the end of time. But in the meantime, we know this: our minds are extraordinarily good at deducing and inferring cause and effect by watching things happen around us.

Examples of "how" problems include the following:

- I'm a software programmer, and I can't nail down what these two interface buttons are supposed to do. *How do these buttons interact? How does pushing one affect the system?*

- I'm a consultant, and my client wants to know what it can do to increase market share. *How can we get a better understanding of the market and how it functions? How can I create a market response? What business action triggers what market response?*

- I'm reading this workbook, and I'm trying to figure out how to best apply what I'm seeing. *How will getting better at visual problem solving really help me solve problems? How can I integrate all these models into what I do every day?*

This ability to see, deduce, and record cause and effect is the business of the visual "how" pathway. It works like this: we see lots of things all the time. As we see them change in quality, number, and position, we see that time is passing and that things are happening. After watching these same things change in the same ways over and over again, we see patterns of interaction emerge. In other words, by collecting enough "whens" we finally begin to see what causes what—we eventually see "how."

What better way to illustrate how "how" works than with a flowchart? Here our initially confused self can observe things changing over and over. After a while, the patterns of interaction become clear, and we see how it all works.

Hmm... How "How" works:

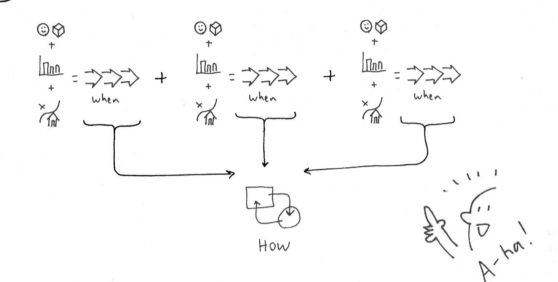

How

A-ha!

Of course that's an oversimplified model, but for understanding how we see "how," it works pretty well. Let's look at some examples.

Yum: apples again!

Imagine that Tom is just a baby, and he's crying. How can we stop Tom's crying? As every parent knows, crying means one of three things: baby needs to eat, baby needs to sleep, or baby needs to be changed.

We begin unsure of what is going on, but as we watch things interacting repeatedly, over time, we collect enough "whens" to build a model of cause and effect. We see "how."

There are three possible options: ▶
eat, sleep, or poop.

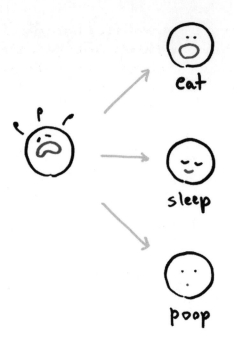

We know from having seen these interactions many times before that *when* we address each of these options in the appropriate way (feed counters eat, bed counters sleep, clean diaper counters poop), we'll get a happy baby. In other words, each cause requires a different approach to achieve our desired effect.

Each cause requires a different ▶
approach to achieve the desired
effect.

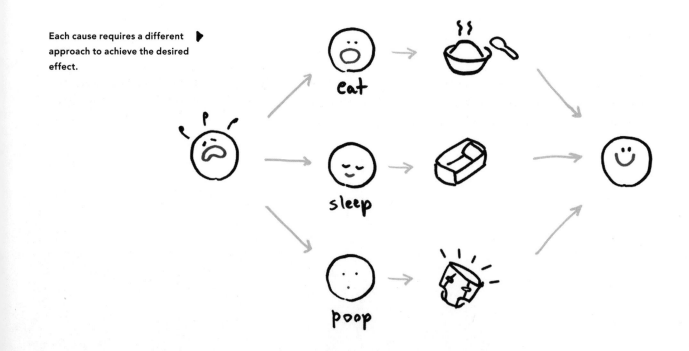

How do we know what Tom needs to do? Let's make a flowchart to see what causes have what effects. If baby has recently eaten, then he won't be hungry. If baby has recently slept, then he won't need the bassinet. If baby has recently pooped, then we *will* need a new diaper.

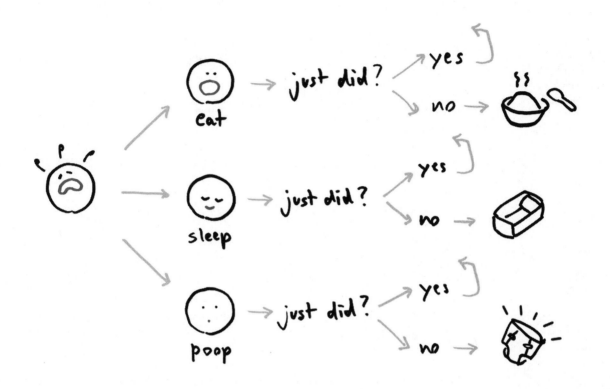

In Tom's case, if we know that he just had a nap and we just changed his diaper, then we can deduce that the only cause for crying is hunger. If we want to stop the crying, it looks like we had better feed him.

▲
Our flowchart illustrates the various "hows": the effects for each of the three causes.

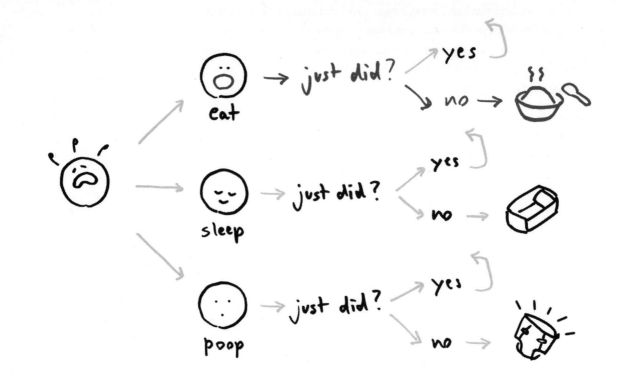

Now we know how to stop Tom's crying: make him something to eat.
Lucky we still have that apple!

YOUR FIRST "HOW" PICTURE

FLOWCHART 1: APPLE SAUCE

Draw a flowchart to show how we'll use an apple and a grater to make Tom stop crying. (Hint: you might want to add a few other items like a spoon, a bowl, and a bib.) For my solution, see the appendix, page xxx.

How to increase market share

Let's imagine that we're the business consultant and our client wants to know how to increase its market share. We know from experience that there are several ways it could potentially do this. If it dropped its product price then it might attract more buyers. If it improved its product quality it might push out the competition. If it expanded into a new market it might have it all to itself.

We've just identified three possible "how" options, each of which reflects a potential cause-and-effect model. How can we help our client decide which is the best one or best combination? Let's start with a simple flowchart show-ing these options side by side.

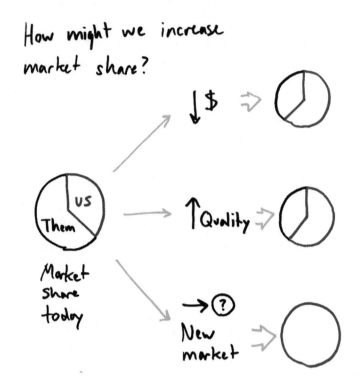

We've just identified three possible ways to increase market share. (There are many more.) How can we help our client select the best options? ▶

Another series of flowcharts will help us understand how to decide which is best. (We're only going to draw one of them, but that will be enough for us to see how this works.) In this flowchart we'll start with just one of the options above and test its viability for our client's market.

We'll start with the price-dropping option. First, we have to determine whether this market is price sensitive. If our client sells milk, a lower price might be the major customer purchasing consideration. If our client sells dia-monds, price might be the last thing the buyer is thinking about, or it could be that the buyer actually *wants* to pay more.

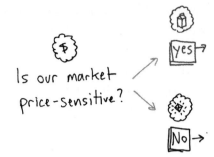

◀ First we show if our market is price sensitive. Milk probably is and diamonds perhaps not.

If price is not an issue, lowering it doesn't make sense. In that case we've already shown that it's better to step back and look at another option. On the other hand, if price is the main consideration, then we next ask whether our price is higher or lower than our competition's.

◀ If price is a factor, we next have to show whether our price is higher or lower than our competition's.

If our price is higher, then dropping it is clearly a good option. There will be a lot more involved in making that decision, but we've shown how it is a valid possibility. On the other hand, if our price is already lower than our competition's, we've got two further options.

First we could drop our price even more and see if that generates more sales. Then again, if our price is already lower than our competition's, our initial assessment that price matters in our market may be wrong. After all, if a lower price isn't helping sell more, perhaps there's something else we should be looking at, like product quality or even whether we're in the right market.

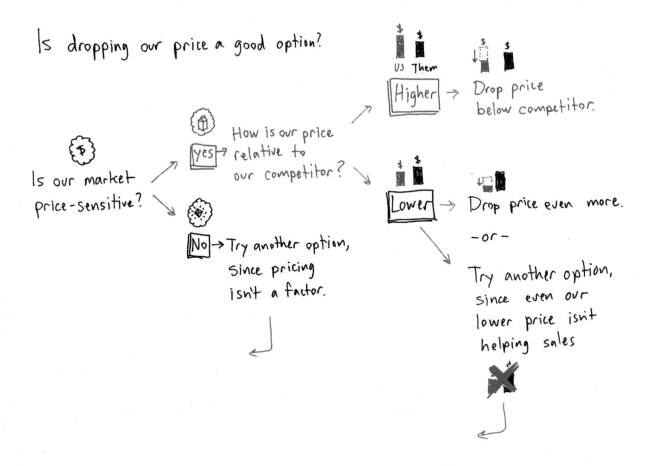

These little flowcharts (which in this case some people might call "decision trees") show how we help our client make a good decision by visually showing how one factor impacts another. If we made similar flowcharts for the other two market-expanding options, we'd come away with a clear idea of what is worth trying and what it not, and without needing anything more than a pen and paper.

YOUR SECOND "HOW" PICTURE

FLOWCHART 2: ONE CLICK

Rearrange these pieces so they create a logical flowchart, then write down the "how" problem that you've solved. For my solution, see the appendix, page 274.

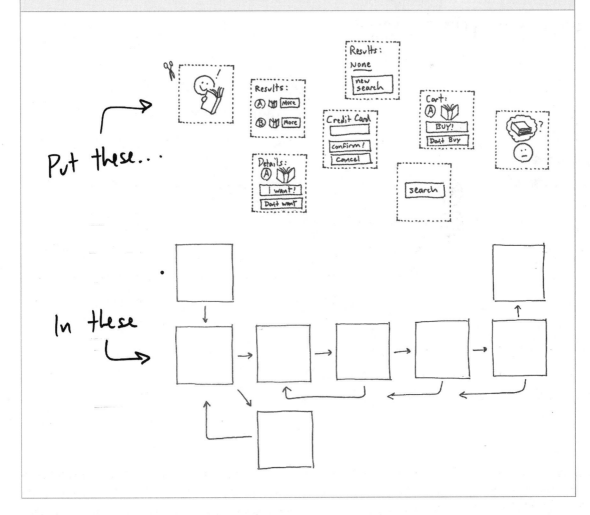

You'll notice that in these examples we've used the terms "if" and "then" a lot: if Tom is hungry then we feed him; if we want to help a client increase market share, then we have to understand its market; etc. All a flowchart does is make these if-then dependencies visible so that we can see what is impacted by what—and so we can compare several of these cause-and-effect options at the same time.

That's all our flowcharts for the time being, so let's add the flowchart picture to the "problem pizza" napkin.

The picture we draw to show a ▶ "how" problem is a flowchart.

EXTRA-CREDIT FLOWCHART: YOUR "HOW" PROBLEM

Can you think of any challenge you or your business faces that could be considered a "how" problem? To help clarify it, what flowchart could you draw?

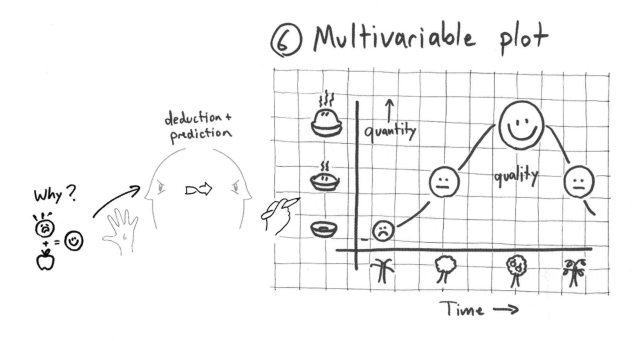

We've finally come to our last slice, and this is the big one. "Why" is the ultimate problem-solving question. If we can answer "why"—why things work this way, why this happens and not that, why certain things seem inevitable—we've probably got much of our problem already solved. We might not clearly see the solution yet, but if we understand the underlying reasons why the pieces interact the way they do, it's just a matter of time.

For example, if we know *why* Tom, Dick, and Harry are here (they're hungry), and we know *why* they're hungry (they've been in a workshop all afternoon), and we know *why* an apple makes a good snack (it's tasty, healthy, and filling), our solution is at hand.

"Why" is more than how something works, or when it happens, or where it takes place, or how much is required, or who needs it for what: why is the summary of all those things rolled into one underlying *reason*.

The way we see "why" is by collecting enough "how": one cause-and-effect situation stacked on another and another until we're no longer surprised by the way things around us work out. We get used to the way things occur and believe that we can pretty well anticipate what's likely to happen in most circumstances. We've got the "whys" of the world figured out, good enough to get along anyway.

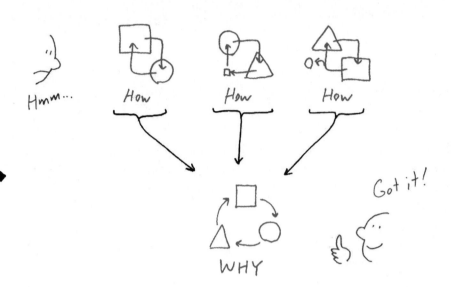

WHY things happen ("Good-enough" approach)

Hmm... How How How

WHY

Got it!

Over the years, we combine all our "hows" to build a good-enough model of "why."

Examples of "why" problems are

- I'm in HR and have been told to plan for layoffs, but I don't know what to tell people. *Why are we downsizing now—there's got to be more to it than just the numbers, right?*

- I'm the CEO, and I want to let everyone know about some big changes we're going to make around here. *Why are global market forces pushing us out of the manufacturing business? Why can't we keep going with business as usual?*

- I'm four years old, and I want to know why the sky is blue, why I can't watch TV all day, and why I get in trouble when I keep asking. *Why can't I get a break?*

As these examples show, there are two ways to answer "why" questions: the "good-enough" way (because we need to save money, because of globalization, because I said so) and the real underlying answer (better sit down because this is going to take a while), which we're going to call the "scientific" way.

Because there are two ways to answer "why," this final slice gets two pictures:* a simple one for the "good-enough" answer, and a complicated one for the "scientific" answer. We're going to give the scientific picture the horribly

✳
Yes, I'm breaking my own rule—but only for a second. In a moment, you'll see why.

scientific (but accurate) name "multivariable plot," and we're going to give the simple picture a name we're already familiar with from earlier today: portrait.*

Let's start with that simple one.

Hey, Microsoft. Why buy Yahoo!? (part I)

Last year, Steve Ballmer, the CEO of Microsoft, and Jerry Yang, then CEO of Yahoo! got into a very public scuffle around a simple question that neither could answer very well and that made both of these extremely smart men look pretty dumb. The simple story is that Microsoft offered to buy Yahoo! for $38 billion, an offer that Ballmer considered a generous price. Yang felt it was not a generous offer at all and said no. Ballmer offered more, and again Yang said no. Then Yang changed his mind and asked for a lot more, at which point Ballmer said no and took Microsoft's offer off the table.

All this happened over a period of many months, at the end of which Yang lost his job and Ballmer's Microsoft lost several billion dollars in market capitalization.

During the time this was going on, you couldn't pick up a newspaper, read a business or technology blog, or watch the TV news without seeing something about the Microsoft-Yahoo! story. The media buzz focused on the bigger-than-life personalities, the monstrous budgets, and the boardroom hysterics, which admittedly were a lot of fun to watch. But what was missing in the frenzy was any truly insightful analysis of why Microsoft made the offer (the largest corporate buy in Microsoft's history) in the first place. There was some talk of Microsoft needing to beat Google at the search game, but for all the "who and what," "how much," and "when," we got almost no "why."

During that time I gave a workshop at Microsoft. As one of the exercises (similar to those we're doing in this workbook), I asked the attendees—none of whom had any direct knowledge of the deal—what picture they would draw to explain why they thought Microsoft was willing to spend $44 billion dollars to buy Yahoo!

A lot of great pictures were drawn by the participants, and when we voted for favorites, two rose above the rest: one showed a Microsoft ice-cream cone with a Yahoo! cherry on top; the other showed a big MSFT fish about to eat a small Y! fish. We called the first one "tastes better together" and the second "in their nature."

✱

Yes: the "why" question—the biggest question of the day—can be shown with the first picture we created, bringing our entire "problem pizza" right back to where it started. Isn't it wonderful when things work out that way?

Why MSFT buy YAHOO?

The "Good-Enough" approach

"Tastes Better"

"In Their Nature"

Two views of why Microsoft would buy Yahoo! "Tastes better together" and "in their nature." Both are perfect "good-enough" portraits of "why."

For their insight and simplicity, both of these are magnificent "why" pictures. Just looking at them gives you a sense of the reality left out of the news. First, Microsoft needs Yahoo! like ice cream needs a cherry; what could be a better description of a bland mega-brand needing a zippy flavor change? Second, because Microsoft is bigger it simply must eat the smaller Yahoo! What could be a better description of the nature of corporate America's appetites?

But insightful as they are, "good-enough" pictures are just that: good enough. And good as our "good-enough" portraits might be, as succinctly as they might show "why," they're rarely good enough to keep us from being whacked on the back of the head by the unexpected.

Just when we've got it all figured out...

The trouble with believing too much in our "good-enough" model is that it might be missing something important.

WHY.

These "good-enough" models are based on what we've seen before. We've been collecting information and building "why" models our entire lives, so why not rely on them? Assuming that the world around us remains the same, our "why" models should keep working, same as always. The problem is that the world around us changes all the time: "who and what" doesn't stay the same, quantities vary, locations shift, timing falters. The same cause might even, one day, have a different effect, for reasons we can't see.

How could we ever draw a "why" picture to account for the interaction of so many different variables? Getting all those things into one picture is tricky, but it can be done, and that's what we are going to do now. As with everything we've drawn so far, though, it's not as hard as it sounds. All we have to do—just as we've done for every visual slice so far—is turn the "why" deduction process around: *to see how lots of things interact, draw a picture that maps together lots of things.*

Meet the scientific "why" picture: the "multivariable plot," an excellent way to visually see the relationships between many different types of data and ideas.*

✻

This shouldn't look unfamiliar; the Thomson strategy chart from this morning was a good example of a multivariable plot.

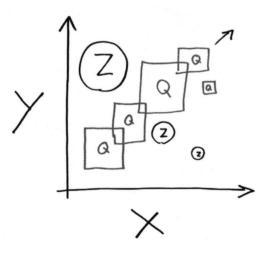

The Multivariable Plot

◀ As the name suggests, a multivariable plot maps together many different types of data (X, Y, Q, Z, etc.) so that we can see hidden relationships that might otherwise have gone undetected.

One way to think of a multivariable plot is a big stew. We select the best of a bunch of different flavors of information (our variables) and toss them together into a pot (our coordinate system), then turn up the heat as we wait to see how they mix and what rises to the top. If we want a simple meal, we've got our "good-enough" portrait. Here we're looking for something more.

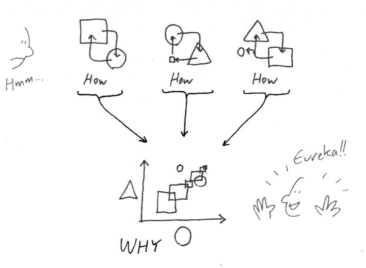

The "scientific" model (the multivariable plot) stews together many "hows" and data variables. Once we see what rises to the top, we have a good sense of "why."

The beauty of a multivariable plot is that once we've got the pot going, we can continue to add in new variables as they appear. We may have to change our coordinate system to accommodate the new arrivals, but that's the beauty of this picture's flexibility. We might be surprised by unexpected input suddenly arriving, but we've now got the ability to catch them before they bonk us—and a place to put them safely.

A good scientific "why" framework gives us the flexibility to deal with unexpected input.

Hey, Microsoft. Why buy Yahoo!? (part II)

Let's use a multivariable plot to see more "why" in this story than ice cream and fish. In many ways this is a repeat of the Thomson Corporation exercise from this morning, but now that we have the 6×6 framework behind us, it should be easier to create. As before, we know we're going to be plotting together:

- "Who and what": Microsoft, Yahoo!, and Google; technology companies and their products.

- "How much": $44 billion price tag plus the market caps* of Microsoft ($282 billion), Yahoo! ($35 billion), and Google ($181 billion).

- "Where": what part of the market do they each occupy?

- "When": today and—since this is clearly a long-term strategic play by Microsoft—at least a few years into the future.

- "How": money, and lots of it.

✳

These are the market capitalizations of the three companies during the second week of the media furor.

With those pieces identified, let's create a coordinate system. Let's start by asking ourselves what big things we already know about these companies. One thing we know about these companies is what they offer. For example, Microsoft offers a lot of applications (Word, Excel, Windows, PowerPoint, Outlook, MSN.com, etc.), Yahoo! offers fewer (Mail, Finance, Photos, Travel, etc.), and at this point Google offers only a few (Search, Docs, Maps). We also know that Microsoft charges people to purchase and use its software, while most everything Yahoo! and Google offer is free to users.

We can easily create a coordinate system using those variables, with "number of applications offered" as our x and "price to user" as our y.

A coordinate system comparing "number of applications" offered to "price" might show us something interesting. ▶

For a third variable, we map "who." And let's kill two birds with the same stone by making a circle around each, representing the companies' relative market caps (just like we mentioned for "how" charts). We end up with a big Microsoft, with lots of applications for pay, and archenemy Google, a smaller circle offering few applications but for free.

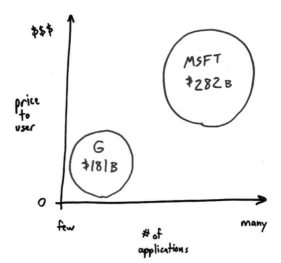

Here's one way to compare Microsoft and its archenemy Google: Microsoft is bigger, offers lots more software, and—since Google's applications are effectively free to the user—charges vastly higher fees. ▶

We don't even have to plot Yahoo! to see that according to this model of the software market, Microsoft and Google aren't even in the same business. How could they be competitors? That's where time enters the picture. While at present Google doesn't offer many applications, every couple of months it launches another one (Google Earth, Android, Finance, Spreadsheets, etc.) What that tells us is that over time Google's ball is going to roll closer and closer to Microsoft's.

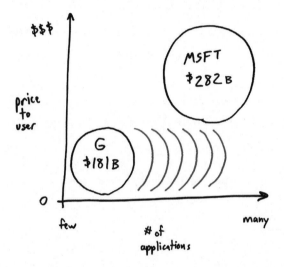

Why would MSFT buy Yahoo?

◄ As Google launches more applications, it's going to start rolling in Microsoft's direction . . .

Wait a minute: if Google starts offering the same kinds of applications as Microsoft and still gives them away for free, how is Microsoft going to stay in business? I mean, who would pay for software when they could get it for free? We have no reason to suspect that Google is going to start charging users for its applications, so the Google ball won't go up. And I can't imagine Microsoft suddenly giving away all its applications for free; that ball isn't moving down anytime soon.

So as more software becomes freely available, what can Microsoft do?

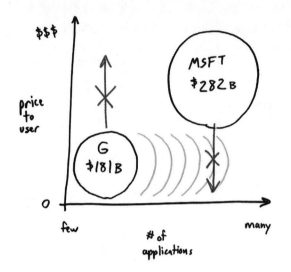

Why would MSFT buy Yahoo?

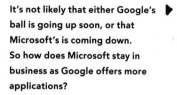

It's not likely that either Google's ball is going up soon, or that Microsoft's is coming down. So how does Microsoft stay in business as Google offers more applications?

Okay, let's stop a moment. I got so intrigued about what I was seeing that I forgot to map little old Yahoo! Let's plot it: a few more applications than Google but also all free.

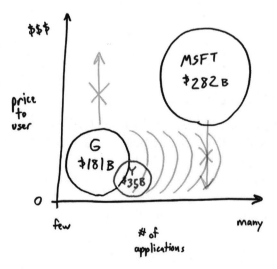

Why would MSFT buy Yahoo?

Now Microsoft's $44 billion strategy begins to make sense. If it can buy Yahoo!—even at a price way above market—Microsoft buys a way to directly block Google's rolling ball. Maybe all Microsoft needs is to buy time to figure out what to do with its big ball.

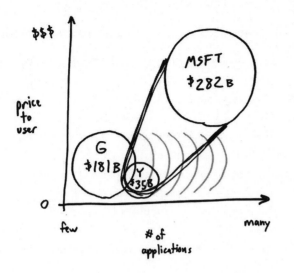

Why would MSFT buy Yahoo?

$$$

price to user

MSFT $282B

G $181B

Y $35B

0

few

# of applications

many

If Microsoft buys Yahoo! it buys a way to block Google's roll—at least for a while.

I have no idea if any of this was in Ballmer's mind when he made his play last year. But based on this picture, I now know why I'd have done it if I was in his shoes.

That's my last example for the day. Now it's your turn; then we can hit the beach.

YOUR "WHY" PICTURES: A THEME AND VARIATIONS

1. A SIMPLE TRUTH

Draw a simple "good-enough" portrait to show why visual thinking is a powerful way to solve problems. For my solution, see the appendix, page 275.

2. A SCIENTIFIC PLOT

Create a basic multivariable plot that illustrates a connection or two among the following data:

- Percentage of people in a typical business meeting who are Black Pens (I can't wait to draw): 25 percent.
- Percentage of people in the same business meeting who are Yellow Pens (I can't draw, but . . .): 50 percent.
- Percentage of people in that meeting who are Red Pens (I hate drawing): 25 percent.
- Information seen is twice as likely to be recalled as information heard.
- Information both seen and heard is four times more likely to be recalled than information heard.
- Number of text-only pages in a typical one-hour business presentation: forty.
- Number of picture-dominant pages in a typical one-hour business presentation: six.

(Hint: let me get you started with a suggested coordinate system. It's not the only one; if you don't like it, go ahead and draw your own.)

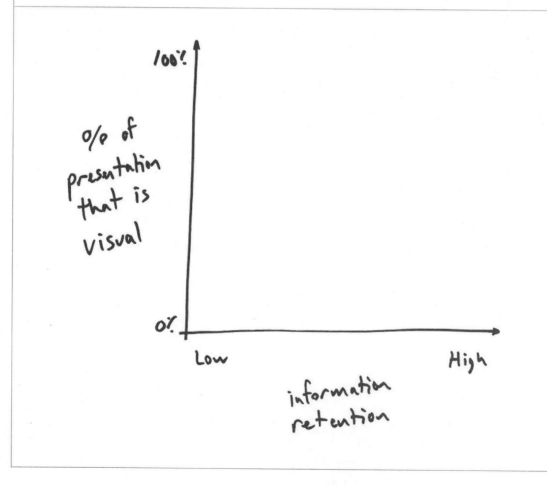

Let's add the last picture to our "problem pizza." If the problem we face is a "why" problem, the picture we draw to clarify it is a multivariable plot. Then again, if "good enough" is good enough, we can just draw a simple "why" portrait. Either way, we've brought the full circle to a close.

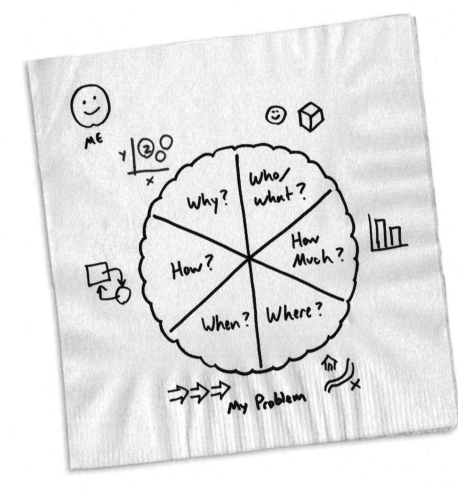

When we have a "why" problem, we draw a multivariable plot (or if "good enough" is good enough, we can draw a simple "why" portrait, bringing the circle back to its beginning).

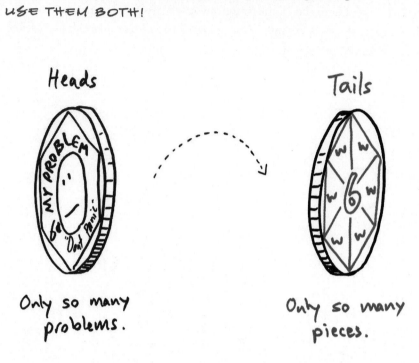

Heads

Only so many problems.

Tails

Only so many pieces.

The 6×6 rule tells us that if we can identify the type of problem we have, we should be able to draw the most appropriate of the six simple pictures that might describe it. Fine, that makes sense.

But what if we can't figure out what kind of problem we have? What if our problem is so fuzzy that we can't tell if it's a "who and what" problem or a "when" problem, or any of the others—how, then, do we know which picture to draw?

This is the real beauty of the 6×6 rule: if at first we can't see what kind of a problem we're facing, we can just "flip the coin" and start drawing each slice one by one. As we move from drawing a portrait (who is involved in the problem) to a chart (how many of them are there) to a map (where are they located) to a time line (when do they interact) to a flowchart (how do they interact), we will see the problem emerge clearly enough to discern which aspects of it are most interesting to explore further. In effect, we've using the six pictures to illuminate the six problem types.

Whichever way we flip the coin, the 6×6 rule is our most useful tool for beginning to solve any problem with a picture.

Now go enjoy the rest of your afternoon outside: tomorrow we're going to put all this into practice.

Welcome to Day 3

I didn't want tell you while we were still knee-deep in portraits, charts, and maps, but yesterday was our workshop's toughest day. Now that we're familiar with the 6×6 rule, everything from this point on will be downhill. Here's why: as we continue to master the 6×6 rule and the basics of visual problem solving, our visual confidence will continue to grow, and we'll begin to really see the potential of our visual capabilities.

I said at the beginning of this workshop that we can clarify *any* problem with a picture, and I mean it. I hope you're beginning to see how. Our three "built-in" tools, the four-step process, and the 6×6 rule are all a big part of it, but there's still one more blade we haven't opened yet in our visual-thinking tool kit. So far we've been focused on the world in front of us, learning to look carefully and see its patterns. But now we're going to blow the doors off all that: we're going to start using our mind's eye to imagine problem-solving options that aren't in front of us at all.

Let's take a break from the 6×6 rule and look for solutions in a completely different direction: let's tap into our mind's eye for a while and see what we can see.

Our mind's eye

In business meetings, books, and magazines and in conferences, off sites, and brainstorming sessions, we're told to "be innovative" and to "use our imaginations" and to "think outside the box." That's all wonderful—anything that reminds us to think differently and encourages us to look for unexpected solutions is to be encouraged. But there's a big problem: in the real world how many of us have been taught how to drop everything and suddenly think differently? I mean, wow, that's a lot of pressure: talk about "deer in the headlights"!

Today's "imagining" step goes straight to the heart of that challenge. After all, we've got the most powerful innovation machine on the planet sitting right inside our heads: our imagination. All we need is an imagination ignition; a guaranteed way to turn on our mind's eye and kick it into gear—on demand, anywhere, anytime.

I think we've got such an ignition, and guess what? (You knew this was coming.) The key is pictures.

Today we're moving on to step ▶ three: imagining.

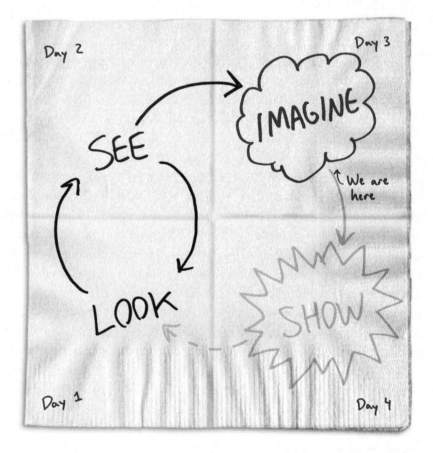

UNWRITTEN RULE 3

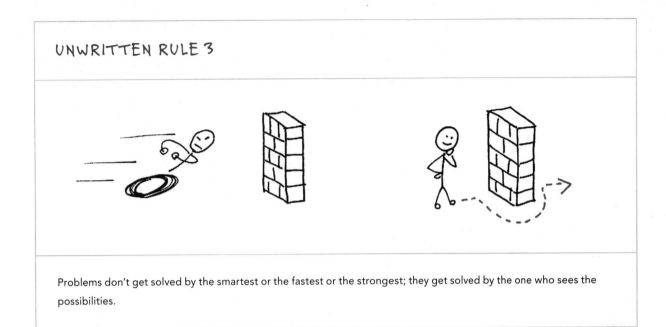

Problems don't get solved by the smartest or the fastest or the strongest; they get solved by the one who sees the possibilities.

We've looked at a lot of problems already, everything from corporate rebranding to buying bananas. If through all that it still hasn't become clear, let me state the real underlying premise of this book: *to see a problem is to see how to solve it.*

This is really important, so I want to be super clear: seeing a problem does not automatically mean we solve it. Lots of people see the impact of global climate change, for example, but that does not mean we're solving it yet. What it *does* mean is this: if we can see the pieces that make up our problem, see the patterns within them, and see how to manipulate the patterns for a different outcome, then all that is needed to solve the problem is the decision to do it.

Yes, we need to have the intelligence to pick the best option; yes, we need the speed to get it done on time; yes, we need the strength to make it happen and to stay on course. But the hardest part of all—finding the solution—depends only on our ability to see what's in front of us and imagine as many ways as we can to deal with it.

The subtext of this unwritten rule is this:

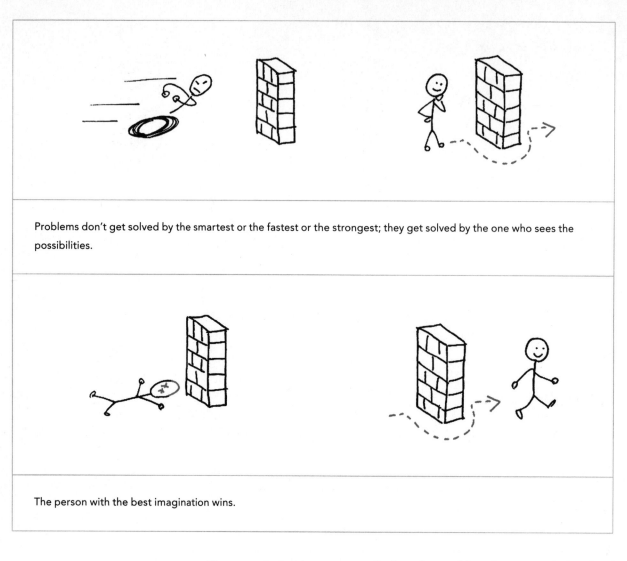

Problems don't get solved by the smartest or the fastest or the strongest; they get solved by the one who sees the possibilities.

The person with the best imagination wins.

I'm an optimist. Any way you look at the world, we've got a whole pile of problems to address every day. But we've been on this planet for a long time and have managed to muddle our way through this far and still come up smiling, so I choose to believe we can keep that track record going.

If we work at it, we can imagine our way past anything thrown in our way, and once we've seen the solution in our mind's eye, all we have to do is make it happen.* Okay, so what about that? How do we see solutions to the impossible? How do we kick our imagination into gear on demand? Back to Day 1 and the "look, see, imagine, show" process.

If we've looked well at what's in front of us and seen what kind of a problem we face and what pieces make it up, we've now got all the raw materials of the solution in mind, ready to go. All we need to do is close our eyes, which brings us to this rule's *second* subtext:

✳

No small undertaking, that "just make it happen" thing, that's for sure. But if we can keep the process going and break it into a series of steps we can see, maybe we can get the impossible done. It's been done before.

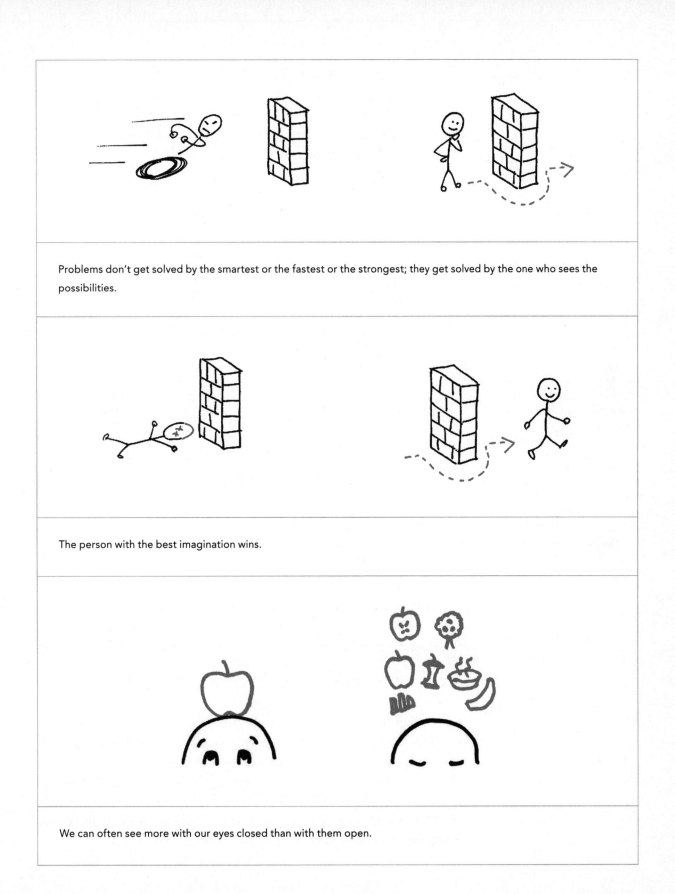

Problems don't get solved by the smartest or the fastest or the strongest; they get solved by the one who sees the possibilities.

The person with the best imagination wins.

We can often see more with our eyes closed than with them open.

The next set of blades

It's finally time to pull out our Swiss Army knife napkin again and add the last blade: the corkscrew. As we draw it in, make sure it has five twists and go ahead and label them with the letters *S*, *Q*, *V*, *I*, and *D*.

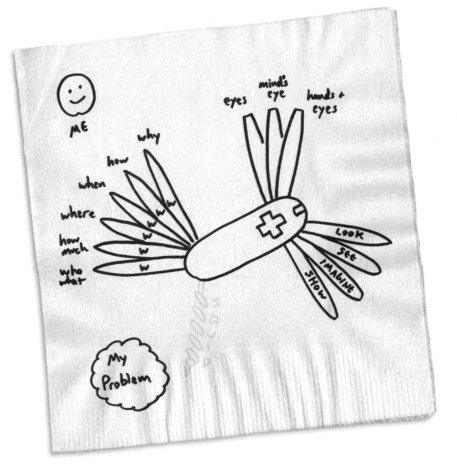

Back to the Swiss Army knife and the last blade: the corkscrew. Give it five twists and label them S-Q-V-I-D.

How to uncork a bottle

Rather than explain how this strangely spelled "SQVID" opens up our mind's eye, let me first show you an example. Here's our scenario: imagine that you've invited me over for dinner, and I bring a bottle of wine. When I arrive, your hands are full so you ask me to open it. The trouble is that I'm a total bumpus (that's part bumpkin, part doofus) and have never seen a corkscrew before, so I have no idea what to do. Luckily, I've got an imagination, and we're going to activate it with the five letters S-Q-V-I-D.

First, I look at the two items I'm holding. I have a full bottle in one hand, and a swirly metal thingy in the other. My mind starts imagining the possibilities.

◀ I have two items in my hands: a bottle and a swirly thing. Looking at them, my imagination kicks into gear.

The first possibility I see for opening the bottle is a *simple* one: obviously I use the corkscrew like a hammer to crack open the bottle:

◀ The *simplest* solution is to use the corkscrew to break open the bottle.

But that seems overly simple: there must be some reason for the screw part of the corkscrew, and, besides, I'm going to end up with broken glass in our wine. That can't be right. There must be a more *elaborate* process involved. I know: I'll drill a small hole in the side of the bottle and catch the wine as it leaks out:

Elaborate

A more *elaborate* solution would ▶
be to drill a hole in the bottle.

But it's going to be really tough to drill through glass. In fact, I can't even scratch the glass with this thing. As I continue to look, I see another possibility: oh, I get it, I'm supposed to drill in from the top where the softer cork is! *Qualitatively*, that looks much better, but it's still going to be tough to pull that cork out:

Qualitative

URG

I can only imagine how ▶
qualitatively difficult it's going to
be to pull that cork out.

If I were a structural engineer, I could probably come up with a *quantitative* way to measure the torque and twisting forces required to open the bottle this way. Plotting them on a graph would show me the exact point at which the cork would pop:

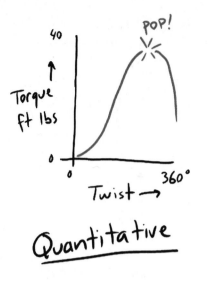

Quantitative

> ◀ **Quantitatively,** I could measure the forces required to get the cork to pop.

But hold on a moment: I'm getting a little lost in the weeds here. It's time to remember why I'm even doing all this. My *vision* is simple: we just want us to have a glass of wine while watching the sunset. Numbers aside, I still know what I'm after: an open bottle and a fine glass of wine:

Vision

> ◀ I can still see my *vision*: an open bottle, a glass of wine, and the sun setting over the horizon.

I've already established the basics of the process, the question now becomes how exactly do I achieve that goal; to put it in business parlance, how do I *execute* the maneuver?

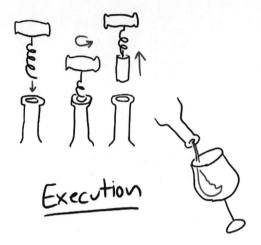

Execution

I see that *executing* my vision ▶
will require a number of discrete
steps, each taken in the right
order.

Before I commit to this course of action, I'd like to confirm that it's correct. If I look at my tools one more time *individually*, I can see what is supposed to happen:

Individual

Looked at *individually*, this seems ▶
like the appropriate course of
action.

To confirm, I can use my imagination to quickly *compare* other possible options and make sure I've chosen the one that looks likely to produce the best outcome:

Comparison

◀ A comparison lets me quickly check my selected option against other possibilities.

Yes: I'm on the right track. When all is said and done I'm going to see a *change* (Δ or delta, as it's known to Greeks and geeks) in the form of the objects now in my hands. If I do this right, in a rapidly approaching future I'm going to have an empty bottle and an almost empty glass:

Δ Change

◀ In a short period of time, I'm going to see a *change* from what I have now: my bottle will be empty and my glass nearly so.

But I don't have that yet. In the present time—in the *status quo*—I still have work to do. At least now I know how to do it.

◀ My *status quo*: a still-full bottle and a corkscrew. Time to get to work.

Status Quo

Presto: the bottle is open. And so is my imagination. That's the SQVID.

Meet the SQVID: a practical exercise in applied imagination

The SQVID is a simple mnemonic device composed of the five letters S-Q-V-I-D. Each of the five stands for one of the five questions we can ask ourselves about any idea to kick our mind's eye into gear and force ourselves to imagine the possibilities. I used the example of opening a bottle, but the SQVID works to open our minds wide open when we want to imagine anything.

Think of the SQVID as a corkscrew for our imagination: a guaranteed way to open up multiple ways of thinking about something. The next time someone asks us to "think outside the box"—when we need to see possibilities that are not directly in front of our eyes—the five questions triggered by the five letters of the SQVID are all we need to ask.

The five SQVID questions

The five SQVID questions are

1. Am I more interested in a *simple* or an *elaborate* view? What might each look like?

2. Am I more interested in seeing *quality* or *quantity*? What would I see in a picture of each?

3. What's more important to me now: the *vision* of where I'm going or the *execution* of how I'm going to get there? How do they look different?

4. Is it more important for me to see my idea *individually* or in *comparison* with something else? Can I come up with a picture for both?

5. What am I more concerned about: how my idea might cause *change* or maintain the *status quo* (how things are right now)? What do each of these look like?

Summarizing that with a picture, we see the SQVID as a framework of five categories, each of which has two distinct and opposite settings:

S. Q. V. I. D.

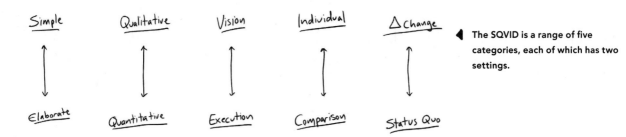

The SQVID is a range of five categories, each of which has two settings.

If we mapped in our corkscrew episode, we'd end up with a visual record of our complete imagination process: from seeing what we had in front of us all the way through nine different ways of looking at it—all generated by our own mind's eye. All the pictures show the same thing—how to open a bottle of wine—but they all look different.

The complete SQVID is a visual record of our entire thinking process. Although all the pictures show the same thing—how to open a bottle of wine—they all look different.

S. Q. V. I. D.

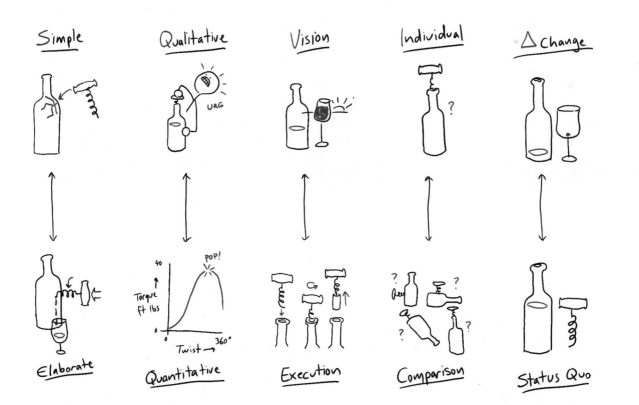

What makes the SQVID a powerful framework for activating our imagination is that these five categories cover most of the ways we can think about things, period. For example, as we shift from quality (feelings, emotions, sensations) to quantity (numbers, amounts, measurements) or from vision (goals, direction, purpose) to execution (process, time, linear steps), we can almost feel our brain shifting gears.

Our imagination has a five-speed transmission

Remember the portrait yesterday that showed an automatic transmission compared to a manual? I like to think of our mind's eye as a powerful engine that is running all the time, but we leave it in automatic too often. We expect our imagination to do the mental-image gear shifting for us since most of the time that works just fine. But when it comes to actively seeing possibilities, that's not enough. We need a manual override: a simple, on-demand way to force our mind's eye through all the gears and see all the possibilities. That's the real purpose of the SQVID.

The SQVID is a manual five-speed transmission for our imagination: shift from "qualitative" to "change" and you can almost feel your brain changing gears. ▶

To test this out, let's go through the five gears of the SQVID one more time, only this time we'll do the shifting together.

SQVID DRILL 1: APPLES AND ORANGES

To make this easy the first time out, we're going to use the SQVID to compare two simple things: an apple and an orange. I'll take the apple through the gears and you follow along with the orange.

We'll start with a simple side-by-side comparison: whatever I do with the apple, you do the same with the orange.

Simple vs. Elaborate	Simple vs. Elaborate
Here's my simple apple:	Now you make a simple orange.

To make a more elaborate version, maybe I can show a whole orchard:	How might you make your orange more elaborate?

Qualitative vs. Quantitative	**Qualitative vs. Quantitative**
What are the visual qualities that make an apple an apple?	What are the visual qualities that make an orange an orange?
How can I create a "quantitative" view of an apple? How about its nutrition?	How can I create a "quantitative" view of an orange?
Vision vs. Execution	**Vision vs. Execution**
What is the perfect "vision" of an apple?	What is the perfect "vision" of an orange?
How do I "execute" to achieve that vision?	How do I "execute" that orange vision?

Individual vs. Comparison	Individual vs. Comparison
What details do I see when I look at an apple all by itself?	What details do I see when I look at an orange all by itself?
What do I see when I compare it to other fruit?	What do I see when I compare it to other fruit?
Change vs. Status Quo	**Change vs. Status Quo**
What might my apple look like in the future?	What might my orange look like in the future?
Remind me: what do I have now?	Remind me: what am I looking at again?

The first way to use the SQVID: opening our mind's eye and stretching our imagination

When you thought about those different ways of looking at an orange, did you feel your mind shifting gears? This exercise is an amazing opportunity to see the variety of ways our brains like to process ideas. What we've witnessed is nothing more than our mind's eye at work; our imagination just doing what comes naturally. Yes, we had to kick it a bit to get it going, but that's only because most of us are out of practice. The engine is running, but we've been letting it idle too long.

When we run our idea through the SQVID questions, we're tapping into processing centers located throughout the brain. We're bouncing our idea between the temporal lobes and the parietal lobes, between the visual cortex and the superior colliculus, and so on. We don't need to know what all those pieces are or do—indeed, neuroscientists are only beginning to understand the roles of the hundreds of distinct processing centers—but we do know that the more of them we activate, the more possibilities we can see.

As we move through the questions posed by the SQVID, we're also passing our idea back and forth between the right and left hemispheres of our brain, forcing our mind's eye to seek alternative images that we might not otherwise have conjured up. Over the past twenty years, scientific evidence has been building to indicate that the right side of our brain is more comfortable with spatial and conceptual processing, while the left side is better at verbal and linear processing.

Evidence suggests that our brain is of two minds.

No it's not. Yes it is.

Debates rage on in academia about how specific and measurable this brain split may be, but the SQVID is a great way to hedge our bets. No matter which side of the debate you fall on, the fact is that whenever we look at anything we see both the "warm," emotional aspects of that idea and the "cool," rational aspects. We need to see both in order to really make sense of what is there.

The SQVID accounts for this by the arrangement of the questions it asks. The "top" side of each question (simple, qualitative, visionary, individual, change) forces a more "right-brained" synthetic view. The "bottom" side of each question (elaborate, quantitative, execution, comparison, status quo) produces a more "left-brained" analytic view. We need to intentionally bounce between both extremes to put our mind's eye fully to work.

The questions along the top of the SQVID force a more synthetic view. Those along the bottom trigger a more analytic view. Both are needed for a full workout of our imagination.

▼

S. Q. V. I. D.

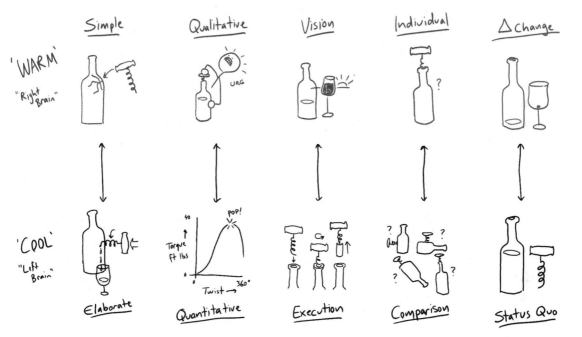

A journey along the SQVID

Let's take a quick tour of the SQVID and look at examples of various ideas along the way.

SIMPLE OR ELABORATE?

There is always a simple way to look at anything. It may not represent an entirely correct and accurate view of the idea,* but we should at least be able to quickly "get it"—whatever "it" is. That's the beauty of the simple view:

✻
Just because something is simple does not make it a good idea. Napoléon's march was an extraordinarily simple idea: *in early summer we collect half a million men at the Russian border, we march during the warm months, and in early autumn we take Moscow.* That's hubris: a simple idea, but a disastrous one.

because we can understand it quickly, we should be able, equally quickly, to discern whether it makes sense or not.*

Simple, but BAD.

Simple, but GOOD.

That's also the challenge of the "simple" view: it's often a lot harder to make something appear easy and effortless than to make it complicated. Making an effective—and not disastrously misleading—simple picture requires stewing lots of parts together for a long time until the good stuff rises to the top.

Just because an idea is simple ▶ does not mean it is good. But making a simple view means we can see what makes it bad.

There is also always an elaborate way to look at anything. That's the picture that contains the details and the nuances; the picture that gives us a deeper sense of what is really going on and what is involved. The challenge with the elaborate picture is that at first glance it can appear so complex that it makes no sense to anyone but an expert. We'll talk about this conundrum in detail after lunch, so for now let's just recognize the two ends of this pictorial spectrum: the simple on the one side, and the elaborate on the other.

Speaking of spectra, here is a series of simple-versus-elaborate comparisons: light (a rainbow and the electromagnetic spectrum), a lock (a sketch of a lock and key and a schematic of lock tumblers), and life (a flower and Krebs cycle).† Think about how appealing each picture is, based on your expertise in the subject.

†

Depictions of Krebs cycle usually combine a time line and a flowchart (a "when" and a "how" picture) to illustrate the process by which a plant converts light into energy.

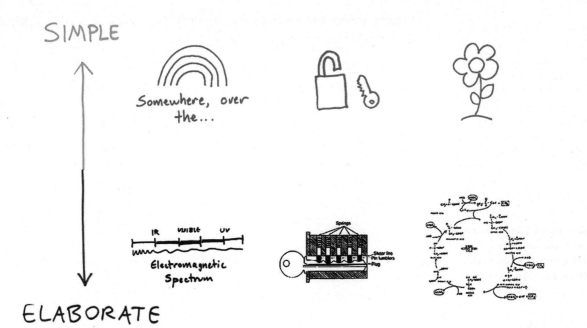

Three samples of "simple" versus "elaborate" pictures: light, locks, and life.

DRAWING DRILL: SIMPLE VERSUS ELABORATE

Pick one of the following items and draw a simple version and an elaborate version.

- An airplane
- Business process management
- A Web site
- Language

QUALITATIVE OR QUANTITATIVE?

The good, the bad, and the ugly: everything we can conceive of has qualities. What is it like? What does it feel like? What does it look like? How does it act? These are all qualitative questions. Although these attributes can't be measured or counted, they are the essence of what makes something itself and not something else.* As we saw yesterday with portraits, these qualitative pictures provide the visual keys we need to distinguish one idea from another.

Quantities are a completely different animal:† they reflect those aspects of an idea that can be measured and counted—all the attributes that can be associated back to and represented with a "how much" picture. As we discussed back when we were buying bananas yesterday, both qualities and quantities are needed to fully describe an idea: qualities provide the visceral feeling and quantities measure amounts.

Look at the following pictures of the qualitative and quantitative attributes of a gem (brilliantly shiny on the one hand, a measurably perfect combination of atoms on the other), love (the indescribable feeling of a parent for a child or the specific interaction of hormones interacting in precise quantities), and a ship in full sail (a beautiful manifestation of wind, sea, and energy, or an engineering calculus of exactly sized materials moving at precise speed and in a specific direction). Imagine which is the "better" picture and according to what context.

✳

If that sounds like existential crap, it is. All "existential" means is that something exists, as itself and in its own place. That's not the kind of description businesspeople usually feel comfortable with, which is too bad, since it is these "qualities" that make one product more appealing than another. Since these qualities can be hard to measure—and therefore hard to duplicate in a chart—we don't frequently see them in business presentations.

†

We've already seen the difference between qualities and quantities when we discussed "who and what" portraits versus "how much" charts. We're going to see it again.

QUALITATIVE

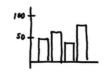
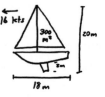

Qualitative vs. quantitative ▶ pictures: a diamond, love, and sailing: there is a time and place for both kinds of pictures, and both are needed to fully describe an idea.

QUANTITATIVE

VISION OR EXECUTION?

Leaders are meant to be visionary: they are supposed to be able to see where we're going even while the rest of us have our heads down and are heaving at the oars. Having a vision for our idea, whether it's going to the moon or making an apple pie, means having our target clearly in sight. Being able to convey that vision to others is the hallmark of a successful leader.

Then again, being able to point people in a specific direction isn't of much use if there is no way to get there. That's where execution comes in: defining the steps along the path that take us from where we are now to that distant place of magic out on the horizon. Sure, we can see our destination, but without project managers and detailed plans, we might as well bag the whole journey right here at the door.

As with the previous SQVID questions, there is a time and a place where we need one or the other or both. Here are contrasting vision-and-execution pictures of football (our objective is the goalpost at the Super Bowl; we get there by making our way step-by-step through the playoff grid), Mt. Fuji (the perfect expression of the forces of nature; one we realize by following the same path pilgrims have followed for centuries), and landing on the moon (planting our flag there was a driving national goal; getting there demanded the organized participation of the hundreds of thousands of people who built the machines).

If you were the leader, which picture would you draw for your team? If you were project manager, which picture would you draw?

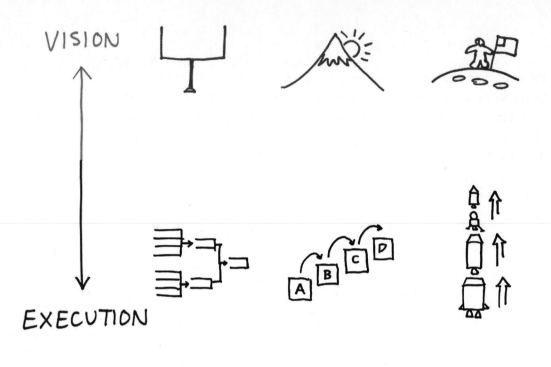

VISION

EXECUTION

▲

The vision is the goalpost, the shining mountain peak, or planting a flag on the moon. The execution is the playoff grid, the steps we take up the mountainside, and the stages of the rocket.

DRAWING DRILL: VISION VERSUS EXECUTION

Pick one of the following items and draw a "vision" and how to execute it.

- The Federal Reserve Bank
- The U.S. Open
- French fries
- The French Revolution

INDIVIDUAL OR COMPARISON?

Often the best way to see our idea clearly is to purge our vision of all other issues. Without the distraction of extraneous elements, we can focus on the details that matter most and consider them in isolation. In pursuit of a singular idea, there is often no other way to make progress. Think about the Wright brothers' first airplane: the brothers not only shut down their bicycle shop in order to focus on their Flyer, they moved halfway across the country to a lonely patch of sand to catch the winds and to escape the distractions of home.

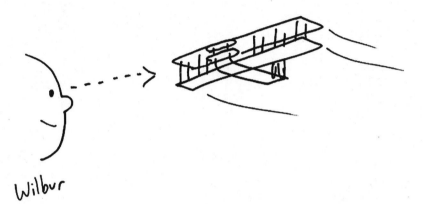

Wilbur

◀ Only by traveling to a deserted beach and cutting out all distractions were the Wright brothers able to "see" their plane into life.

Other times, the only way we can make sense of our idea is to compare it to other ideas and look for the similarities and differences. The genius of the Wright brothers' design was that they compared the nuances of flight to those of riding a bicycle. No aircraft designer before them had successfully flown a powered plane, largely because all designers assumed a plane had to be inherently stable to be controllable. The Wrights took the bicycle path: like a bike, they intentionally designed their plane to be unstable and thus made the critical breakthrough in aeronautical thinking.

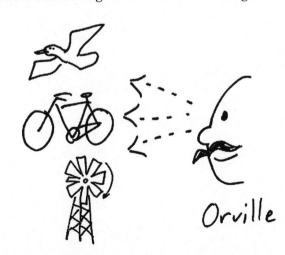

Orville

◀ Only by comparing their plane to other ideas were the Wrights able to conceive of how to make it fly.

As before, neither the individual view nor the comparative view is always right. We need to be able to conjure up both to fully see our idea. Look at these examples of individual and comparative pictures and think about situations where each might be more appropriate. We can see a baseball (distinguished alone by its stitching and autograph or by size and shape when compared with a football, soccerball, and basketball), a man (identified by his size, clothes, and haircut or by side-by-side comparison to everyone in a crowd), and a chart of "us" (located alone in a particular place on a plot or identified by our position relative to "them.")

▲

This ball, that man, us: these are individual concepts that allow us to see one thing clearly. Those balls, all those people, us *and* them: these are comparisons that become clarified by showing similarities and differences.

Pick one of the following items and draw it by itself and in comparison to something else.

- A hammer
- Watching a movie
- My company
- The bottom line

CHANGE OR STATUS QUO?

"The only thing that stays constant is change." Yesterday we said that the way we see time passing is by noting change in the world around us; quite literally, if there were no change, time would cease to exist. When we want to imagine a better world, or imagine what things would look like after we've worked hard to improve them, we need to be able to see those changes before they've taken place; we need to find a way to see a different world: one that doesn't yet exist.

That's what "change" pictures do: they show us what something—the weather, our finances, our market space—will look like after we've taken action. Simple "change" pictures are the pure expression of our imagination's ability to see beyond what is right in front of us. Every businessperson makes decisions, not to change where he or she is right now, but to change where he or she will be.

Then again, it's also true that we can't know where we're going unless we know where we are. Pictures of the "status quo" give us the platform from which to leap: without an understanding of our present position and the forces that put us here, we have no ability to change anything. After we've seen the vision of where we'd like to be, we always need to come back to where we are in order to see what we need to change.

Look at the following set of "change" and "status quo" pictures, and think about when one or the other (or both) would give the most useful information. First, we have the weather (tomorrow will be better than today, but today is pretty nice), our market share (it could go up, it could go down; today it's holding flat), and our financial position (tomorrow could be a penny or a dollar; today we have a quarter).

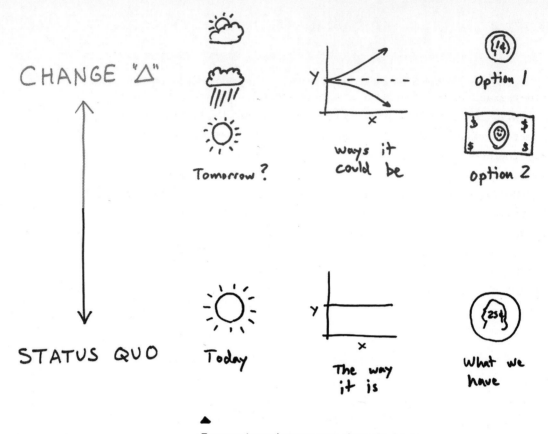

CHANGE "△"

Tomorrow?

ways it could be

Option 1

option 2

STATUS QUO

Today

The way it is

What we have

▲
Tomorrow's weather prognosis, alternative futures, the money we could have: these all show change—the way things could be different. Today's sun, the path we're on, the money we have now: these all show the status quo.

DRAWING DRILL: CHANGE VERSUS STATUS QUO

Pick one of the following items and draw how it is now and how it might be later.

- A side of beef
- The stock market
- The price of oil
- My mood

Putting the SQVID back together again

In these examples, we've pulled from a lot of different ideas, which is great to illustrate how the SQVID works. But to put the SQVID through its paces and see the magic it sparks in our imagination, we need to use it to explore a single concept—something that we might often think about but rarely *really* think about.

In this last exercise of the morning, I'd like you to pick a single familiar idea and see if you can't come up with five, six, seven, or more new ways of looking at it by running it through all the SQVID questions.

You can pick your concept from my list below or pick something from your business that you'd like to see illustrated in something more articulate than the usual way.

FULL SQVID DRILL 1

Fill in the blank SQVID framework on the next page with ten pictures describing
(Pick one or pick your own)

- Leadership
- HR
- IT
- Manufacturing
- Marketing
- Profit
- _____

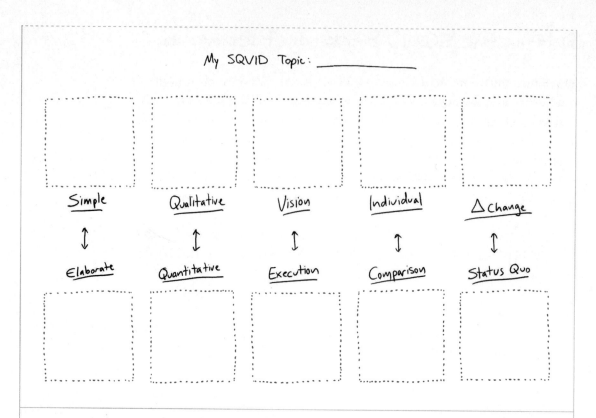

My SQVID Topic: _____

Simple	Qualitative	Vision	Individual	Δ Change
↕	↕	↕	↕	↕
Elaborate	Quantitative	Execution	Comparison	Status Quo

If you find yourself getting stuck, try these hints:

- Look back at the examples throughout this section: does the orange trigger any ideas?
- You don't have to start with "simple": Profit, for example, is most easily drawn starting with "quantitative."
- When you think of your topic, what's the first image that comes to mind? Make that your "simple" and go from there.
- Remember Day 1? Start with a circle and give it a name.
- We don't care how "good" the pictures are: it's the ideas we're after.

Above all, remember this: we are giving your entire brain a workout: it *will* be tiring, but *you can* do it, and *you will* be amazed at what your imagination comes up with.

We're not done with the SQVID quite yet

That's the SQVID: an on-demand way to get the most out of our imagination. The next time someone says, "Let's think outside the box," we'll say, "Okay: stand back."

The SQVID is a surefire way to stir up our imagination and generate an explosion of ideas.

It's time to break for lunch. But before we do, think about this: so far this entire book has been about us—how we see the world, how we can better look at problems and solve them, how we can improve our visual thinking. All that is critical, but it's not enough. In order to make any of this truly useful, we have to start thinking about what others are going to see. We have to learn to put ourselves into someone else's eyes and see what they see. That's where the SQVID is taking us next.

What is a solution worth?

We spent this morning popping open our imaginations and coming up with many different ways to look at a given problem. "Different ways" are exactly what we wanted: remember that our third rule told us that the one who sees the most possibilities wins.

Now here's the tricky part: just because we can see many possibilities does not mean that anyone else can or will even try. The simple business truth is that our solution, no matter how brilliant we think it is, is only as good as someone else's willingness to look at it and support it. That's important. Let's say it again:

> **Our solution is only as good as someone else's willingness to support it.**

Non-QWERTY?

The most common example of something we interact with daily and that needs a rethink but will never get one is the QWERTY keyboard. When Christopher Sholes finalized this typewriter layout in 1873, his main concern was placing the keys in such a way that would minimize jamming in his patented "hidden carriage" typewriter design. He intentionally placed frequently used keys so the typist would alternate hands as he or she wrote, thus keeping keys on the same side from bumping into one another. Sholes's design worked well, and E. Remington & Sons bought the manufacturing rights. The rest is history, and QWERTY has remained the standard English keyboard ever since.

Christopher Sholes designed his QWERTY keyboard to force the typist to alternate hands and thus avoid jams. It became the universal standard for English keyboards more than one hundred years ago and will likely stay the standard forever. ▶

But worldwide adoption doesn't make QWERTY the best design. Because it was intended to minimize crashes on a specific machine, QWERTY was never intended to be the easiest or most intuitive typing layout. By the 1930s typewriter designs had evolved to be less prone to jams, but the standard was already set. In 1936 educational psychologist August Dvorak patented a much more efficient keyboard. His design moved the key placement to increase typing speed and make it easier to learn to type.

DVORAK 1936

Dvorak's idea was, by any contemporary measure, better than QWERTY. But because so many typewriters were already in use, and so many people already knew how to use them, typewriter manufacturers turned down his "better" design, and it was never adopted.*

What people?

The lesson from Dvorak is this: if we can't convince others to support our "better" idea, it isn't really any better.

What does that have to do with our pictures? Lots. All the tools we've looked at give us powerful ways to describe problems and see solutions. But if we can't get other people to look at our pictures and see the same things, they're no better than an endless list of forgettable words.

We already know that the 6×6 rule helps us create pictures that align well with the way our brains see the world, and that also goes for the brains of anyone we're likely to show those pictures to. Creating 6×6 pictures that are easy to "get" is a good starting point, but if we really want to make sure our audience understands what we're showing, we have to put ourselves in their mind's eye and see what they see in our pictures, which brings us back to the "what people?" question from Day 1 and back to the SQVID.

▲

August Dvorak's 1936 keyboard was easier to learn and made for faster typing, but it never replaced QWERTY.

✳

That's not entirely true: several teletype and technology companies tried to adopt the Dvorak design but it was already too late. QWERTY was so widespread that no increase in efficiency was deemed worth the effort to replace it. If you want to see this keyboard in action, Dvorak is supported on most versions of Windows.

Let's be clear: this does not mean we become visual chameleons, changing our ideas to pander to the closest audience. On the contrary, the goal here is to make sure that we're so confident in our idea that we're willing to let it be flexible in presentation. Not all audiences are going to understand every view of our picture, but let's make sure we know enough about what they're willing to look at that we give them the best possible shot.

The equalizer: seeing with our audiences' eyes

We're going to use the SQVID again but now in a completely different way. Rather than running through the five questions to come up with alternate ideas, we're going to use it as a graphic equalizer, moving virtual sliders up and down along each question until we find the settings that will make our picture most accessible and relevant to whomever we show it.★

S. Q. V. I. D.

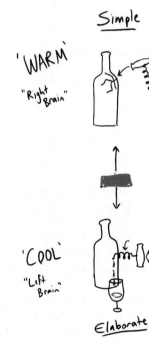

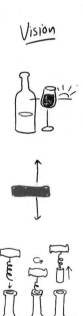

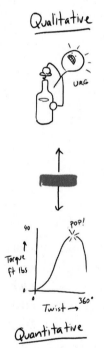

▲
Now we're going to use the SQVID as a graphic equalizer, finding the ideal settings for conveying our picture to different audiences.

To see what I'm talking about, let's run through setting the equalizer for the first SQVID question: simple or elaborate?

Newbie versus expert

We can take any of the 6×6 pictures we drew yesterday as a starting point to demonstrate the SQVID equalizer concept. Let's select the technology-architecture map as a starting point—it's clear enough to get us started, and we can elaborate on it all day if we need to. (Don't worry: we won't.)

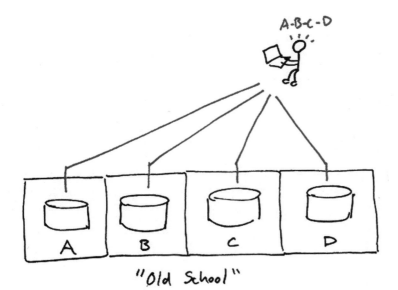

For this example, we'll use our previously drawn "technology architecture" map as a starting point.

Here's the drill. Imagine you're such a whiz at technical architecture that you've become a bit of a celebrity with your employer. One day the local elementary school calls your company, requesting someone to come over for "bring an expert to school day" and explain to the kindergartners how the Internet works.* You've been volunteered.

Look back at that map. It's a solid representation of where the pieces of a technical system like the Internet fit, but how appropriate would it be as a starting point for a bunch of six-year-olds? Perhaps it would be better to start with something even simpler, something that they could see themselves in. Maybe a drawing of two people looking at each other through the wires of the Internet, like this:

This might be a better starting picture for the six-year-olds; they can immediately get it—largely because they can see themselves in it.

The Internet

As you think about this, let's add another variable. On the way to the school, you get a message from your company's head of sales, asking you to join her on a sales pitch later this afternoon. She's been asked by the IT department of Megacorp Inc. to bring along an expert and pitch your new services-oriented-architecture offering. It's a potential multimillion dollar deal and, once again, you've been volunteered.

Look again at that original map. Same routine: it's still a solid representation, but how appropriate would it be as a starting point for a bunch of forty-year-old techies? In this case perhaps it would be better to have a more elaborate picture: something that shows the multiple layers and components that make your company's system so robust.

This might be a better picture for the forty-year-old techies: it shows that we know exactly what we're talking about.

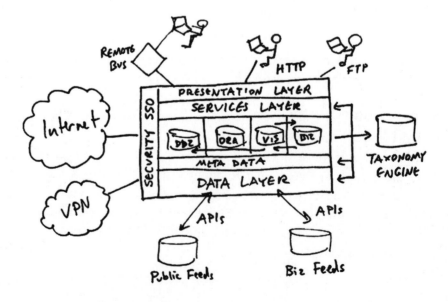

Here is where the equalizer comes in. Even on the single spectrum of "simple versus elaborate," we can see that there might be any number of possible pictures.

The "simple versus elaborate" conundrum and the simplicity principle

In a situation like this—in fact, in any situation where we have to describe an idea to anyone—there is a rule of thumb we can follow. Let's call it the "simplicity principle":

> **Our audience's willingness to look at an elaborate picture is directly proportional to its experience with the subject.**

In other words, if we will be showing our picture to someone unfamiliar with our subject, we must start with a simple picture. If not, we'll once again trigger the deer-in-the-headlights effect. This time it won't be *us* that seizes up (we know exactly what our picture shows—we drew it, after all); it will be our audience. When they see a picture that overwhelms their vision, they'll stop looking.

On the other hand, if our audience is made up of a bunch of experts in our subject, we must start out with an elaborate picture—otherwise they will think we don't know what we're talking about and then *they* will stop looking.

If we first show an elaborate picture to a group of nonexperts, they will stop looking. Similarly, if we show a simple picture to a group of experts, they will stop looking too!

▼

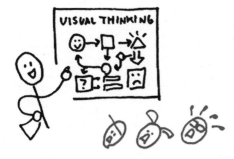

"Non Experts" ≠ Elaborate

"Experts" ≠ Simple

When we show a simple picture to nonexperts first, they will keep looking. Similarly, it's only when we show an elaborate picture to a group of experts that we convince them we know what we're talking about.

To draw our nonexpert audience in, we need to start with a simple picture; once they "get it," they will stay with us as we increasingly elaborate. The opposite is true of experts: only after we've convinced them of our competence by showing them an elaborate picture will they be willing to stay with us as we simplify.

"Non Experts" = Simple

"Experts" = Elaborate

PUTTING THE EQUALIZER TO WORK, PART I: THE CEO

Let's push this equalizer model and see where it takes us. In the following scenario, I want you to think through where you would set all the sliders on the SQVID equalizer.
(Remember: our goal is to try to get into the mind of our audience so that we can create the view they'll be most willing to look at.)

THE SETUP

We're in the business process management (BPM)* group at a major teapot manufacturer. We're responsible for coming up with ways to streamline the manufacturing process so the company can be more efficient and survive in this difficult economic climate.

✸

If you're in business and you're not familiar with BPM, you better get on it. BPM is the latest fancy buzzword for making business systems more efficient by better understanding them through mapping and modeling. Especially in times where companies are looking for ways to operate faster, better, and cheaper, BPM is only going to get bigger. Plus, it uses lots of pictures.

THE CONCEPT

A couple of days ago, a few of us were sketching out some process thoughts on a napkin at lunch, when we were struck with a brilliant idea: why not manufacture teapot lids on the same assembly line as the pots? It will save money, boost R & D, and possibly save the company.

THE BACKGROUND

In the past we'd always created the lids and pots on separate lines and put them together just before packaging. That required two assembly lines running nearly identical processes with identical materials. Given that orders are scaling back, why not consolidate on one line, leaving the second idle with a skeleton crew for the people in R & D to use to test their new breakthrough teapot designs?

THE BENEFIT

We keep the business running on a smaller scale, and the money we save by operating only one line can be used to support new product development. Yes, we will have to lay off some assembly line workers, but it's a lot better than shutting down operations completely.

THE CHALLENGE

Somehow Marge, our CEO, got word of our concept and was intrigued. She is leaving on a plane in an hour, to visit the managers at our manufacturing facility in Atlanta, but wants to hear more about our idea before she goes. Marge is giving us five minutes to convince her that we're on to something before she heads out the door.

Without drawing the picture, fill in the boxes below to indicate where you'd set the SQVID equalizer sliders for the picture that would be most compelling for the CEO *in this situation.* If Marge needs a simple picture, fill in the top box; if she needs an elaborate picture, fill in the bottom.
(Remember: she's only giving you five minutes, and her mind is already in Atlanta.)

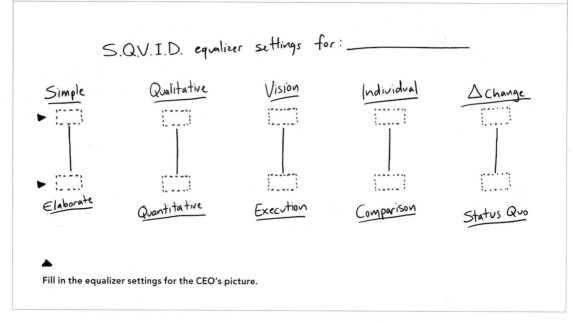

S.Q.V.I.D. equalizer settings for: _____

Simple	Qualitative	Vision	Individual	△ Change
Elaborate	Quantitative	Execution	Comparison	Status Quo

Fill in the equalizer settings for the CEO's picture.

PUTTING THE EQUALIZER TO WORK, PART II: THE PROJECT MANAGER

THE SETUP

Using exactly the same scenario, assume the CEO loves your idea. As she's walking out the door, she says to you, "Take this concept to Bob in project management and tell him I want to implement it. He'll argue with you because it's so different from what we've been thinking, but see if you can't convince him of your idea."

THE TASK

Set the sliders for the picture you'd show to Bob in projeact management.

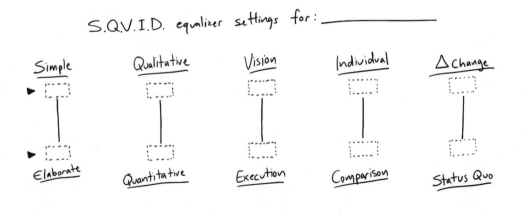

S.Q.V.I.D. equalizer settings for: _____

Simple	Qualitative	Vision	Individual	△ Change
Elaborate	Quantitative	Execution	Comparison	Status Quo

Fill in the equalizer settings for the picture for Bob in project management.

PUTTING THE EQUALIZER TO WORK, PART III: FINANCE

THE SETUP

You've convinced Bob to back you. Now you need to get Mary in finance to start thinking about the money side of your idea.

THE TASK

Set the sliders for the picture you'd show to Mary in finance.

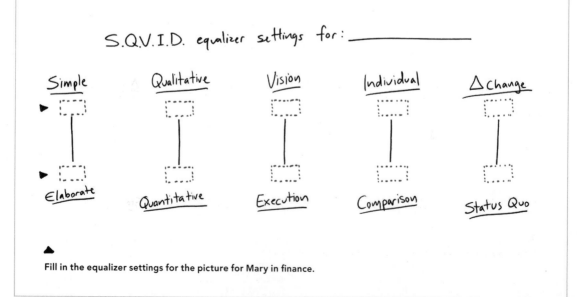

S.Q.V.I.D. equalizer settings for: _____

Simple	Qualitative	Vision	Individual	Δ Change
Elaborate	Quantitative	Execution	Comparison	Status Quo

Fill in the equalizer settings for the picture for Mary in finance.

PUTTING THE EQUALIZER TO WORK, PART IV: THE ASSEMBLY LINE

THE SETUP

Marge, Bob, and Mary like your idea. You've got executive support, an emerging plan, and some money. Congratulations: you've now got an *initiative*. Next, you've got to let Steve, who runs the assembly lines, know what you're thinking. If he doesn't buy into your initiative, it's dead on arrival.

THE TASK

Set the sliders for the picture you'd show to Steve, who runs the lines. Remember: aside from Steve's neck being literally on the line, he is also ultimately responsible for hiring and firing the assembly line workers.

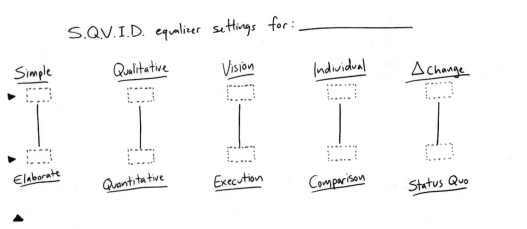

S.Q.V.I.D. equalizer settings for: _____

Simple	Qualitative	Vision	Individual	Δ Change
Elaborate	Quantitative	Execution	Comparison	Status Quo

Fill in the equalizer settings for the picture for Steve on the line.

PUTTING THE EQUALIZER TO WORK, PART V: THE BOARD

THE SETUP

You've done it: your initiative has support throughout the company. Marge is so pleased with your ability to use pictures to get everyone on the same page that she has asked you to make the presentation to the board next month.

THE TASK

Set the sliders for the picture you'd show to the board.
(Remember: only the future of your company, your colleagues, your products, and your job are on the line. No pressure.)

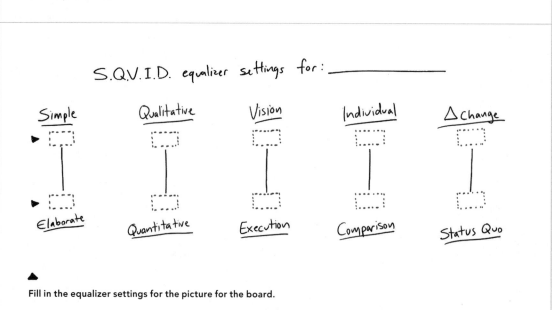

S.Q.V.I.D. equalizer settings for: _____

Simple	Qualitative	Vision	Individual	△ change
Elaborate	Quantitative	Execution	Comparison	Status Quo

▲
Fill in the equalizer settings for the picture for the board.

Reviewing our equalizer settings

I hope the rationale for the last exercise is clear: the initial sketch we created at lunch might signify our breakthrough, but we might not want to start waving that napkin around until we've thought about whom we're showing it to and what *they're* going to see when they look at it.

There are no absolutely right answers: CEOs, PMs, finance jockeys, assembly line workers, board members—they're all people, and they're all different from one another and from everyone else who shares their job title. There is no standard personality type for CEO; just as there is no standard personality type for teapot makers.

That said, we can still use the SQVID to help us get behind their eyes and glimpse the world the way their job makes them see it. That's the key: by taking even a moment to set the equalizer sliders, we're forcing our mind to imagine a world that looks a little different from our own.

Based on my experience with people in each role, here's the way I would set the sliders. It's stereotyping, but as they say, stereotypes come from somewhere.*

MARGE, THE CEO

As CEO, Marge is above all else responsible for setting the "vision" for where the teapot company is going. Although she's very smart, she knows she's not an expert in all aspects of the business. She needs to know the numbers but relies more on her trusted business intuition. She likes ideas that are expressed clearly and prefers to know where the company *could* be rather than where it is. Marge is always in demand and always pressed for time.

For all these reasons, I'd slide everything to the top for our Marge picture: "simple," "qualitative," "vision," "individual," and "change."

✻
Yes, this is an exercise in "profiling," and in this case it's exactly the right thing to do. In fact, it's the only thing we can do. For good or bad, our brains are wired to look at people and make decisions about them based on our previous experience, either with that person or with someone who looks like him or her. It's an imperfect system, so using SQVID can help. By taking just a moment to ask ourselves what would *likely* be most compelling to that person at each step along SQVID, we force our brain to *try* to see the world the way they do.

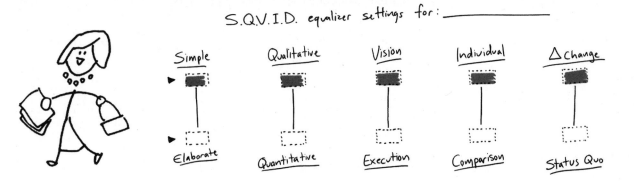

S.Q.V.I.D. equalizer settings for: _____

Simple — Elaborate
Qualitative — Quantitative
Vision — Execution
Individual — Comparison
Δ Change — Status Quo

BOB IN PROJECT MANAGEMENT

Bob lives in the details; he has to keep the trains running on time but knows that he can't drive every one of them himself (although if he could find a way, he'd be in heaven). Bob is interested in the numbers only to the extent that they impact his procedures: tell him how much he's got available and he'll build his plan around that. Above all, Bob is the process guy: his greatest concern is *how* to do whatever the company's decided to do. He loves to compare new approaches to those he already knows—if only to rip apart the newcomers. Bob lives completely in the present and hates change, but if change is coming, he wants to be the first to know, so he can start preparing his next plan.

We set Bob's equalizer to "elaborate," "qualitative," "execution," "comparison," and "change."

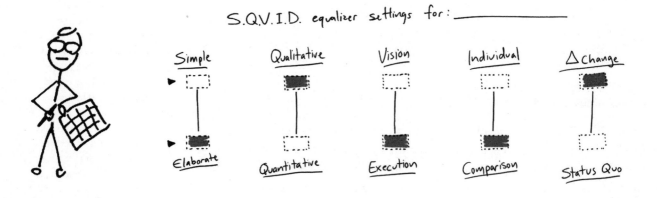

S.Q.V.I.D. equalizer settings for: _____

Simple / Elaborate — Qualitative / Quantitative — Vision / Execution — Individual / Comparison — Δ Change / Status Quo

MARY IN FINANCE

Vision—ha!—what's that? Mary manages the money. She lives by the details of her spreadsheets and the numbers on her charts. Mary is all about getting things done, and as long as those things are in the black and not in the red, she's not too particular about what they are. Mary loves to run the numbers side by side to see how much she could save by shaving off a little here and a little there. But when it comes to making decisions about who to pay and how much, Mary lives totally in the here and now.

Mary's sliders would be all pushed down: "elaborate," "quantitative," "execution," "comparison," and "status quo."

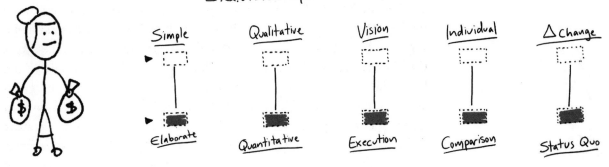

STEVE ON THE LINE

Steve and his people drive the trains. He doesn't mind Bob throwing the switches as long as Bob stays up in the control room and out of the way. Steve has to choreograph a lot of people, moving a lot of pieces, so he needs instructions to be simple. Steve likes to run things by the numbers and likes to know exactly what he's supposed to do next. And until change impacts his people, Steve isn't interested in the way things might be; he wants to know how they are now.

Steve's settings are "simple," "quantitative," "execution," "individual," and "status quo."

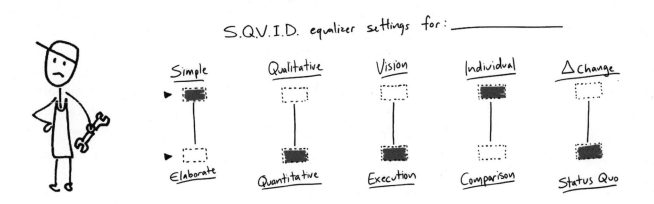

THE BOARD

The board wants to know one thing: *are we making money?* Keep it simple, keep it short, and show us the numbers. The board's settings: "simple" and "quantitative." *Basta!*

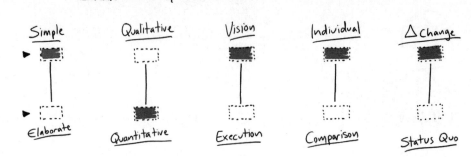

That's it for the SQVID exercise. We've seen that one picture isn't going to be enough to convince everyone we need to support us, and, more importantly, we've figured out which sorts of pictures we need to create to get their support.

So when do we draw the picture?

You might have noticed that we've been through the SQVID several times now and still haven't drawn anything. That's okay: half the value of the SQVID is to get us thinking about visual options. The workout we've just completed has shifted so many gears in our mind's eye, and fired off so many neurons, that we're more than ready to put pen to paper and start pictorially persuading people to support us.

Before we do, let's review the tools so far. Either the 6×6 rule or the SQVID is alone enough to clarify a problem. If we're stuck in the headlights of an onrushing problem, we can slow it down by breaking it into its six visual elements and addressing them one by one. If we're stuck with one idea in mind, we call upon the SQVID to uncork our imagination and let new ideas flow.

6×6
slows problems down

SQVID
shows us possibilities

In many ways, we're done. We can apply those two tools on a case-by-case basis and be extraordinary visual thinkers, sometimes using the 6×6 rule, sometimes using the SQVID. But let's push it one step further and imagine what might happen if we combined these tools: not only could we draw out a way to explain *anything*, we could also tailor that picture to *any* audience. Whoa! Now, that would be amazing.

By themselves, our two main tools help us visually solve problems: 6 × 6 helps us slow down what's coming; the SQVID helps us accelerate the possibilities.

Imagine if we could combine them

For the rest of the day, let's amaze ourselves.

Pulling it all together: the visual-thinking codex

To see the places where the 6×6 rule and the SQVID overlap, we'll do what we always do with a "where" problem: we'll create a map.* As we remember from yesterday, we can start any map with a coordinate system. In this case we're going to be comparing the six pictures of the 6×6 rule to the five questions of the SQVID, so we draw a grid that holds thirty pieces (6 × 5 = 30):

Remember that the 6×6 rule tells us that for a "where" problem we draw a map, a "when" problem a time line, etc. I hope it's becoming clear how these few simple pieces fit together. We really can use these tools to visualize anything we can imagine.

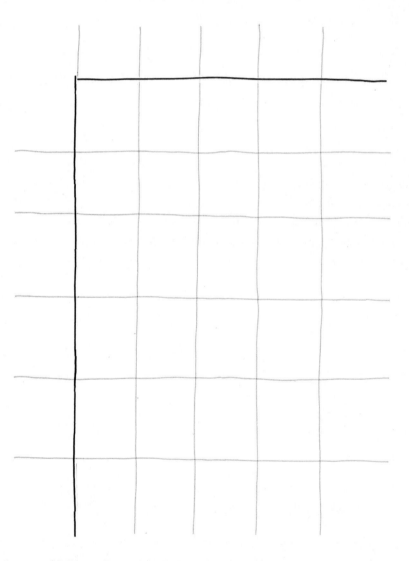

Here is the underlying grid for mapping our six pictures to our five questions. ▶

Into our blank grid we add the first component of our coordinate system, the six pictures from the 6×6 rule: "portrait," "chart," "map," "time line," "flowchart," and "plot."

We add the first component of our coordinate system, the six pictures of 6×6.

▼

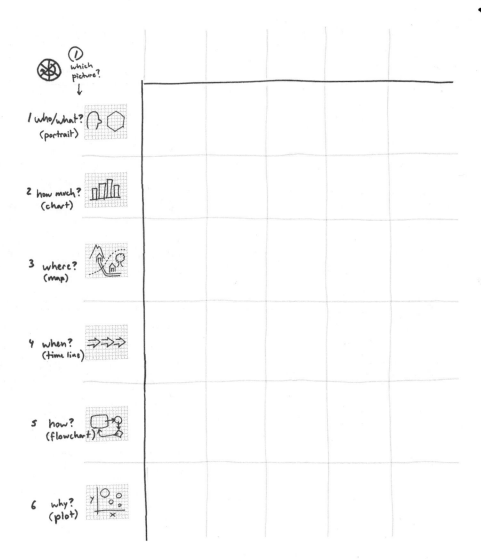

which picture?

1 who/what? (portrait)

2 how much? (chart)

3 where? (map)

4 when? (time line)

5 how? (flowchart)

6 why? (plot)

Now we add the second component of the coordinate system, the five SQVID questions: "simple," "qualitative," "vision," "individual," and "change."

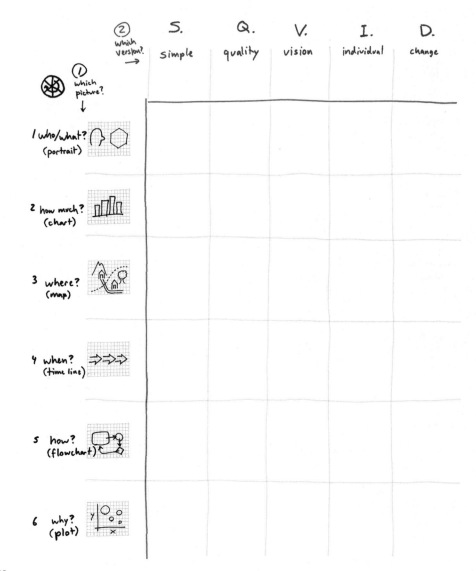

Adding in the five SQVID
questions completes our
coordinate system.

✳

Four of the five SQVID versions
of a portrait are the same;
the "change" version is an
exception because by definition
it must show two images: one
for what we have now and one
for what we will have.

With our coordinates plotted, we map the pictures that would result from combining the basic six with the various versions from the SQVID. In some cases the SQVID versions look the same for each 6×6 picture.* In other cases there may be significant variation as we move along the SQVID.* In either case we see that we can readily derive many possible pictures from our original six.

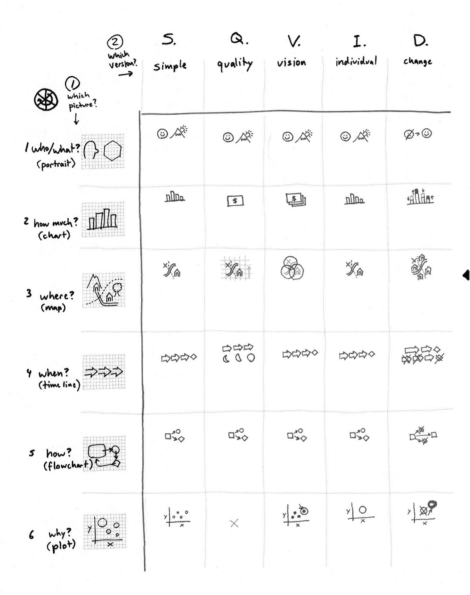

✳

The multivariable plot for each SQVID step is slightly different, depending on what we want to emphasize. And there is no "qualitative" plot at all, because it would just be a "portrait," like the Microsoft-Yahoo! fish we saw yesterday.

◀ This landscape is made up of the pictures that result from combining the basic six with the various SQVID comparisons.

That's a lot of pictures—all of which we know how to create by starting with one of the six basic formats, and then asking how we might modify it to account for the SQVID. But keep in mind that so far we've only accounted for the top side of the SQVID sliders. Now let's add in the flip side of those SQVID questions, doubling the number of picture variations available to us.

This is the "visual-thinking codex": a diagram of diagrams that shows us how to easily create more than forty simple pictures of almost any idea.

The resulting map is the "visual-thinking codex," a diagram of diagrams that shows us forty-plus pictorial variations of almost any idea and shows us how easy they are to create.

Using the visual-thinking codex: teapots revisited

Think of the visual-thinking codex as a simple cheat sheet that we can turn to when we need inspiration or guidance. We already know, from the 6×6 rule, which picture to draw, and we know from the SQVID which version is most appropriate to any circumstance. All the codex does is visually summarize what we already know.

To show how we can use the codex for guidance, let's go back to the teapot scenario and start drawing. Remember that the whole episode began at lunch as we were sketching out ways to modify our company's manufacturing process.

Here we see our original napkin sketch. It shows one solid line, representing a fully operational assembly line, and a dotted line, representing a switched-off line. They both end in a box, which represents a product. It doesn't get much simpler than that.

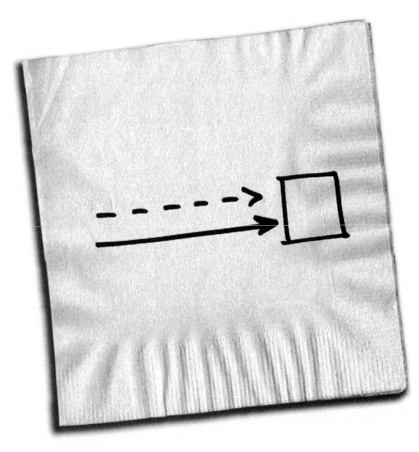

◀ Our original napkin: a fully operational assembly line and a switched-off line. They both end with a product. That's about as simple a portrait as we can make.

We didn't need our codex to create that. But if we did plot it in our codex, we would see that we had created a "simple," "qualitative," and "individual" picture of our "vision" for the assembly line. In other words, this one picture covers four of the top five slots that make up the codex.

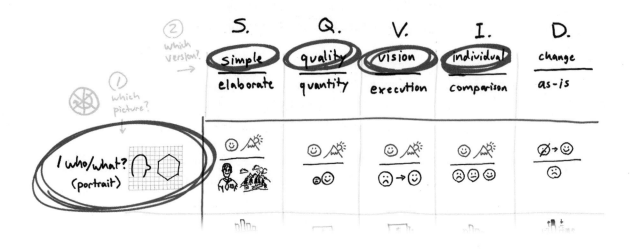

▲
Our napkin sketch covers four of the top five pictures on the codex: it's a "simple," "qualitative," and "individual" portrait of our assembly line "vision."

Hey: that's pretty close to the picture we wanted to show Marge. Our napkin sketch doesn't show change, but with the addition of a few more lines and an *x*, it easily could. Now we've got a simple, qualitative, visionary picture of *change*: exactly what the SQVID ordered for the CEO.

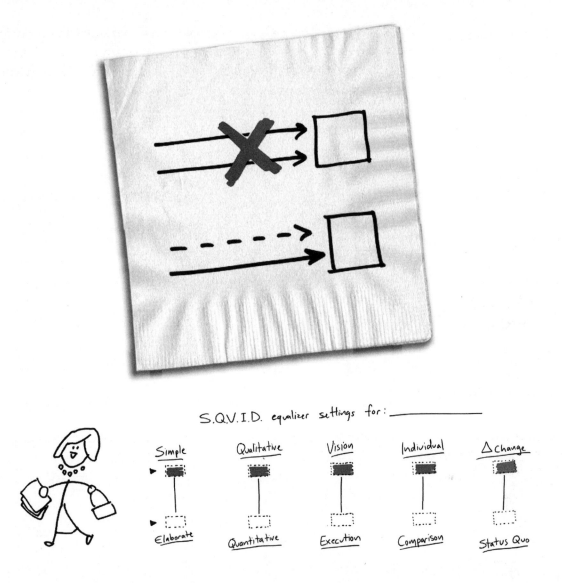

S.Q.V.I.D. equalizer settings for: _____

Simple	Qualitative	Vision	Individual	△ Change
Elaborate	Quantitative	Execution	Comparison	Status Quo

That's how the codex works: by showing us the possible combinations of basic pictures and their audience-appropriate variants, the codex guides us towards the right visual for any situation. To test it, let's keep going and see if we can't use the codex to create pictures for the rest of the teapot crowd.

The addition of a couple of more lines and an *x* gives us the CEO-level picture of change that we needed to show to Marge on her way out the door.

BOB'S BACK

Bob the project manager wanted something more elaborate. Let's start by adding details to the napkin assembly line portrait, things like pots, lids, and people. Before we know it, we're going to end up with a more elaborate map of our existing assembly line.

	S. simple / elaborate	Q. quality / quantity	V. vision / execution	I. individual / comparison	D. change / as-is
1 who/what? (portrait)					
2 how much? (chart)					
3 where? (map)					
4 when? (time line)					
5 how? (flowchart)					
6 why? (plot)					

① Which picture?
② Which version?

When "where" everything fits is combined with the "elaborate" side of the SQVID . . .

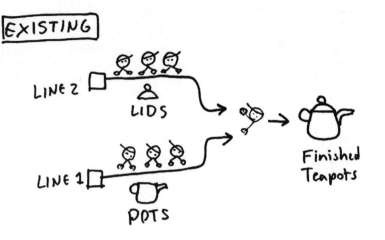

... it gives us (and Bob) a more elaborate map of the existing assembly line.

That's a start, but Bob really wanted to see what was going to change, so he could compare it to his existing process. If we mark up the map to show the changes we we're thinking about, we've got most of Bob's "elaborate," "qualitative," "comparison," and "change" picture.

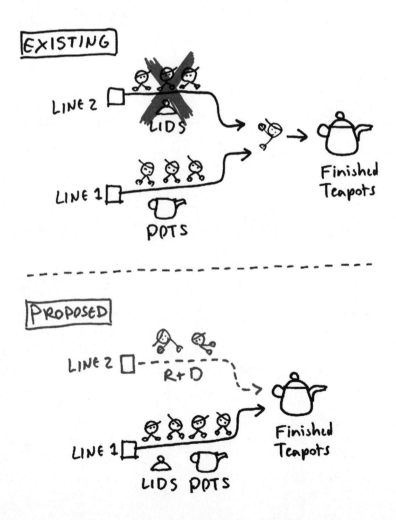

Now we've got most of Bob's "elaborate," "qualitative," "comparison," and "change" picture complete.

That's most of what Bob wanted, but let's remember that Bob is the execution guy: he's all about getting things done. He can now see from our picture what we're talking about, but it would help our cause enormously if we could show *how* to make it happen. Sounds like we could use a flowchart.* Let's rearrange the pieces and add arrows to indicate how the change could happen. That's it: we've got the pictures to show Bob.

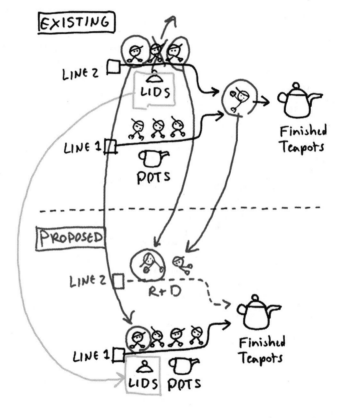

An "elaborate," "qualitative," ▶
"execution," and "change"
oriented comparative
flowchart: we've pretty well
covered everything Bob was
looking for. We'll leave the
"when" time line to him.

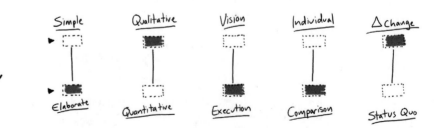

Now we've given him the context, details, and steps, Bob is happy. As a project manager, he lives for deadlines, so let's leave the "when" time line to him.

MARY 11

Let's do one more run through the codex. Remember that the SQVID settings for Mary from finance were exactly the opposite settings from Marge's: Marge is all up, Mary all down. Where Marge is interested in the big-picture vision of where we could go, Mary wants detailed numbers to let her compare the financial possibilities of tomorrow with those of today.

For Mary to run an elaborate cost-benefit analysis of our proposal, she has to see potential for our company's financial gain, so let's create a quantitative picture to motivate her. We know from the 6×6 rule that "quantitative" means "how much," and that means charts. What kind of quantitative data have we seen in the pictures we've created so far?

How about salary reductions? The whole reason we created our sketch in the lunchroom was to look for ways to operate more efficiently, which means ways to save money. Looking at the flowchart we made for Bob, we already see that closing an assembly line eliminates one line worker position.* That's a short-term money saver and an easy picture to draw: today we have seven workers, tomorrow we'll have six.

*
We can also see that we shifted three of the line workers to other positions: two to R & D, where they can help develop new products, and one to the still-running line, the better to help with the increased manufacturing load on that line.

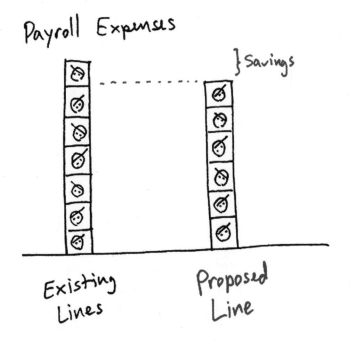

◀ Our first "how much" chart compares status quo payroll to decreased future payroll.

But if we shut down an assembly line, aren't we eliminating four jobs? No, because by keeping the line available for R & D we're increasing our ability to develop new products. So we shift two of the line workers to the R & D team, and another to help out on the line now manufacturing lids and pots. We can show that in another similar chart.

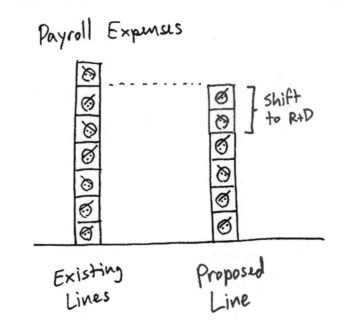

Two of our displaced workers are shifting over to R & D roles. ▶

The interesting quantitative aspect is that previous investments in R & D workers in the long run paid off three times higher than an equal investment in assembly line workers. That's an easy one to draw as well: we create a chart comparing the ROI of the two types of workers.

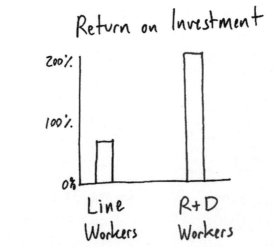

In the long run, an investment in R & D workers has always paid out three times higher than an investment in assembly line workers. ▶

Putting those two concepts together—reduced short-term payroll costs combined with better long-term investment returns—shows that in the short term profits will decrease as the company reduces manufacturing capacity to one assembly line, but that profits will increase long-term as it launches new products. That's the picture we needed for Mary all along: an "elaborate," "quantitative," "execution"-oriented "comparison" with the "status quo."

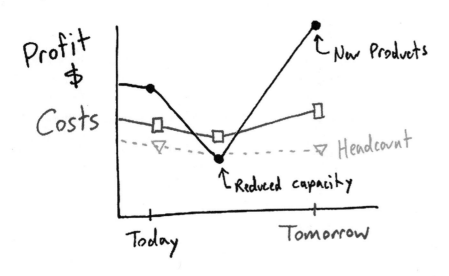

Here's Mary's picture: an "elaborate," "quantitative," "execution"-oriented profit-and-cost "comparison" to the "status quo."

Now Mary can see what we're talking about too. After we share equally appropriate pictures derived from the codex with Steve and the board, we should be good to go.

YOUR CODEX MOMENT: STEVE AND THE BOARD

Choose either Steve, from the line, or the board, and use the codex to help you create the picture (or pictures) you'd show them to convince them to back you. (Hint: whomever you pick, we've already just drawn almost everything you need.)

That's it for today. One closing thought, and we can head to the beach.

We started the day with the SQVID, five simple questions to help open our imagination, and we ended the day with the codex, the visual cheat sheet that gathers everything we've learned in the past three days. Tomorrow is our last day, and we're going to wrap this all up with a simple way to tell anyone a business story with the pictures we've made.

Quick review

Since this is our last day, let's quickly look back at how far we've already come. On Day 1, we looked at the world as visual problem solvers do: we looked for patterns, processes, and tools that we could rely on to feel visually competent and confident. On Day 2, we saw problems in six ways and then saw six equivalent ways to make pictures of those problems. On Day 3, we imagined five ways to vary those pictures in order to further open up our mind's eye and to help us imagine the way the world looks to other people. Today we're going to put all those ideas together as we complete the visual-thinking process: today we're going to *show*.

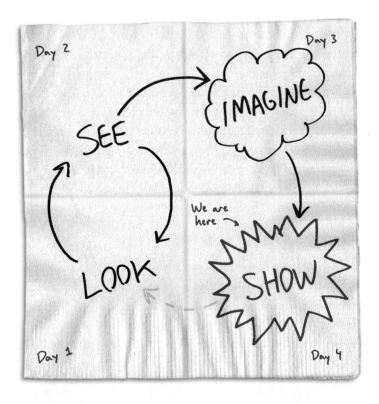

◀ It's Day 4, and we've reached the last step in the visual-thinking process: it's time to *show*.

Show-and-tell

✱

Chelsea Hardaway is the author of *Why Businesspeople Speak Like Idiots*, one of the great books on clear business communications.

†

In one of those ironies of the personal-computing tech boom of the last thirty years, Bill Gates's first version of Excel was designed to run exclusively on the then one-year-old Apple Macintosh computer. It's hard to imagine that, these days.

I'd like to start today with a quick show-and-tell story—this one taking us back to Microsoft. Last year Microsoft asked me and my colleague Chelsea* to help clarify a data-visualization challenge. As anyone who has ever used Microsoft Excel knows, a spreadsheet is a fantastic tool for collecting, comparing, and calculating vast amounts of data. Not surprisingly, many of the greatest spreadsheet whizzes on earth work at Microsoft—after all, they invented Excel†—and many of these Excel masters are clustered in the Microsoft finance group responsible for running the numbers that power the company's business decisions.

The finance group asked us up to Redmond, Washington, to help them think about how to make the financial insights generated within spreadsheets easier to spot, and to see if there were visual ways to make data analysis quicker and more intuitive. Tactically speaking, the finance team was asking us to help them design a blue-sky prototype for an upcoming conference on data presentation—a conference that would help determine the future of financial software design. It was an awesome challenge.

The only problem was the timing: we had just a couple of months before the conference, and we would need most of that time for coding and testing the prototype. If you've ever designed software—actually, if you've ever created anything that someone else is supposed to use, whether a Web site, a map, or a recipe—you know that the right way to start is to first find out what your potential "users" already know. In the case of software, that demands a requirements-gathering exercise that consumes months, followed by additional months of user testing.

We had no time for the right way, so we did it another way. We invited twelve of the top data analysts from the financial group into a conference room and locked the doors. Standing in front of enormous whiteboards with pens in hand, we announced that nobody was leaving until we'd mapped out the most frustrating problem facing a spreadsheet jockey today.

Here, stick figure for stick figure, is what we drew.

ANALYSIS PARALYSIS: STEP 1

Just as we did with the first napkin, on the first day, in this book, we started with a circle and gave it a name. And just as we did with the second napkin, on the second day, we made that circle a "who." Because everyone ultimately reports to him, the CFO was the foremost "who" in the financial analysts' minds, so we named our first circle "CFO." Next, we drew the two division presidents, since the analysts report directly to them. Then we added "portrait" details to make it visually clear who was who. With three simple portraits drawn, the casting for our business scenario was complete.

THE FINANCIAL ANALYSIS - PARALYSIS CYCLE   CAST: ☺ CFO   ☺ President 1   ☺ President 2

The analysts told us that the whole process begins when the CFO asks for a quarterly report on financial status, the so-called ROB, or "rhythm of business." That means he wants to see the numbers.

We drew our first circles and gave them names: "CFO," "President 1," and "President 2." Then we made them into portraits.

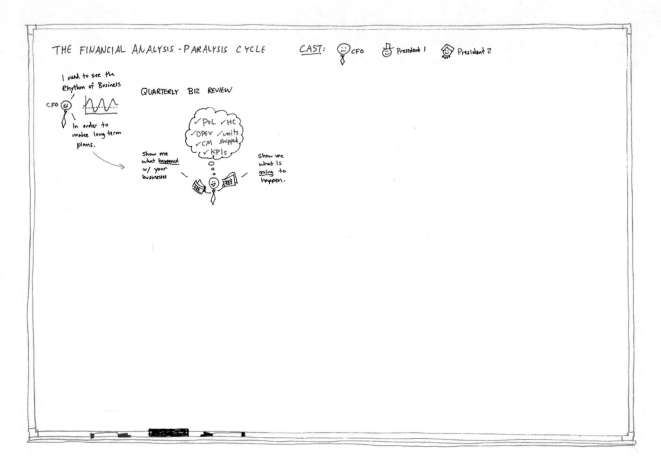

▲

Each quarter, the CFO wants to see the rhythm-of-business report; he wants to see the numbers.

✻

Just to be clear, this scenario is an illustration of what might happen in a hypothetical situation. No one in the room was projecting anything about any particular company, division, or quarter.

In the ROB meeting, President 1 happily reports that the previous quarter was great, then sadly reports that the next quarter is shaping up badly. President 2 reports the opposite.*

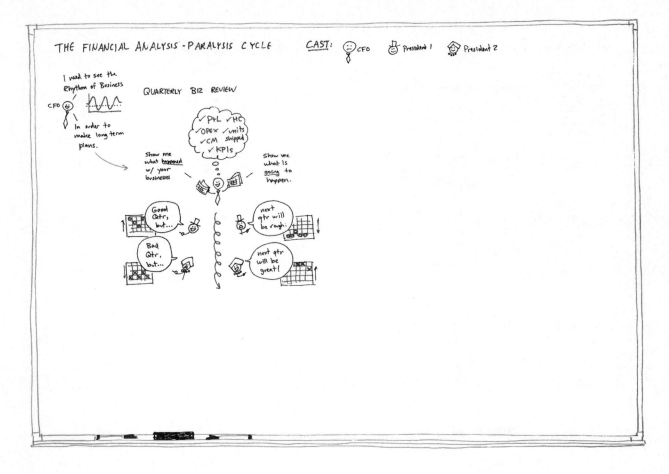

The CFO looks over the numbers and realizes that the two presidents are reporting on different financial metrics. The CFO tells them to come back when their reports are in synch.

▲

President 1 reports a great previous quarter but a bad next quarter. President 2 reports the opposite.

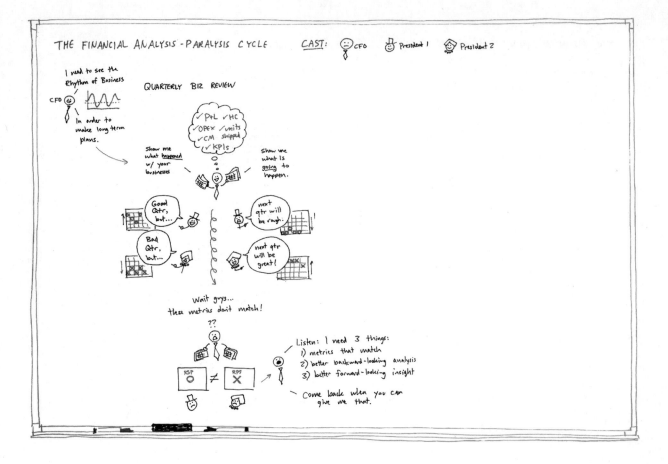

▲

The CFO sees that the presidents are reporting differing metrics. He tells them to come back when the metrics match.

Now the presidents are frustrated too. Their choice is to try to guess what is most important to the CFO *this quarter* and provide those metrics (in matching form) or simply to give him everything. To be safe, they choose the latter approach. At which point the whole process starts over again.

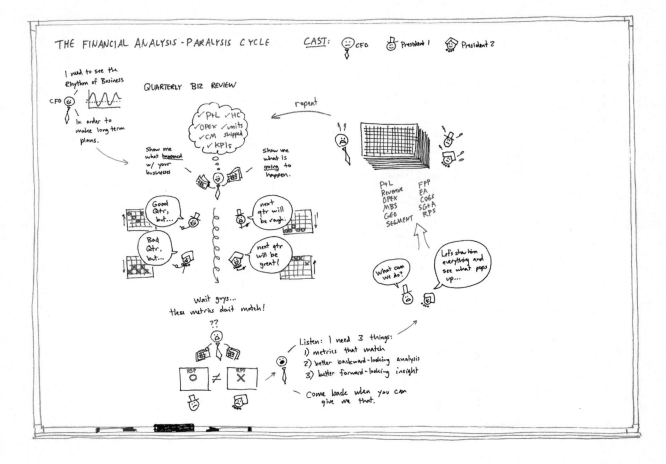

The circle now complete, our analysts agreed that we'd mapped out their greatest source of spreadsheet angst: their inability to predict precisely what data their bosses—and their bosses' boss—would most need to see during the quarterly review. We then let them out of the room for lunch with instructions to think about how we could best solve the problem.

▲

Unsure about which metrics are most needed, the presidents deliver everything their analysts have collected, and the process starts over again.

ANALYSIS PARALYSIS: STEP 11

Upon returning to the room, we went back to the whiteboard with this question: *If there were one step in the process that we could change with a better spreadsheet, which would it be?* After going around the table, we agreed that if we could give the presidents a more fluid way to select and present data *during the meeting with the CFO*, we could avoid the "let's show everything" crisis. We drew a big red X through that step, marking it as the area to change.

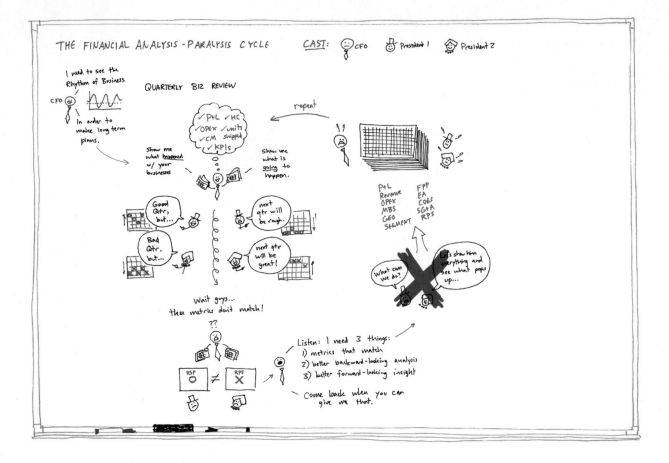

If the presidents had a more fluid way to select and present data during their CFO meeting, they could avoid the "let's show everything" crisis.

Having decided which step of the cycle to fix first, we then drew out a potential spreadsheet interface that would allow for real-time selection of data from multiple sources, with visual representations presented side by side. That would please our entire cast, and if we could create a prototype of it, our conference demo would be a hit.

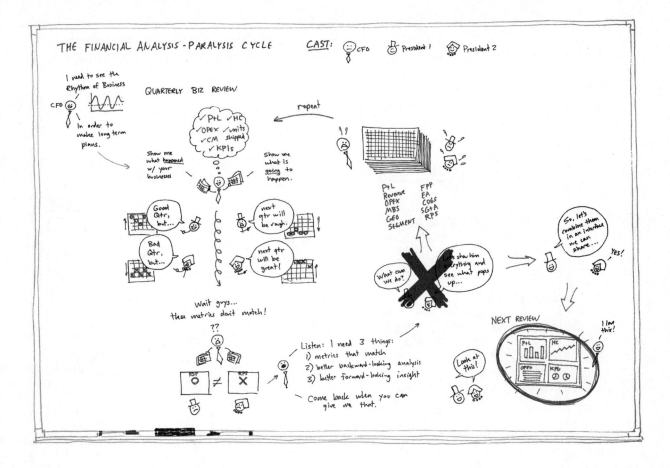

ANALYSIS PARALYSIS: STEP III

Our first day of whiteboarding complete, we went home thinking about potential interface designs. The next day we erased everything (after photographing it in detail),* and then sketched out ideas for what the spreadsheet might look like, based on the team's collective best guess of where technology might be a few years down the road.

▲

If we could design a spreadsheet interface that allowed for the selection and visual presentation of multiple data sources in real time, our demo would be a hit.

✳

Documenting your work during a process like this is critical—we'll talk more about that this afternoon. Also be aware that, for the sake of brevity, I have not shown all the whiteboard sketches it took to get this far. Nevertheless, these images are the actual drawings created during the sessions. All I have done is clean them up in Photoshop for clarity.

✳

I received Microsoft's approval to share this level of work, and I appreciate their openness enormously.

I can't show the final designs we chose, but I can show a sample we did not select.* As you look at this sketch, you can see the simultaneous presentation of multiple data types, several side-by-side data visualizations, and many tools for selecting and interacting with the numbers.

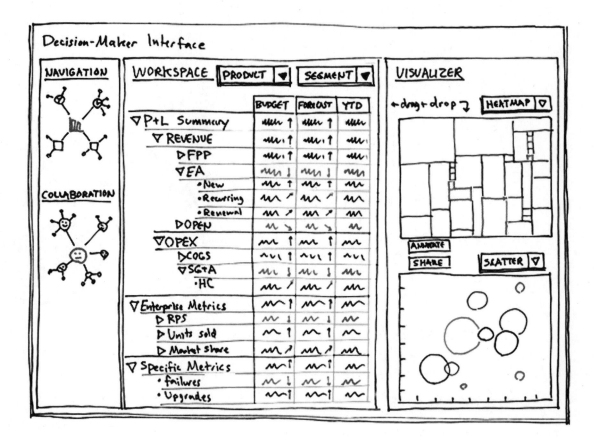

▲

Although it shows a rejected design, this screen sketch includes many of the data-selection and presentation elements we eventually included in the final prototype.

†

Who knows? Perhaps one day you'll see elements of that prototype in a future version of your favorite spreadsheet program.

IF I CAN'T SHOW YOU THE FINAL PICTURE, WHY THE SHOW-AND-TELL?

The most important part of this story—and to me, personally and professionally, this is one of the breakthrough stories in this book—is not what the final prototype looked like.† The breakthrough came in the pictures the team drew to get there, the very same pictures we have just looked at in detail.

Like in the McKinsey-Lego story, I was afraid to show these rough sketches to the executives at Microsoft during our review meetings. Although I knew they looked "unprofessional" there simply wasn't time to re-create them using a computer-drawing program. So we presented them as is.

Something amazing happened in the review meetings as we walked the execs through the whiteboard scenario and the interfaces: everyone immediately "got" what we were showing. In years of senior-level presentations, I'd never seen anything like it. Nobody complained that we'd used the wrong typeface, nobody questioned our choice of colors, and no one got caught in the weeds of the accuracy or relevance of the data we'd selected.[*]

On the contrary, the discussions stayed on a high conceptual level, exactly where we needed them to get the green light to proceed. The level of participation in the meetings was high, the comments insightful, and the conclusions quick.

When the meetings were over, two senior executives from Microsoft came up to me and said, "We really like the way those meetings went, and we think it was due in large part to the quality of the images you presented. What software did you use to create them?"

I thought it was so obvious that they'd been drawn by hand that I suspected the execs were pulling my chain, so I answered in the same spirit. "I created them," I replied, "using 'gray matter 1.0' and 'pen and paper 1.0.' "

The executives replied in unison. "Who makes them?" they asked.

Unwritten Rule 4

This brings us to Unwritten Rule 4. When the execs asked me who created the software that allowed me to draw pictures that looked "human," I knew that they weren't thinking about a divine being or about 300 million years of visual evolution. They were betraying one of the most prevalent beliefs of our time: that without computers we are poor thinkers. It was a shock to them that business ideas could be represented and business decisions made without software.

Well, they can.

And they must.[†] When we need to show our ideas to others—*when what really matters is getting the idea that's in my head into yours*—nothing is more powerful than our eyes, our mind's eye, and the cognitive magic of a little hand-eye coordination. That's what this last rule is all about.

The important lesson from the show-and-tell story isn't that we can improve spreadsheets (we can) or that insightful financial analysis is critical to business success (it is): the real lesson is that polishing our pictures actually makes them worse for problem solving. Unwritten Rule 4 states this way:

[*] Go back and look at the "data" in the interface sketch: it's not real numbers—in fact, it's not numbers at all: it's a bunch of squiggles! Yet no one complained. On the contrary, the conversation stayed on the high level where we needed it.

[†] I'm no Luddite. As a hobby I create three-dimensional computer renderings of spacecraft for the National Space Society, and I find it difficult to come up with anything more techno geek than that. But it's important to note that, with the exception of the Thomson story, not a single image in this book was created using anything other than a pen and paper. When we need to think, especially visually, we do much better without the artificial constraints put upon our minds by menu, mouse, and keyboard.

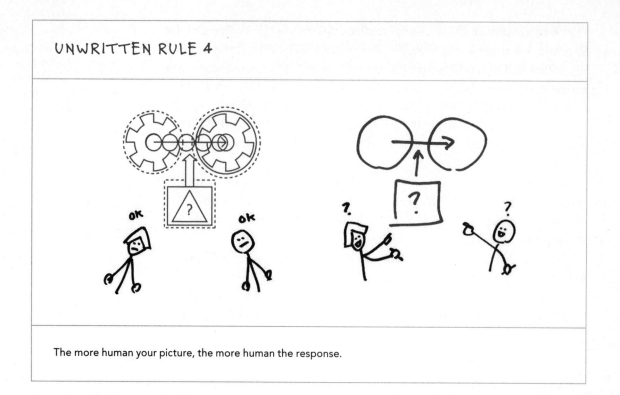

The more human your picture, the more human the response.

Countless meeting-room experiences before and after have confirmed it: if we really want to explore an idea, we're better off with a less-than-perfect picture, which is much more likely to get a thoughtful reaction. When we polish our pictures to make them look "finished"—when we clean up the corners, straighten out the lines, round out the circles; in other words, when we create them on a machine—we're decreasing the likelihood that other people are going to "get" them.

I can think of three reasons why this is so.

1. IT'S DONE? I LOVE IT. IT'S DONE? I HATE IT.

If we see a picture that looks finished, we assume there is nothing left for us to add. We either accept what it shows and agree wholeheartedly or find a single flaw and reject it outright—neither of which is the desired reaction in a problem-solving session.

2. I DON'T WANT TO HURT YOUR FEELINGS, SO I WON'T SAY ANYTHING.

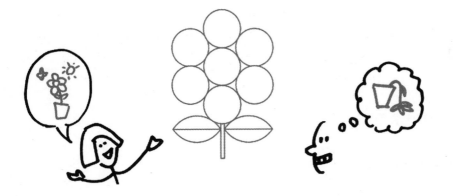

If we see a picture that is highly polished, we see that someone worked it again and again. Our instinctive "golden rule" gene (treat others as we'd like to be treated) kicks in and tells us not to criticize it.* So we either say "I like it" or say nothing. Again, neither helps improve the idea.

3. WHAT, DO YOU THINK I'M DUMB? I ALREADY KNEW THAT.

If we see a picture that looks unequivocally complete, we instinctively assume that it represents a proven fact. And if we recognize it as a fact we

* For anyone who has ever suffered through an art-school critique or a product-design review, you know what I'm talking about. Students or professionals who normally can't keep quiet suddenly struggle for words when asked what's "bad" about someone else's work. The fix? Intentionally make it look like it's still in progress; then people can't wait to chime in.

already know, we feel smug. If we don't, we're offended that the creator thinks we're too stupid to already know about it. Once again, neither is a reaction conducive to good thinking.

PROFESSIONAL IS MANDATORY; IT'S POLISH THAT KILLS

Let's be clear: like wearing a suit to a job interview, there is a time and a place to look buttoned up. But a suit alone does not make us professional, nor does a picture with straight lines. People whose real interest is in solving the problem will always react better to a rough picture that shows the truth than a polished picture that makes no sense.

"HUMAN" PICTURES DRILL

Look over the following machine-drawn pictures and see if you can determine what the essence of each is. Pick two and draw a "human" version for each.
(Refer back to any of the 6×6 pictures or SQVID if you need help. I don't think you will.)

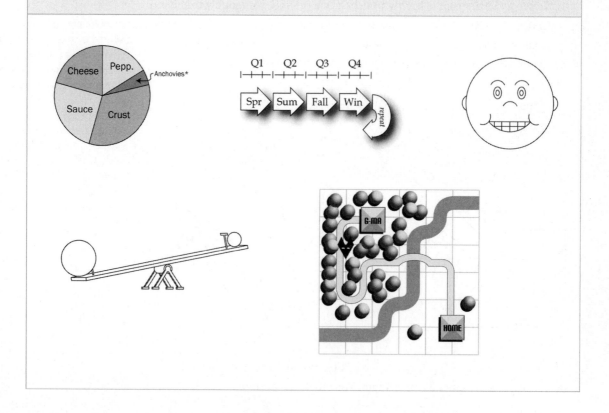

THE FLIP SIDE

That's enough of the "what *not* to do"; I think we got the picture. Let's look at the positive side of Unwritten Rule 4, because that's where everything we've learned these last days comes together.

The more human your picture, the more human the response.

We like to look at things that match the way we think.

We've already applied this in several ways: the 6×6 rule showed us how to make pictures that align with our visual pathways. The SQVID helped us think through variations of a visual idea by bouncing it among our mental processing centers. The simplicity principle told us that we react best to a simple view when we see something for the first time and prefer elaboration once we become expert.

This all supports the notion that we like to look at things that match the way we think, but these are not the underlying reason why hand-drawn pictures are so compelling. Hand-drawn pictures are compelling precisely because they are imperfect. In other words, they work because they invite interaction; human-drawn pictures work because they're human.*

The easiest way we can make our problem-solving pictures interesting to look at is simply to leave them as we drew them. Mistakes and all, they make our thinking visible to anyone who looks at them, and, in the end, that's the whole point of this book.

We're so attracted to pictures that were obviously created by hand that we'll pause in front of a scrawl-covered whiteboard just to try to make sense of it—something most of us would never do with a computer-generated image on the same wall. For the same reason, we'll pay to see a musician in concert when we know we can download her music for free or fly around the world to see a friend when we could easily chat with them online. We're still people, and we love to see what other people think.

✸

It's in our nature to humanize the things we see around us. We can't help but "anthropomorphize": from a car's twin headlights (eyes) to the pointers of a clock (hands) to the posts of a chair (legs), we constantly look for human connections in inhuman things.

▲

We're still people and are drawn to pictures where we can see other people's thinking at work.

How can we draw "human" pictures in business?

As we reach the end of this workshop, what we're talking about is doing something in our business meetings that nobody does: tossing aside our prepared bullets and showing a bunch of hand-drawn pictures instead—or even better, drawing them right there in the meeting. Ye gads! Meetings aren't supposed to be done that way!*

That's true: modern meetings aren't designed that way, which is why business tools aren't intended to help us draw. Then again, we're not here to talk about what tools were designed to do—we're talking about what they *can* do. Our basic business tools can help us be visual; we just have to think about them a little differently.

"PERSONAL," "PARTICIPATORY," AND "PERFORMANCE": THREE DRAWING TOOLS FOR THREE KINDS OF MEETINGS

There are three sets of business drawing tools we're going to look at, one for each of the three kinds of meetings we typically engage in: "personal" meetings with ourselves or another person, "participatory" meetings intended to generate discussion among a few people, and "performance" meetings where it's us in front of a crowd. In all these situations the same simple pictures work, but we'll be drawing them on a different surface.

A "PERSONAL" DRAWING SURFACE FOR PERSONAL MEETINGS

When we want to think about an idea on our own or with another person, most of us prefer a drawing surface that is small and personal—it's less

Say that to the general on the battlefield as he sketches plans with a stick in the dirt; say that to the coach as she scrawls Xs and Os on the chalkboard during halftime; say that to Arthur Laffer in that bar in D.C. The very best meetings are those where someone has the guts to draw what they think—that's how big ideas get conveyed and that's how they get understood.

intimidating that way, and it feels like we're closer to the idea. A personal lap-sized whiteboard is my favorite tool: because it's easy to erase, we're willing to experiment on it without the concerns of publicly committing to our idea. To save an idea we really like, we just take a photo of it with our cell phone and e-mail it to ourselves. Then we erase the board and start over again.

Anything easy to carry and draw on works just as well, from a notebook to a napkin. I drew the pictures in this book on plain bond paper with a pencil and a Sharpie, scanned them on a basic desktop scanner, then beefed up the contrast in Photoshop so they would print better.

Personal meeting drawing surfaces include

- Napkins (front or back)
- Sheets of paper
- Personal whiteboards

A "PARTICIPATORY" DRAWING SURFACE FOR PARTICIPATORY MEETINGS

Every time we have a team meeting, a brainstorming session, a weekly project update, or a problem-solving discussion, we're in a participatory meeting; the intent is to get ideas on the table and to get everyone heard and *seen.* The drawing surface we need should be big enough to be seen from any corner of the room and have space for everyone to draw. In most cases, a big whiteboard is perfect: we just need to make sure there are plenty of erasers around and that the markers aren't the permanent kind.

Flip charts are a distant second in utility: large as they seem, they're still too small for use by more than five or six people and are almost impossible to manage beyond a couple pages. The exception is a flip chart with an adhesive strip along the back. The best way to use this kind is to tear off several sheets and cover the walls with them before beginning to work. When the canvas in front of us appears boundless, we're much less inhibited about drawing.

But a whiteboard or flip chart only work if everybody is in the same room, which is becoming less likely as teams go global, as more employees work remotely or from home offices, and as businesses cut down on travel to save money. Many brands of "smart boards" are now available that allow drawings created in one location to be seen and modified in real time at another location. I'm sure the technology will continue to improve dramatically, but at present these boards are expensive to purchase, challenging to install, and less than seamless to use.

A less-expensive and, presently, more user-friendly option is to use any one of "desktop-sharing" applications now emerging. When combined with a conference call, these tools allow one person to share their computer screen with others via the Internet. They require everyone to download the same software, install and test it in advance of the meeting, and still have some technical issues, but assuming everyone has access to a decent computer and high-speed connectivity, they work reasonably well.

Participatory meeting drawing surfaces include

- Wall-mounted whiteboards
- Flip charts (especially the sticky-back type)
- Smart boards
- Computers with desktop-sharing software and Internet connectivity

About that last option, one big question remains: assuming the technology for sharing computer desktops is all set, which drawing program can we use to draw, broadcast, and edit our pictures with other people? There is a gloriously simple answer, and it's the same one we'll use for the next type of meeting.

A "PERFORMANCE" DRAWING SURFACE FOR PERFORMANCE MEETINGS

Although few businesspeople are willing to admit it, meetings of more than ten or twelve people are always performances. These meetings aren't intended for open discussion or the shared exploration of an idea; on the contrary, they are the platform for one individual or small group to perform for another. And our performances usually stink.

There are lots of reasons, from lack of preparation to nervousness to over-reliance on the bad parts of PowerPoint to simply not having anything worthwhile to say. Those are all real issues and need to be addressed on their own, but we're here to talk about pictures. Assuming we've dealt with all those other challenges and have made it this far in the workshop, the real question is: how can I draw pictures in front of a crowd?

The answer, I'm happy to report, is already in your computer.

THE BEST COMPUTER DRAWING TOOL IS ONE YOU ALREADY OWN

When I give a presentation, I bring along a small tablet PC and a projector. The beauty of the tablet is that I can draw directly on the screen, "live," and everyone can see exactly what I'm drawing while I'm drawing it. This means that my prepared presentation is often a series of nearly blank slides;* when I want to make a particular point, I draw my circles and stick figures right on the screen. This creates a level of live performance and interaction rarely seen in business meetings. Believe me, when your audience sees you drawing a picture right in front of them—regardless of how ugly or simple it is—they pay attention.

After meetings, people often ask what specialized software I used to make the drawings. They can't believe it when I show them: it's nothing but plain vanilla Microsoft PowerPoint. That's right: the very best on-screen drawing software I know of is built right into the most commonly available business tool. Nobody knows about it because the drawing tools are only available in "slide show" mode, and nobody composes their slides in "show" mode.†

HOW TO ACCESS THE "LIVE" DRAWING TOOLS IN POWERPOINT

Although the tablet PC I use allows me to draw directly on the screen—making it much easier to draw—we could just as well use a regular mouse. The fact is that anybody with any version of PowerPoint released within the past five years can draw on-screen without buying anything new. Here's the process:

1. Create your slides as you normally would (and since we've just spent four days talking about this, always use simple pictures: *no long text and no long bullet lists!*)

2. Leave blank areas on pages where you will be drawing live.

3. Save your file as usual.

4. When it comes time to present, open your file and go into "slide show" mode.

5. Using your pointer (whether tablet PC stylus or mouse), move over the lower left corner of the screen. A drawing palette will appear. Select the type of pen you want and the ink color.

*At many conferences, the sponsor requests the slides in advance so they can print them up as handouts for the audience. After I send my slides in, I always get a call back letting me know that something is wrong with the file—half the pages are blank! When I explain, the meeting sponsors invariably tell me that they have never heard of someone drawing on-screen before. That's how I know I'm doing something the audience will find compelling; they've never seen it before either.

†It's another of the mysteries of Microsoft that it has added the nicest and simplest on-screen drawing tools right into its most ubiquitous business application, and then buried the tools in a place where nobody knows they exist. Redmond, hello?

The Back of the Napkin
Workshop

These tools only appear in PPT Slide view!

Problems with Pictures

This is the BEST onscreen drawing tool on any platform!

*

We can use this approach with any of the desktop-sharing applications mentioned earlier, which means we can turn any conference call into a free-form drawing exercise with all attendees participating.

6. Move your pointer off the corner and start drawing.

7. Presto! You've got a modern-day overhead projector with global reach!* The best part is that you can draw directly on top of pictures or words you placed on the slide previously. You don't have to draw everything live—in many cases just using the pen to indicate where on the slide you'd like to draw people's attention is enough to make your (visual) point.

8. When you're done, close the file. PowerPoint will ask if you want to save your notations. Say no if you want to use the same blank pages again. Say yes if you want to save your live sketches for further editing.

Performance meeting drawing tools include

- A PC running PowerPoint and a projector (a tablet PC makes the drawing much easier but isn't required)

That's it: the tools we need to make our problem-solving pictures come to life are simple. In most cases we don't need anything we don't already have.

The foolproof business outline: the third use of the SQVID

We're almost done. I want to leave you with one last tool that you can use immediately for the very next meeting you attend, whether personal, participatory, or performance. It requires the SQVID one more time,* and using it means we never have to think about how to outline a business presentation again.

To put this into practice, let's imagine we're that surprisingly visual politician who drew the world-saving Venn diagram back on Day 2, and we've been asked to visually explain what's going on in the auto industry. We'd start by asking what kind of a problem we're looking at—"who and what," "how much," "where," "when," "how," "why"—and then create a series of pictures to clarify each of those aspects. When we were done, we'd have several pictures we could show, but what order should we show them in?

Here's where the SQVID helps us one more time: if we use its five questions as a outline, we can tell any business story in a way that will make sense to any audience, taking them from the simplest possible introduction right through all the details. Let's try it.

We start with a *simple* "what" portrait: a tombstone showing that Detroit is dying. Having established our premise, we then *elaborate* with a quick series of portraits showing the decline of Ford, GM, and Chrysler.

✱

Some people who otherwise loved the concept of SQVID have complained to me that it's a terrible mnemonic: it's not a real word, it's not self-explanatory, and it's not "sticky." I don't mind: perhaps because it is unexpected and a little "off" I find "SQVID" easy to recall and put into practice. You still may not like the spelling, but now you know where it comes from.

SQVID as outline:

(S) What's the problem? (Simple) / RIP Detroit ? / More detail...? (Elaborate) GM⅂ Ford⅂ Chrysler⅂

◀ A *simple* portrait shows that Detroit is dying. We *elaborate* by showing each of the Big Three heading down.

Then we show what this *qualitatively* feels like: like we fell off a cliff and are hanging on by our fingertips. Then we back that up by *quantitatively* showing the numbers that lead us to feel that way.

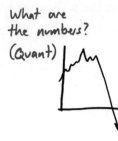

Q What does it feel like? (Qual)

What are the numbers? (Quant)

Qualitatively, it feels like we've fallen off a cliff. We then back that feeling up *quantitatively* with the numbers. ▶

Then we come up with a *vision* for what might save us. Perhaps manufacturing high-quality hybrid cars might do the trick. To *execute*—to make that happen—we'd need to react to the global forces at work, retool to build a new generation of cars, and reinvest to get the lines running again.

V What's the big-picture solution? (Vision)

Hybrids

What does it take to make that happen? (Execution)

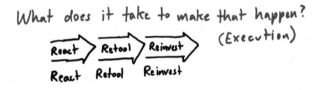

React → Retool → Reinvest
React Retool Reinvest

▲

Our *vision* might be mass-produced quality hybrid cars. To *execute,* we'd have to react, retool, and reinvest.

Then we show what that would mean all by *itself*: people lining up to buy our great new hybrid cars. That's a pleasant scene (especially if you live in Detroit where we make them or California where we consume them), but how does it *compare* to the options? Well, nobody is buying monster gas-guzzlers and fewer are buying expensive sports cars.

I What does that mean by itself? (Individual)

How does that compare to other options? (Comparison)

▲

Individually, we see people lining up for our shiny new hybrids and *compare* that to nobody buying our expensive gas-guzzlers.

Then we'd show what *change* would look like: employed workers and a reinvigorated national economy. Finally, we'd close with the *status quo*: if we do nothing, we've got mass unemployment and a worsening economy.

① What will we have in the future? (Change)

What do we have now? (Status quo)

▲

Whether we all agree with this approach for saving Detroit is for another discussion. What matters is that by using our simple pictures and the SQVID, we've made our case crystal clear, and that should be the point of every performance meeting.

The *difference*? If we make this change, we employ people and get our economy back. If we don't—if we stay with the *status quo*—we see massive unemployment and a worsening economy.

Last lunch: working style

For our last assignment, we're ordering in lunch. While eating, use the SQVID outline to create a three-minute presentation on what visual thinking is and why it works.

Practice makes picture perfect

Now we're really done. Equipped with the basic tools of visual problem solving, we're ready to take our whiteboards and pens and put them to work in the real world of business. If you're concerned about how to get started, let me suggest the mantra I scratched out on a Post-it ten years ago and have kept above my desk ever since:

Whenever I can use a picture at work, I will.

Just start practicing, and watch what happens. You'll quickly see all kinds of new ways to solve problems.

One last thought: the real magic wand

My daughter recently finished reading her first Harry Potter book, and she was intrigued by the magic wands. One day when she was drawing at the kitchen table, she casually mentioned that when she put pencil to paper it was like holding Harry Potter's magic wand: her ability to instantly see ideas form in front of her eyes was pure magic.

That was the best description I'd ever heard of what happens when we let our mind's eye go free with a pen in hand. So, with hats off to Sophie, here is our workshop's closing thought: the best way to bring the infinite ideas that exist in our imagination into the real world is to simply pick up a pencil, rest the tip on a sheet a paper, take a breath, draw that first circle, and then let the magic happen.

I hope this workshop helps the magic happen for you.

APPENDIX:
MY VISUAL ANSWERS TO PARTICULARLY CHALLENGING EXERCISES

P. 48. Active Looking, Exercise 2

The data table shows the total "carbon footprint" of all Wal-Mart stores worldwide in 2005. This data was collected by Wal-Mart to kick off the company's sustainability initiative. In 2006, I created a set of visuals based on this and other data to help people understand Wal-Mart's approach to business and environmental sustainability. This is the chart I created from the data on page 48.

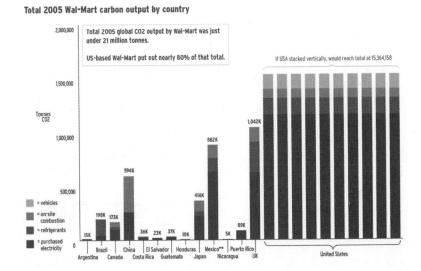

Total 2005 Wal-Mart carbon output by country

P. 117. Your next portrait:
Make a list and check it twice

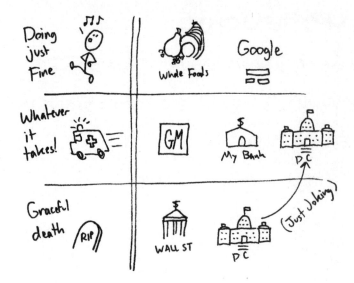

P. 129. Your turn to draw a chart

Option 1: Who sees how? ▶

Option 2: Taking temperature ▶

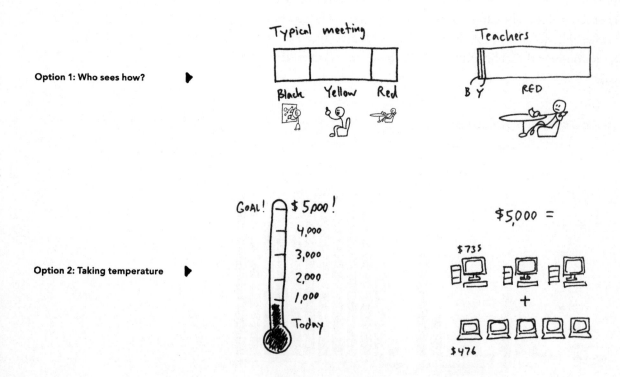

P. 141. Map option 2: What to keep; what to chuck

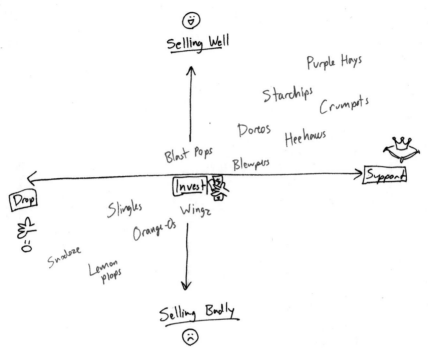

P. 157. Your first "how" picture

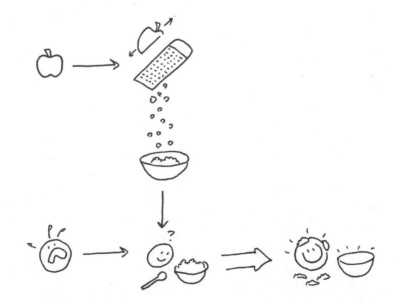

P. 161. Your second "how" picture

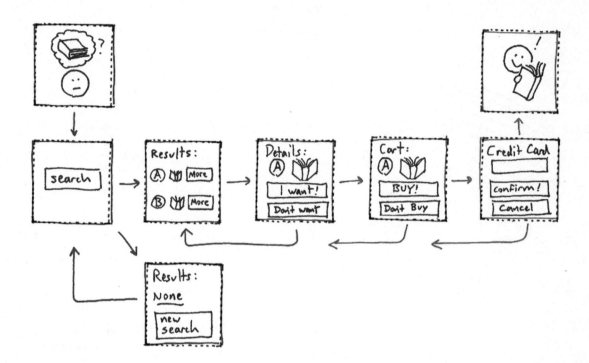

P. 173. Your "why" pictures: A theme and variations

Why Visual Problem-Solving Works

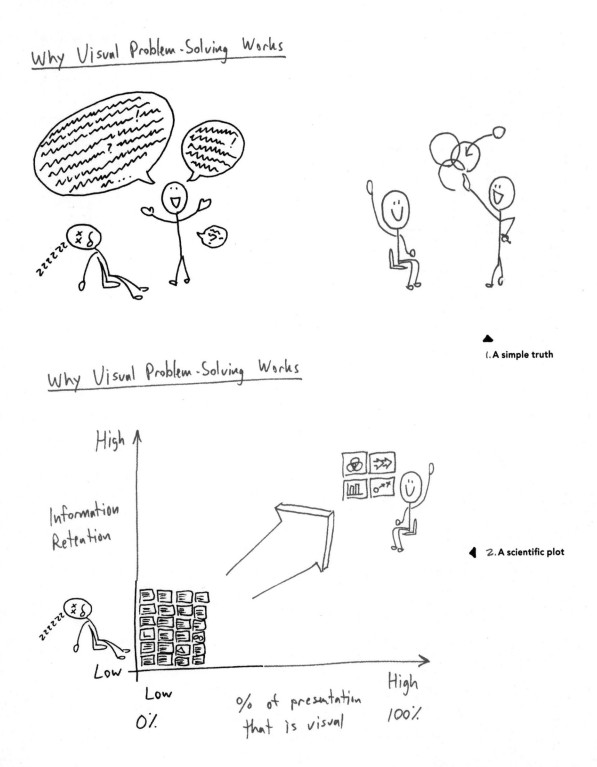

1. A simple truth

Why Visual Problem-Solving Works

2. A scientific plot

INDEX

Absolute quantities, versus comparative
    amounts, 122–124
Accenture, 58
Active looking, 35–48, 57
Airlines, 11, 45, 51
Air Transport Association (ATA), 45
Apple Macintosh, 246

*Back of the Napkin, The: Solving Problems
    and Selling Ideas with Pictures*
    (Roam), x–xii, 3, 31, 35, 36, 89
Ballmer, Steve, 165, 173
Bar charts, 121
Biological clock, 143
Black Pen people, xxvi, 24–27, 30, 38, 129
Bloomberg, 91–93, 97–103
Boeing, 3, 51
Brain hemispheres, 50, 196–199
Brand pyramid, 94–99
Bubble charts, 121
BusinessObjects, 52
Business process management (BPM), 216

Cause and effect, 85, 86, 152–161
Change, versus status quo, 189–191,
    195, 197, 205–206, 208, 218–226,
    230–242, 268–269
Charts, 105, 119–131, 176
Cheney, Dick, 15
Cognitive science, 49
Color, 78
Communication channels, 51
Comparative amounts, versus absolute
    quantities, 122–124

Coordinate system, 38–42, 45, 62, 95–96,
    136, 167–170, 228
Corporate-brand recognition, 94–102

Data visualization, 36–48
Decision trees, 160
Dow Jones Industrial Average, xiv–xv
Drawing drills
    change versus status quo, 206
    draw "me," 567
    how much is 75 percent, really?, 22
    individual versus comparison, 205
    name three problems (S,M,L), 5
    the pictures we need, 56
    qualitative versus quantitative, 201
    simple versus elaborate, 199
    6×6 problem-solving napkin, 74
    vision versus execution, 202
Drawing surfaces, xxxi, 4, 262, 263
Dvorak, August, 211

Einstein, Albert, 29
Emotions, in portraits, 110
Excel, 45, 52, 246
Eyes, as visual-thinking tool, 21–22, 24

Financial crisis (2008), xiv–xvi,
    137–140
Flip charts, 263
Flowcharts, 105, 145, 151–162, 176
    examples of, 153–156
    exercises, 157–162
Ford, Gerald, 15
Frito-Lay, 94

Gantt charts, 145
Garage-sale principle, 38
Gates, Bill, 246
Globalization, 51
Good-luck coin, 64
Google, 3, 165, 169–173

Hand-eye coordination, as
    visual-thinking tool, 21–22, 24
Hardaway, Chelsea, 246
Harrington, Dick, 101–103, 145
Histograms, 121
How much problems, 62, 63, 66, 67, 74–77,
    79–80
    in case example, 92–94
    charts and, 119–131
    examples of, 119
    visual-thinking codex and, 229–242
How problems, 62, 63, 67, 74–77, 101–103
    examples of, 152
    flowcharts and, 105, 145, 151–162
    visual-thinking codex and, 229–242
"How" vision pathway, 69, 84–85
Hypothalamus, 143

Imagining (Day 3), xxix, 7–8, 30, 32–34,
    179–242, 245. (*see also* SQVID)
Individual attributes, versus comparison,
    188–191, 195, 197, 203–205, 208,
    218–226, 230–242, 268
Information overload, 51

Kennedy, John F., 12
Krebs cycle, 198

Laffer, Arthur, 12–15, 261
Laffer curve, 15
Left brain hemisphere, 50, 196–199
Life cycles, 145
Limbic brain, 69
Linear progressions, 145
Looking (Day 1), xxix, 7–52, 30, 31, 33,
    34, 245
    active, 35–48, 57

Maps, 105, 132–143, 176
    examples of, 134–140
    exercises, 141–142
Market share, 157–160
McGraw-Hill, 91–93, 97–103

McKinsey & Company, 58–60
Microsoft, 3, 28, 165–166, 169–173, 246,
    254–255, 265
Mind's eye, 179–183. (*see also* SQVID)
    as visual thinking tool, 21–22, 24, 32
Multivariable plots, 105, 163–175
    example of, 169–173
    exercises, 173–174

Name recognition, 94–102
National Education Association, 129
National Space Society, 255
Neocortex, 50, 69
Neurobiology, 49

Occipital lobe of brain, 69

Parietal lobes of brain, 196
Participatory drawings/meetings, xxxi,
    261, 262–263
Pattern recognition, 56–58
Pearson, 91–93, 97–103
PepsiCo, 94
Performance drawings/meetings, xxxi,
    261, 264–266
Personal drawings/meetings, xxxi,
    261–262
Pfizer, 3
Pie charts, 121
Poker, visual-thinking process and,
    31–33
Portals, 58–60
Portraits, 105, 107–118, 165–166, 175, 176
PowerPoint, 28–29, 265–266
Problems (*see How* problems; *How much*
    problems; *When* problems; *Where*
    problems; *Who/what* problems;
    Why problems)
Profiling, 223

Quality, versus quantity, 186–187,
    190–192, 194, 197, 200–201, 208,
    218–226, 230–242, 267–268
QWERTY keyboard, 210–211

Radar charts, 121
Reagan, Ronald, 12, 15
Red Pen people, xxvi, 24–27, 30, 129
Reed Elsevier, 91–93, 97–103
Reptilian brain, 50, 69

Retina, 69
Reuters, 91–93, 97–103
Right brain hemisphere, 50, 196–197
Rumsfeld, Donald, 15

Seeing (Day 2), xxix, 7, 8, 30–34,
    55–176, 245
Sense processing capacity of brain, 23
Shape, 78
Sholes, Christopher, 210
Showing (Day 4), xxix, 8, 30, 32–34,
    245–270
Simple, versus elaborate, 185–186, 190,
    191, 193, 197–199, 208, 213–216,
    218–226, 230–242, 267
Simplicity principle, 215, 260
6×6 rule, 39, 68, 78, 91, 104–108, 176, 179,
    211, 226–227, 260
6-W system (see How problems; How
    much problems; When problems;
    Where problems; Who/what
    problems; Why problems)
Size and proportion, 78
Sleep patterns, 143
Southwest Airlines, 11
Split-brain structure, 50
Spreadsheets, 38, 44, 45, 146, 246, 255
SQVID, 184, 260
    change versus status quo, 189–191,
        195, 197, 205–206, 208, 218–226,
        230–242, 268–269
    combined with 6+6, 227–232
    as graphic equalizer, 212–226
    individual attributes versus comparison,
        188–191, 195, 197, 203–205, 208,
        218–226, 230–242, 268
    quality versus quantity, 186–187,
        190–192, 194, 197, 200–201, 208,
        218–226, 230–242, 267–268
    right brain/left brain activation and,
        196–197
    simple versus elaborate, 185–186, 190,
        191, 193, 197–199, 208, 213–216,
        218–226, 230–242, 267
    vision versus execution, 187–188,
        190–192, 194, 197, 201–202, 208,
        218–226, 230–242, 268
    visual-thinking codex and, 228–242
Steiger, Doug, 11, 12
Stereotyping, 223

Superior colliculus, 196
Supplies, xxx–xxxi, 262
Supply-side economics, 15
Suprachiasmatic nucleus, 143
Swim lanes, 145, 148
Swiss Army knife visualization, xxvii,
    19–21, 30, 63, 74–77, 184

Tableau, 52
Techical-architecture maps, 134–135, 213
Temporal lobes of brain, 196
Texture, 78
Thomson Corporation, 89–94, 97–103,
    145–147, 169
Thomson Reuters, 103
Three-dimensional space, 61, 62
Time lines, 105, 143–150, 176
    example of, 145–147
    exercises, 149–150
Time series, 121
2×2 (quad) map, 136

U.S. Senate, 3, 11
Unwritten rules of visual thinking,
    x–xiv, 8–11, 57–58, 64, 181–183,
    255–260

Venn, John, 138
Venn diagram, 138, 142, 267
Vision, versus execution, 187–188,
    190–192, 194, 197, 201–202, 208,
    218–226, 230–242, 268
Vision system, 61–62, 68–69
Visual cortex, 196
Visual lists, 115–117
Visual-thinking codex, 228–242
Visual-thinking process (see Imagining;
    Looking; Problems; Seeing;
    Showing; SQVID)
Visual-thinking tool kit (see Swiss Army
    knife visualization)

Wal-Mart, 3
Washington, George, 12
"What" vision pathway, 69
When problems, 62, 63, 66, 67, 74–77,
    100–101
    examples of, 144
    time lines and, 143–150
    visual-thinking codex and, 229–242

"When" vision pathway, 83
Where problems, 62, 63, 66, 67, 74–77
  in case example, 94–100
  examples of, 133
  maps and, 94–100, 132–143
  visual-thinking codex and, 229–242
"Where" vision pathway, 69, 81–82
"Who and what" vision pathway, 77–78
Who/what problems, 62, 63, 65, 67,
    74–77
  in case example, 91–92
  examples of, 108
  portraits and, 105, 107–118
  visual-thinking codex and, 229–242

Why Businesspeople Speak Like Idiots
    (Hardaway), 246
Why problems, 62, 63, 66, 74–77
  examples of, 164
  multivariable plots and, 105, 163–173
  visual-thinking codex and, 229–242
Wolters Kluwer, 91–93, 97–103
Woods, Tiger, 58
Workshop-location fantasy, xxvii–xxviii
Wright brothers, 203

Yahoo!, 165–166, 169–173
Yang, Jerry, 165
Yellow Pen people, xxvi, 24–27, 30, 129

YOUR SCRATCH PAPER